DELTA ECHO!

Experiences in a Bush Hospital in Papua

Ruth Archer

Honeybee Books

Honeybee Books

Published by Honeybee Books
Broadoak, Dorset
www.honeybeebooks.co.uk

Cover illustrations ©Anna Reali
Photo of Ruth's Nautilus shell taken by Helen Scoging

Photo of Ruth taken by Wendy Hilton

Printed in the UK.

ISBN: 978-1-910616-04-8

This book is dedicated to the memory of my friend,
Elizabeth Stella Smith, 1941-1977.

And to my mentor, Revd Ravu Henao,
1927-2007.

CONTENTS

About the Author

As a youngster growing up in rural Essex, Ruth – the daughter of an agricultural labourer – attended the Congregational Church in Ingatestone. Here she heard many accounts of missionary endeavours in different parts of the world. In her early teens she experienced what she felt was a call from God to work overseas. With this is mind she trained as a nurse and midwife, and after spending time at the Selly Oak Colleges in Birmingham, she was appointed by the London Missionary Society to Papua (today's Papua New Guinea). She worked there from 1966 to 1976. This book is an account of the first three years of that time, spent at Fife Bay in southeast Papua.

When Ruth returned to UK she worked part-time in the NHS, whilst training as a psychotherapist at the Westminster Pastoral Foundation. She eventually gave up nursing but continued to work at the WPF as a therapist and manager, where she worked with a team of therapists, counselling people who were seriously physically ill. In 2006 she edited a book Dual Realities, published by Karnac Books, which documented this work. She is now retired and lives in Dorset.

ACKNOWLEDGEMENTS

I am greatly indebted to the people of the Territory of Papua and New Guinea for welcoming me into their country and culture. Especially the Suau people amongst whom I lived in the 1960s. In particular, I would like to thank the pastors, nurses, patients, villagers and church members, with whom I had close contact during my stay at Fife Bay. Specifically I would like to thank the following who played a large part in helping me to adapt to living in a different culture: Mary B, Walo I, Rev Ravu Henao, and Rev Kwalahu M.

My thanks go also to a number of people who assisted me on my journey: my English, Australian, New Zealand, Samoan and Papuan colleagues, with whom I lived and worked, many of whom are mentioned in this book, and specifically Rev Norman Williams, Stella Smith, Rev Alan Dunstone and Wendy Dunstone, Margaret Cole and Rev Norman Cocks.

I would like to thank the staff of LMS/CCWM for supporting me through sometimes difficult times, enabling me to work for ten years in the exciting country of Papua.

I am indebted to many people for their help in the production of this book, in particular Dr Helen Scoging for the central part she has played in every aspect of this book - editing, proof reading, enhancing the photographs, drawing maps 1, 2 and 4, and photographing my shell collection. It is likely that without the generous giving of her time and expertise this book would not have been completed.

My thanks to Rev Bernard Thorogood for writing the Introduction; Dr John Kadiba, for checking and advising on the historical details and the Rev Dr YakHwee Tan at CWM for her support and encouragement.

Thank you also to Anna Reali for the cover artwork and general advice, to Sally Green for jogging my memory and clarifying points, and to Dr Nick Thomson for his helpful suggestions.

I would like to thank my family and friends and the people of Dorchester United Church for their encouragement and support during the writing of this book.

Lastly, my thanks and appreciation go to my publishers, particularly Chella Adgopul of Honeybee Books for designing the cover and for her help and advice.

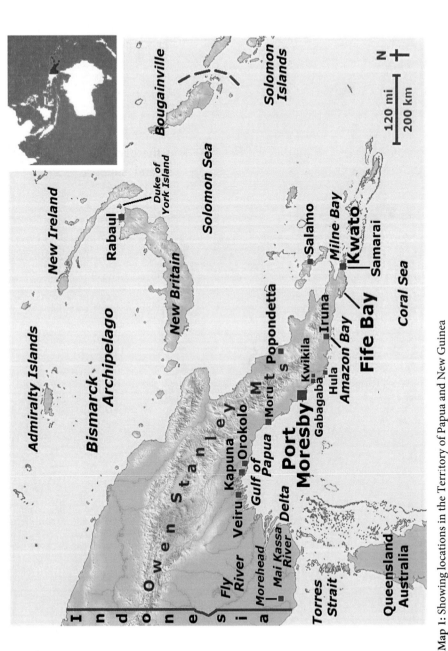

Map 1: Showing locations in the Territory of Papua and New Guinea
©Helen Scoging   Base map: Map of Papua New Guinea Demis
Licensed under Public domain via Wikimedia Commons
http://commons.wikimedia.org/wiki/File:Map_of_Papua_New_Guinea_Demis.png#mediaviewer/File:Map_of_Papua_New_Guinea_Demis.png

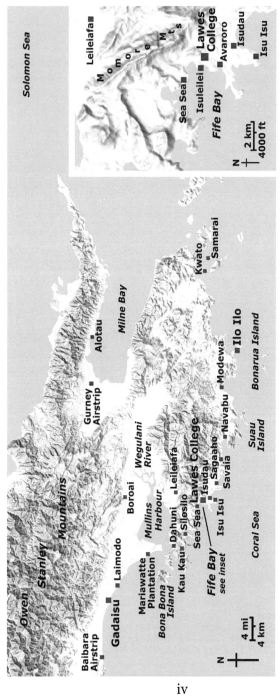

Map 2: Relief Map of Ruth's District, Gadaisu to Ilo Ilo, with inset of Fife Bay
©Helen Scoging
Base map: ©2014 GBRMPA, Google, MapIT   www.maps.google.co.uk

Inset (Fife Bay):

Solomon Sea

Leileiafa

M o r o m M t s

Isuleilei   Lawes College

Sea Sea   Avaroro   Isudau

Fife Bay   Isu Isu

N

2 km
4000 ft

Main map:

Solomon Sea

Owen Stanley Mountains

Baibara Airstrip

Gadaisu   Laimodo

Mariawatte Plantation

Bona Bona Island   Kau Kau   Dahuni   Silosilo   Leileiafa

Mullins Harbour   Boroai

Wegulani River

Gurney Airstrip   Alotau

Milne Bay

Sea Sea   Lawes College

Isudau   Sagaaho   Navabu   Modewa

Fife Bay   Isu Isu   Savaia

see inset

Coral Sea   Suau Island   Ilo Ilo

Bonarua Island

Kwato   Samarai

N

4 mi
4 km

iv

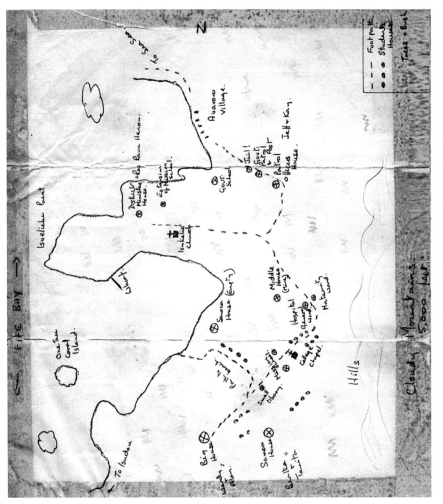

Map 3: Sketch map of Fife Bay. North is to the right
© Ruth Archer 2014

v

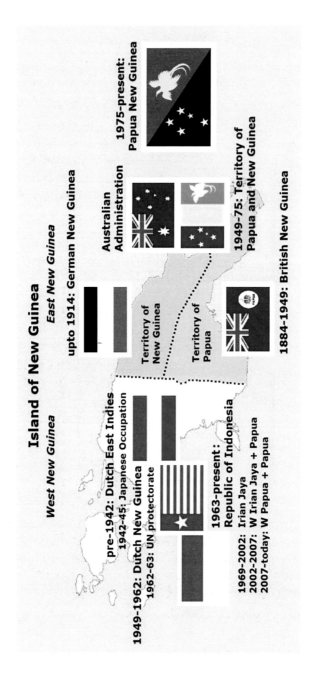

Map 4: Showing the 20th Century colonial history of the Island of New Guinea, including the Territory of Papua and New Guinea up to the creation of the independent state of Papua New Guinea
©Helen Scoging   Base map: Map of New Guinea   www.demis.nl
Licensed under Public domain via Wikimedia Commons
http://commons.wikimedia.org/wiki/File:Map_of_New_Guinea_Demis.png

DEFINITION OF TERMS

The Territory of Papua and New Guinea

The modern country of Papua New Guinea (PNG), occupying the eastern half of the island of New Guinea (see map 1 for locations in the Territory of Papua and New Guinea), along with many outlying islands, is not only one of the most culturally and linguistically diverse, but has had a very complex history before it gained its independence from Australia in 1975, after 70 years of foreign administration. The northern half of the country, having been ruled by Germany in the 19th century as its colony German New Guinea, later to become occupied by Australia after the First World War, eventually became the Territory of New Guinea. The southern part of the country was colonised by the British as British New Guinea, until 1904 when administrative power was transferred to Australia, becoming the Territory of Papua a year later. After the Second World War the two Territories were combined as the single Territory of Papua and New Guinea, which is what it was when I was there in the 1960s. In this book, unless otherwise specified, I shall use the terms Territory and Papua interchangeably, to denote this entity. The word Papua is pronounced Pah-*pooh*-a with emphasis on the second syllable.

The London Missionary Society

I left UK in 1966 under the auspices of the London Missionary Society (LMS). By the time I arrived at Fife Bay, LMS, together with the Commonwealth Missionary Society, had become the Congregational Council for World Mission (CCWM), but it had long been the tradition at Fife Bay to call this missionary organisation the London Missionary Society, because of the big letters, LMS, painted on the roof of one of the Lawes College school buildings (plate 1). This remained the case all the while I was at Fife Bay. In 1977, after major restructuring to become a partnership of over thirty churches, CCWM became the Council for World Mission (CWM, plate 2). I shall use LMS throughout this book, unless otherwise specified, to reflect local usage.

Papua Ekalesia

The LMS had always aimed to establish an indigenous church from its mission work. After several years of consultation with European and local church leaders the Papua Ekalesia was inaugurated on 21st November 1962 on the anniversary of Lawes' landing at Port Moresby in 1874. The church was the first major church to become independent in the Territory.

Introduction

In the popular imagination today, missionaries have a poor image. They are either aggressive fundamentalists or colonial hangovers. After their celebrity status in the 19th century it is quite a let down. Some correction is welcome, for the 20th century story is as varied, and as challenging, as the days of the pioneers. I am prejudiced, having served the London Missionary Society (LMS), and I am grateful that Ruth Archer has written a personal memoir of a vital service in a little known corner of the great island of New Guinea.

Papua, the southern half of the present nation, was the last pioneering venture of the London Missionary Society, and to those who have read the missionary history, the story is full of familiar names. It was a vast shoreline, from the Morehead River in the west to Milne Bay and Kwato in the east, with Motu as the *lingua franca* and a host of languages inland. Communication was slow and risky, without roads or commercial development, until recently, and with the gap between local and imported cultures as wide as the Pacific Ocean. A characteristic of the varied and dynamic people who stayed the course as missionaries in a tough context was their respect for the local cultures. There was surely a stern rejection of tribal killings but in matters of language and arts and crafts, in knowledge of the natural environment, in agriculture and seafaring there was a genuine desire to learn. The number of Bible translations made is a powerful testimony to the effort put into language skills.

The colonial period of about one century included brave attempts by the Australian government officers to bridge the cultural divide, but they were hampered by the scant resources available and the turn-over of staff, so the services provided by government were spasmodic and sparse. When the decolonisation mood swept the world after the Second World War there had to be a very rapid transition to a locally elected parliament for an independent state. This adventure has been a tough journey for Papua New Guinea, for the principles of elections and cabinet government have confronted a strong, treasured tribal culture which still holds the primary loyalty of very many. I wonder whether the Westminster pattern of government has ever been advocated for so different a culture, where clan and language, valley and river, swamp and mountain have divided the people so deeply.

Throughout this period the missionaries of the London Missionary Society were giving signal service to the Papuan people. Ben Butcher, William Saville, Bert Brown and Stan Dewdney were trekking to remote villages and persevering to reduce languages to writing and then translating great passages of scripture. Percy Chatterton was giving care to the growing Port Moresby population and then served in the first independence parliament. Constance Fairhall and Myra Kennedy were creating a healing community at Gemo Island. Samoan and Cook Island pastors – whose predecessors were among the bravest pioneers – were sharing their pastoral gifts. Many more, with varied talents and theologies, gave their service without concern for status or reward.

But through their lives – and those in service of all the missions – something very significant was happening. The gap between cultures, so extreme and so daunting, was crossed by the most personal service. That is how it happens. Not on the grand scale of diplomats or consuls, not by industrial giants or wealthy banks, but by the daily, intimate, loving contact between individuals. This is what changes people, and in both directions. For the best of missionaries have been those who learnt as much as they taught. We have learnt the values of a non-literate society and of the extended family, the power of memory and the bearing of pain. In the extensive medical work we have learnt that traditional medicine is not all superstition but has valuable gifts for us all. Here, in this very personal story of service, Ruth Archer shares what she learnt as well as what she offered in knowledge and skills and faith. Friendship and faith run well together.

One of the valuable effects of steady, personal service has been the encouragement of local leadership. In all the government services this has happened as part of the independence movement, and it is not surprising that the results in such rapid development have been patchy. It has happened with great goodwill in the churches, so that missionaries from overseas have been very ready to serve under indigenous leaders. I was delighted, in Ruth's pages, to meet Ravu Henao. He was deeply rooted in family and village life but became a minister for the new nation, an open-hearted friend who seemed to me a model of what a bishop is called to be. This transition of Christian leadership owed much to the modesty and grace of the missionary teachers who led the way.

The new reality of Christian mission means that life-time service in another culture will be a very exceptional option; short-term service is more likely to meet the needs of the church and the regulations of the government. But I dare to hope that there will always be those who throw in their lot, *totus porcus,* to become sisters and brothers with distinctive gifts in a foreign land, and so reveal the joy of the Household of God.

Bernard Thorogood

Pymble, New South Wales, January 2014

Revd Bernard Thorogood, served with the London Missionary Society, later the Council for World Mission in the South Pacific (Cook Islands and Kiribati) from 1953-1970. He was General Secretary of CCWM/CWM from 1970-1980 and General Secretary of the United Reformed Church UK from 1980-1992.

CHAPTER 1: "SAIL OH!"

I AWOKE AT 5 AM ON 22ND JULY 1966, a little nervous about missing the boat, but I need not have worried, as the cry of "Sail Oh!" was not heard until 7 AM, by which time I was ready. Not that there was a sail, but every ship was hailed in the same way. This time it was the motor vessel (MV) Moturina, who plied her trade up and down the southeast coast from Port Moresby to Samarai (map 1). I did not board the boat in Amazon Bay until around 8.30 AM as people and supplies had to be off-loaded, and copra (the kernel of the coconut used to extract coconut oil) and people taken on.

Amazon Bay, home of the Mailu people, was in the Central District of the Territory of Papua and New Guinea. I had spent a few days there, at Iruna Hospital in order to learn from the resident doctor, Nick Thomson, a New Zealander, as much as possible about treating sick people in this part of Papua. It was an invaluable time, but all too short, as I needed to catch the fortnightly boat when it came through. However, I did manage to fit in two patrols to local villages, one by sea, and the other by tractor to an inland village. Afterwards I felt a little more confident about holding village clinics, although I had found both journeys rather arduous.

I was heading for Fife Bay, further down the coast in Milne Bay District, the home of the Suau people (map 2, for locations in my District, and details of Fife Bay). It was remote and could only be reached by boat, unlike Iruna, which had an airstrip, and was therefore more accessible, although it had not seemed so when I boarded the small Cessna flown by the Missionary Aviation Fellowship (MAF) that brought me from Port Moresby (plate 3). There was only room for

1

four passengers and we sat with our luggage piled up around us. The plane flew over the Owen Stanley mountain range (plate 4) to stop at Popondetta on the north coast, to deliver supplies and refuel. I had an amazing view of the Owen Stanley mountains. They were vast and extensive and far larger than I had imagined. We then flew south to Amazon Bay.

Sally Green, a friend and colleague from the UK, had also been appointed to Papua, and we had travelled out from England together. Sally and I had spent a few days in Moresby, meeting people, attending the government-run Maternal and Child Welfare clinics, and generally trying to acclimatise, before we went our separate ways. Sally headed west to the Gulf area of Papua to work at Kapuna Hospital, that like Iruna was a Nurse Training school. Two doctors, also from New Zealand, a husband and wife team, Lyn and Peter Calvert, staffed Kapuna. Nurses staffed Fife Bay, like so many of the smaller centres and I was to be the Sister-in-Charge. As I was inexperienced and this was my first time in the country, I was a little surprised to be appointed to Fife Bay, because of its isolation, but I assumed correctly, that this was because there was a vacancy there that needed to be filled.

Coastal Boat

There was not a lot of room on the boat, but I managed to find a space near the stern. It was to be an overnight journey and Jan, Nick's wife had provided me with some food, but not long after we left the shelter of Amazon Bay for open sea, I began to be very seasick! The Australian captain took pity on me, his only expat passenger and leant me his cabin, the only one on the ship. The sheets and pillowcases on his bunk were an odd grey colour and looked as if they had not been washed for a long time but I was past caring and fishing out a small towel from my bag, to cover the pillowcase, I laid my head on the pillow and drifted into a fitful sleep.

The Moturina called into several bays to off-load goods and disembark, and to pick up more passengers. It was very well laden, with livestock as well; pigs and chickens were hauled on board in home-made containers, protesting loudly at the indignity of it all. The toilet facilities were somewhat primitive, but as the local Papuans seemed to manage I felt I should also. I was, however, very grateful to the captain for giving up his own space to me. He seemed to sleep very little as he negotiated the vessel through rocks and reefs into beautiful, secluded bays where local people awaited his arrival. He also carried the mailbags and I was to discover that this was the only way mail could be collected or delivered.

After a very rough night of pitching and rolling, which seemed to go on for ever, I realised that although my father and brother had both spent many years in the Royal Navy, I was definitely not cut out to be a sailor. I emerged in the morning to somewhat calmer seas, and Alan, the captain, pointed out a coconut plantation to me. It bordered the black sandy beach and, behind the plantation, mountains covered in tropical rain forest rose up to the skyline.

"That's Gadaisu," Alan said cheerfully, "it's the end of your District."

I must have looked puzzled as he continued,

"You will be patrolling up to here."

I was a little surprised, as the reality of that type of work dawned on me.

"How will I get there then?" I asked, as we drew away from the shore.

"Oh," he said, "You have to walk." I was horrified.

"Is it far from Fife Bay?" I heard myself asking.

"Quite a way," he said, " but if we are in the area, you can always come back on the boat, or travel by canoe," he added as an afterthought.

I felt a tight knot in my stomach; I had proved to be a poor sailor, and I knew I was definitely not a walker. For the first time since I had left Sydney and the safety of All Saints' College, I felt a sense of misgiving. What on earth was I thinking of coming to this country, if I could not meet the demands it would place on me? But there was no going back and by the time we reached Fife Bay about 4 PM on 23rd July, I had begun to feel a little more optimistic.

Arrival at Fife Bay

The boat anchored in the bay, and I stepped off it into a canoe with an outboard motor that took me to the beach. I was glad to be on dry land. Revd Alan Dunstone was there to meet me, as was Revd Ravu Henao, the District Minister to whom I would be accountable during my time at Fife Bay. Alan was feeling unwell, but had got out of bed to come to meet me. In fact he was my first patient, although I only had some aspirin to give him. He was suffering from PUO (pyrexia – fever – of unknown origin) and I was to discover that it was a common problem in Papua.

Alan and his wife Wendy had been at Fife Bay for about six months, having first spent some time at Veiru in the Delta. They had a little boy, Andrew, a two-year old, who called me aunty Loof. I was to stay in their house for a few weeks as the Sister's house was rather dilapidated and needed some repairs before I could move in. Alan was Principal of Lawes College, the theological training college for student ministers and their wives. There were 15 families in the college at that time, with around 35 children between them, coming from all over Papua and speaking many different languages. Also on the staff were a Samoan couple, the Revd Tavita Samuelu and his wife Bertha, who lived in Samoa House. They had a little girl called Miriam, who could speak four languages!

Although Lawes College had a truck and a generator, neither of them worked, so we had no electricity and had to manage with pres-

4

sure and hurricane lamps. As a child I had grown up in the country, with no electricity, so I did not find this too difficult. At Fife Bay there were no roads so we did not really miss a mechanised vehicle, although it did mean that all cargo from the boat had to be carried up the hill by hand, usually by Lawes College students.

Ravu and his family lived at the Head Station at Isuleilei, about half a mile away. He invited me over to tea the next day to meet his wife Lahui and their children. I was disconcerted to find that my predecessor, the Samoan Sister, had already left, but I did meet Mary, the Papuan nurse who was qualified in Maternal and Child Health. Fortunately Mary came from the Suau area, and therefore the local language, also known as Suau, was her native tongue.

Introduction to the Hospital

The next morning I went down to the Hospital, and found it was already busy with outpatients who had come for treatment. There were two wards, a General ward and a Maternity ward (plate 5), that included a separate Labour ward. All were made of local materials, with corrugated iron roofs to catch rainwater. The General ward only consisted of a floor and a roof, but some local men were making new walls from *kipa*, the woven bark of the nipa palm (*Nypa fruticans*). The patients had to be housed in some empty students' houses nearby, until the wards were finished.

The Labour ward also doubled as a theatre for any minor procedures, and contained the DDA cupboard (Dangerous Drugs Act), a high bed for deliveries and a large cot, protected with mosquito netting, for the newborn. There was also a shelf for notes. On the corner of the Maternity ward was the all important water tank that collected rainwater from the roof. There were of course no taps and no running water in the Hospital itself. Adjacent to the Maternity ward was a small space where we could sterilise instruments and syringes in a fish kettle using a primus stove. This was not ideal but it was better

Fife Bay Hospital - Maternity ward on left,
General ward on right

Fife Bay Hospital Maternity ward

6

than nothing. We were unable to sterilise dressings but kept them in clean packs. We made our own cotton wool balls from a cotton wool roll, and we had some open weave bandages and a few crepe bandages and slings.

The Maternity ward had five beds, and the General ward, which was divided into three rooms, had only one bed with a spring and a mattress, but there was floor accommodation for up to 12 patients. Normally, most local people would sleep on a mat on the floor, so this was not unusual, but the addition of relatives meant that space was at a premium. I saw a pile of what look liked parts of wooden beds in one corner and made a mental note to sort them out later. The family usually accompanied a patient to Hospital, sometimes on foot, sometimes by canoe (plate 6), and stayed with him/her throughout their treatment. This added to the overcrowding, but the advantages of this arrangement were that relatives cared for a patient and would cook for him/her and provide psychological support. The nurses were thus freed for more specific duties.

As well as Mary B and myself we had two Nurse Aides, Olinda and Liasa, who had received in-house training. As we looked after Lawes College students, their wives and families, as well as the school children and village people, we were quite busy. Tuberculosis and pneumonia were common illnesses requiring admission, and injuries and axe wounds were frequently seen. Outpatient clinics were held morning and evening on the Hospital veranda. At these clinics we treated the more common ailments, coughs, colds, sores, tropical ulcers, intestinal parasites and ever-present malaria. Although sometimes patients were ill enough to be admitted, most of them were happy to go on their way. Cough medicine was very popular, as was "rubbim", a liniment for aches and pains, but the most popular of all was Gentian Violet (GV), a mauve skin paint that was very good for sores caused by mosquito bites. Most school children sported purple patches on their legs that they were quite proud of. Although Papua Ekalesia (the Papuan Church) did most of the medical work along the

Fife Bay Hospital General ward
Miriam and Andrew on veranda to right

coast, the government supplied drugs, bandages and such like that had to be ordered and brought in by boat.

On that first morning, I looked in the DDA cupboard to see what supplies we had and discovered that not only was it not locked but that it was also full of cockroaches! They had a habit of eating the labels off the boxes, so had to be banished, but it was difficult to keep any cupboard cockroach-free. The main medical store was situated under Sister's house. We had a reasonable supply of basic drugs. As well as penicillin we had sulphadimidine (one of the sulphonamides, a bacteriostatic, used for some infections.) and the antibiotic tetracycline. For pain we had aspirin, codeine and morphine, plus pethidine for women in labour. Malaria was treated with chloroquine and quinine. For asthma we had aminophyline, ephedrine and also adrenaline. Paraldehyde and phenobarbitone were for sedation and in addition we had intravenous fluids.

I also discovered that there were no toilets for Hospital patients. Mary said that the toilets had fallen down and had not yet been rebuilt. It was difficult to get people to build or do repair work, as the Hospital had no funds and all work had to be voluntary, although sometimes patients' relatives would lend a hand (plate 7). As we had village men already at work on the Hospital they agreed to build two toilets, one for each ward. This involved digging a large hole and building a *small house* around it, with or without a seating arrangement inside. Because the water table was quite high it was not an easy job to accomplish and several sites had to be abandoned. We were able to give the men some food by way of payment, and they seemed satisfied with that. Village people often used designated areas of the bush for toilet purposes, but as we wanted to encourage healthy living, I felt quite pleased when I saw the two toilets being used regularly.

Location

I had been told that the further east one travelled in Papua, the more beautiful it became. This seemed to be true of Fife Bay, which though isolated was very beautiful (plate 8). The Bay was large and irregular, as if some giant mouth had taken a large uneven bite out of the land. The Mormore mountain range rose from the foothills above the black-sanded beach. It took about four-and-a-half hours to walk around the bay. Coconut palms swayed in the breeze and coloured shrubs and kapok trees grew in abundance. Isuleilei, the church's District headquarters, and Lawes College were situated somewhere in the middle of the bay about half a mile apart. The Hospital was in between the two. The government Patrol Post and centre of local administration was about ten minutes' walk away, and was staffed by an Australian couple, Kay and Geoff.

Mary said she would show me Sister's house, and took me up the hill. Because it was between Lawes College and Isuleilei, it was known as Middle House. It looked rather large and dilapidated to my uninformed eye. A row of tightly curled heads peered over the veranda to get a better look at the new Sister. The house was built high up on 8 ft wooden piles, and for some reason it reminded me of a shoebox standing on legs, with a roof on. The centre was divided by partitions and these formed the main rooms, with an open veranda running all the way round. The walls were made of local materials, mostly *kipa*, or local bark. Some of the outside walls were hanging off, or missing altogether. There were numerous damp patches on the floor where the roof had leaked. I counted over twenty.

Only half the house was occupied and was shared by three nurses and three schoolgirl boarders. I glanced around, felt discouraged and decided to look at the kitchen, which we would all share. It now occupied part of the veranda. The original building, that had been separate from the house, had fallen down the previous year, so I was told, and would not be replaced. The four concrete piles on which it had been built still stood erect in the back garden. In the corner of the makeshift kitchen stood an ancient wood stove, belching out black smoke. Alongside it, looking rather out of place, stood a stainless steel sink piled high with unwashed dishes. Next to the sink was a rickety table, on which were the remains of a hurriedly eaten meal. A bucket of water stood on a box near by. I could see now why Alan and Wendy had suggested I stay with them for the time being.

I decided to take up Ravu's invitation to tea and was somewhat revived by Lahui's tea and cakes. Their children were very entertaining, and Ravu promised to organise some repairs to Middle House, for which I was glad.

Night Call

I had reason to wish that I had done a tropical diseases course, when on the third night after my arrival someone banging on the door woke me about midnight. I had been late to bed as I had been called out around 10 PM to a sick child and so was reluctant to get up again. At the door stood a man with a hurricane lamp. "Please come," he said, "one man is mad at the Hospital. " I followed him feeling apprehensive. The patient was in the Maternity ward, which fortunately was empty that night. He was a young man, who was being held down by four other young men. I recognised them as Lawes College students, living at Isuleilei. Ravu had come over with them and Mary had also been called.

The patient, Mareko, was raving and violent. Ravu explained that he had had a convulsion and they had carried him over on a home-made stretcher. I was nonplussed. He had no history of epilepsy or mental illness, and as he had a high fever it was unlikely to be a psychotic episode. "He has cerebral malaria," Ravu said to me quietly. I could not recall having heard of that form of the disease, and had little idea of the treatment. I knew we had anti-malarial drugs but was uncertain of the correct dosage. I drew Mary to one side and asked her what she would normally do in such a situation. Mary gave me a quizzical look and I could imagine her wondering what sort of incompetent person she had been landed with. "We don't have malaria where I come from," I said, but it sounded a feeble excuse even to me. I had left all my books behind to follow by sea with my other luggage, as we had been restricted to one small suitcase on the plane to Iruna. But now I wished I had brought my *materia medica* with me.

After consulting with Mary, I gave Mareko ten mls of chloroquine by injection to treat the malaria. It seemed a large dose, but he was very ill. I also gave him a dose of paraldehyde, also by injection, in an effort to sedate him, as he was exhausting himself and his friends with his agitation. Apart from a small amount of phenobarbitone it was the only sedative we had. I prayed silently, "Please God don't let him die, either from the illness or the blunderbuss treatment I have given him." Mary and I took it in turns to sponge him down with cool water in an effort to reduce his temperature and after a couple of hours he became quieter and finally he fell asleep, which I took to be a good sign. He seemed settled enough for Ravu and his three friends to leave. Two of his *wontoks* (a Tok Pisin word, a form of Pidgin, derived from the English *one talk* meaning people from the same language group or village) said they would stay with him for the rest of the night. Mary and I waited a little longer then decided to go to

11

bed as well, as by that time Mareko was sleeping soundly and there was little more we could do.

I told his friends to call me if he got worse and set off home, but it was only after I got outside that I realised that I had no light to see by. I had not yet learnt never to go out at night without a torch or a lamp. It was a cloudy night and very dark. I contemplated going back and asking one of the men to accompany me with the one remaining hurricane lamp, but realised that it would leave the ward in complete darkness, so did not do so. It was not far so I set off, but before long I realised I was hopelessly lost, having wandered off the path into some long grass. I started sneezing, as I am allergic to grass pollen, and tried to recall what Alan had said about the presence of snakes in the area. Suddenly I was seized by a fit of giggles, a sign, I think, of the stressfulness of the situation. I wondered if I would have to stay there till morning, when the moon moved out from behind a cloud and I caught a glimpse of the outline of the Big House, as Alan and Wendy's home was called, on a hill to the right. I walked as fast as I could towards it, and fell in to bed fully dressed in case I was called out again.

I awoke at first light and went down to the Hospital. Mareko was still asleep but he was less feverish, and his friends were cooking rice for his and their breakfast. When I went down later he was awake and although he looked pale, he had had some tea, and was talking and behaving normally. It was with an enormous sense of relief that I gave him some chloroquine tablets and a couple of aspirin for a residual headache. Next day he was well enough to go home. I felt so grateful for answered prayers, to Ravu for his on-the-spot diagnosis, and to Mary for her support. Although everyone thought that my getting lost at night was very amusing, I did not wish to repeat the experience and when Lawes College store opened I bought a hurricane lamp and a large torch!

CHAPTER 2: A LONG JOURNEY

Travelling from the UK to Papua was a journey of over 10,000 miles, but the beginning of that journey stretched back over the years to the time when, as a child barely into my teens, I felt convinced that God was asking me to prepare for work in the church overseas.

I was born and brought up on the outskirts of the Essex village of Ingatestone. My father worked on a farm and we lived in a tied cottage without gas, electricity or running water. My father worked seven days a week for small wages, and my mother was a housewife. She was a good manager but money was always tight. My brother Fred was eleven when I was born and I am told he was very excited at having a baby sister. I loved the countryside and the farm animals. The village, chapel and school were a couple of miles away and as we had no other form of transport, we walked or cycled everywhere. Following in my father's footsteps, Fred left home to join the Royal Navy when he was seventeen and I was six. We did not see a lot of each other after that. I was a regular member of Ingatestone Congregational Church, where my parents and friends worshipped Sunday by Sunday. I went through the usual rebellious period when I wanted to abandon all thoughts of Christianity, but I returned whilst I was still at school and entered fully into the life of the Church.

The minister at that time was Revd Norman Williams and he took what I said so seriously that he accompanied me to London when I was 14 to meet Mrs Francis Bowers, the candidate secretary for LMS. She impressed upon me that to work overseas I would need to be qualified in teaching or nursing or an allied profession "in order to be any use." When I left school at 15, I was offered a job by Essex County Council in a children's residential nursery in Harlow in Essex. I saw this as a first step to becoming qualified and accepted the job as a nursery assistant even though it meant living away from home. So at 15 years and three months, I was launched into the adult world of work.

Nursery Nurse

I enjoyed nursery work but was keen to obtain a nursing qualification. I would peruse the Nursing Times each week and when I was 16 and a half, I answered an advertisement to become a nursing assistant in a London Hospital for mentally retarded children, as they were then known. The Matron at the nursery and my parents were none too pleased, when Averil, my friend and fellow nursery assistant, announced that we were leaving to begin work in London.

Major Conflict

The Fountain Hospital in Tooting in southwest London was to have a profound influence on my life. I was totally unprepared for the numbers of severely handicapped children that lived within its walls. The children were housed in long wards of 60 or more; their beds were at the far end of the ward, whilst the day room, office and kitchen were at the top end. There was a concrete yard outside for more able children to play in. Averil and I were too young to train but the Hospital was so short of staff that almost anyone who applied was taken on. Several overseas people on the staff had very little English and had found it difficult to obtain employment and were therefore glad of any job. We spent the entire day washing, feeding and looking after the children, many of whom were severely physically handicapped as well as being mentally disabled.

I found it difficult to believe that God could allow such innocent children to suffer so badly in what were often far from ideal condi-

14

tions. Many children had no visitors at all; their families, who may have been advised to forget them, had apparently abandoned them. This seemed to have been the prevailing attitude at the time. I was totally shocked by the situation, but I persevered and like so many others on the staff, I did what I could to make the children's lives more bearable. I tried to talk to various people in and outside the church but it was difficult for them to understand the extent of what I felt to be the problem, and I became quite depressed. Eventually, however, after much thought and soul searching I came to an understanding that enabled me to see that God did not intervene to prevent suffering but that He was present in the midst of it all. This understanding allowed me to continue with the work, which was often distressing and difficult.

As soon as I reached the age of 18, I applied to the training department of the Hospital and was accepted by them for the three-year training. So I became a student nurse and, together with Averil and several other friends, I began the training for the RNMD (Registered Nurse for the Mentally Defective) qualification, as it was then known.

In December 1957, Averil left to get married to her fiancé Ray Brown, whilst still in her third year, before taking her final exams. Ray worked for the government of East Africa in Tanganyika, today's Tanzania, and he had to return early in 1958. They got married on 18th January 1958, on a freezing cold day. I was a bridesmaid, and wore a white imitation fur cape over my dress to keep out the cold. After a short honeymoon in Bournemouth, Averil and Ray left by boat for East Africa, in early February 1958.

Tanganyika Visit

I qualified in December of that year, and stayed on to work as a Staff Nurse. However, early in 1959, I received an invitation to spend some time with Averil and Ray in Tanganyika. They were settled in an area near the village of Ngudu, where Ray worked as a veterinary officer, combating tsetse fly, which causes disease in cattle. Averil was pregnant and in need of some friendly company. I jumped at the chance to visit Africa and spend some time with my friends. In March 1959, my brother saw me off at Heathrow when I flew out to Entebbe on Lake Victoria. I had to spend one night in a hotel there, before boarding a plane for Mwanza, the town nearest to Ngudu, the other side of the lake. I was 21 and very excited at the prospect of foreign travel. I had not realised at the time that it was unusual for a young single woman to be travelling alone. I had to fend off a few lone males who were propping up the bar, keen to spend the night with an apparently unattached female!

Staying with Averil and Ray was an eye opener. The place was quite isolated and the people were poor, with many health problems. There was a colonial feel to the set up and expats met at their club for sundowners most evenings, waited on by African staff. Averil and Ray had a houseboy called Afmali, as was the custom. He lived with his wife and children in a little house behind their bungalow. Averil's baby was due in April and in order to be near Hospital when the time came we all three moved to Mwanza to stay with friends of theirs. Mwanza was a sizeable town but there was quite a lot of wild life, including monkeys, which could be seen swinging in the plane trees.

Averil's elder daughter, Linda, was born on 18th April 1959, in Mwanza Hospital. The Hospital had no laundry facilities, and I walked into Hospital each day to return with soiled nappies and clothing. These were washed by hand but at least drying was not a problem. We returned to Ngudu after about 10 days and Averil had to cope as best she could with the difficult conditions of heat and flies and a new baby. Ray went back to work and Linda thrived. Meanwhile I enjoyed getting the feel of life in East Africa.

I did manage to fit in a trip to the Serengeti National Park with a husband and wife stationed at Ngudu. We went in their Land Rover and camped in the rest houses provided for the purpose. I was able to see a lot of wildlife and it was altogether a very exciting experience.

16

Back in England my father became ill following a heart attack and I returned to spend some time with my mother.

Nurse Training

Fortunately my father made a good recovery and I turned my attention to the next phase of my training – General Nursing. I applied and was accepted for a shortened SRN (State Registered Nurse) course at Mile End Hospital in the East End of London. The Hospital had an active Christian Fellowship that I joined. Initially I was resident in the Nurses' Home, but during the second year, five of us rented a house not too far from Hospital. By this time I had passed my driving test and Revd Norman Williams, who had moved to Burnham-on-Crouch in Essex, gave me his old car, a Ford Standard. Friends and I enjoyed getting around London and the country although it was definitely past its sell by date and kept breaking down.

I enjoyed the General Nursing training, and I took the opportunity to learn and observe as much as possible about diagnosis and treatment, knowing that one day I might be on my own somewhere, and be glad of the extra knowledge. I obtained my SRN qualification in December 1961 and stayed on for a few months as a Staff Nurse. Living and working in the East End was an interesting experience because of the different ethnic groups that lived there. There was a big Jewish population who sometimes became our patients and I learnt a lot from some of them who had immigrated to London during the Second World War.

A friend in my set, Merle Johnson, and I decided to do our Part One Midwifery training at Mile End Hospital, as it had a good reputation. We completed this in August 1962, but had to move elsewhere to do our Part Two training as that meant working for some time on the district, doing home deliveries. Merle was keen to go to Sheffield, and as I had little knowledge of the north of England I agreed to go with her. We went to Nether Edge Hospital for the Hospital part of the training, and were there during the very bad winter of 1962-63, when the snow fell several feet deep. This coincided with our three months' district experience. Most of the pupil midwives were housed in a hostel for this period, but another girl and I were asked to live with a training midwife. We were often called out at night, sometimes to women who had had little or no antenatal care, and who lived in poor conditions. Mostly we travelled on the bus or walked, but whatever time of night we got in we had to re-sterilise everything in the midwifery bag in case we were called out again half an hour later. However it was good experience and both Merle and I qualified as midwives entitled to practice in our own right in June 1963.

Carey Hall

During this time I had kept in touch with LMS, who now considered me to be sufficiently qualified to undertake the candidates' procedure. This involved various interviews, medicals, training days and finally an appearance before the LMS Board. They accepted me, and it was agreed that I attend the Selly Oak missionary training Colleges in Birmingham.

There were six theological colleges, four of which received students from the major non-conformist denominations. These were Carey Hall, St Andrews, Kingsmead and Overdale. The Quakers attended Woodbrook, and the Anglicans went to The College of the Ascension. In addition there were two more colleges, Westhill, a teacher training college, and Fircroft, a men's college that had a link with the trade unions. These eight colleges provided us with a rich mixture of people and ideas. Merle was also due to go to Selly Oak as she had been accepted by BMS (the Baptist Missionary Society) to go to the Congo. I did not know at this stage where I would be going but I did express an interest in India, as it was a country that I had always felt drawn to. However I had made an open offer to LMS, which meant I could be sent to any of the countries where LMS worked, if there was a suitable vacancy.

18

Merle and I started at Carey Hall, the college for BMS and LMS candidates and Presbyterian deaconesses, in September 1963. The college was named after William Carey, a missionary well known in Baptist circles. It was an all-female college as our male counterparts were housed in nearby St Andrews, on the same campus. The Methodist missionary candidates attended Kingsmead, the Methodist college. There was a central staff of lecturers and professors, and college students came together for lectures. There was a varied curriculum of theological and Biblical studies as well as a programme of practical subjects such as car maintenance, bookkeeping, hairdressing and emergency dentistry. We also had to take services in local churches and were critiqued on these on a regular basis. The curriculum covered many subjects in an attempt to prepare us for life overseas. I enjoyed it all immensely as I had missed out on a higher education and this seemed to fill in some of the gaps, although I did draw the line at learning New Testament Greek.

For my practical experience I opted to do a placement in the local psychiatric Hospital where I worked in the outpatient clinic with Dr Bob Lambourne, a psychiatrist with unusual ideas. He allowed me quite a lot of leeway when treating his patients, as he encouraged me to talk with them unsupervised. I learnt a lot and was very grateful for the experience. Sadly, after I had left Birmingham I heard that he had died from a heart attack. He had been ill previously and my friend, Stella Smith and I had visited him in Hospital. I have a signed copy of his book, *Community Church and Healing* (Lambourne, 1963) and his thinking influenced my perceptions on mental health issues.

I became very friendly with a Baptist Minister from St Andrews and went out with him for some months, but as he was destined for the Congo and I had by then been told it was likely that I would be posted to Papua, we parted company. My parents and older brother Fred, who by now was married with a family of three boys, realised by this time that I was not going to grow out of the notion of working overseas and were supportive.

After I left Birmingham, I lived at home and worked as a midwife in a small maternity home in Brentwood to get some experience. It was confirmed by the LMS Board that I was to be appointed to Papua and I was commissioned, along with others going to different parts of the world, from the General Assembly of The Congregational Church in England and Wales in May 1965, when I was presented with the Bible in Motu, the language in mainland Papua. We had discussed my going to India but they were in need of Sister Tutors and I did not have that qualification. It was also thought (quite rightly) that I would have problems learning the language. My friend from Carey Hall, Stella Smith, was appointed to South India but was unable to take up the post owing to ill health, but she was supportive of my efforts, and kept in touch with my parents, as did my friends Averil and Ray.

I was commissioned by my local church at Ingatestone on 9th January 1966. My uncle, my mother's youngest brother, Revd Charles Attridge who was a Congregational minister took part, as well as Revd Norman Williams, who had supported me through out the process. Several people representing LMS were present. Revd Maxwell Janes gave the address, and Mary Cumber, who had replaced Mrs Bowers as Candidate Secretary, also attended. A number of my friends from Carey Hall and Mile End, as well as local friends and

INGATESTONE CONGREGATIONAL CHURCH

ORDER OF SERVICE

for the

COMMISSIONING

of

MISS C. RUTH ARCHER,
S.R.N., S.C.M., R.N.M.S.

as a Missionary appointed by the
London Missionary Society
to serve the Church in Papua

SUNDAY, 9th JANUARY, 1966
at 6.30 p.m.

UNTO GOD BE THE GLORY IN THE CHURCH BY CHRIST JESUS

Ruth's Commissioning Service document

neighbours, also came. We had a reception afterwards in the church hall and it was a very meaningful occasion.

Emigration

I left England for Australia on 16th January 1966, at the age of 28, with Sally Green, who was also a nurse and came from Hayes in Kent. We were emigrating under the £10 assisted passage scheme, as it was a cheap way of getting us out there.

When we arrived in Sydney on January 18th, Revd Norman Cocks, LMS Secretary for Papua and his colleague Daphne Watt met us. I stayed with Daphne for a few days whilst Sally stayed with friends. We were to spend six months at All Saints' College in Haberfield in Sydney. The Principal was Revd Frank Whyte, who with his wife Nina had been missionaries in India. We also attended the Australian School of Pacific Administration to learn more of life in Papua.

I enjoyed the six months in Sydney, although I experienced some culture shock. Sally and I were the only two 'poms' at All Saints and sometimes we were teased about our English ways, especially after I mistook a fly swat for an egg slice when I was cooking breakfast! Sally and I both wanted to see something of Australia during our stay, so over the Easter holidays we travelled south with an Australian friend and a New Zealander, ending up camping in Canberra over a very cold weekend. Before we left for Papua we visited Rockhampton in Queensland with the same Australian friend who lived in Rocky. We came back by train to Brisbane in mid-June in time to catch the boat to Port Moresby.

Arrival in Port Moresby

We were at sea for about a week. It was not a very comfortable journey, due to rough seas but when at last we docked in Port Moresby Harbour at about 9 AM on 29th June 1966, there was a feeling of satisfaction that I had arrived at last. Both Sally and I had to complete a three-year probationary period within Papua Ekalesia before being finally accepted. Whilst in Port Moresby we were based at LMS headquarters at Metoreia. The house and a cluster of other buildings, including a church had been built by WG Lawes. When we arrived the house was full, and we both stayed nearby in a Hostel for Papuan girl students, but ate our meals in the house. Metoreia was situated near the village of Hanuabada, which was built on stilts over the sea, inland of the harbour. We were told that the children learnt to swim before they could walk to avoid accidents.

Our first job was to go into town and register as trained nurses with the Department of Health. We went in by bus as we had no other means of transport, but as most Europeans travelled everywhere by car, it caused something of a stir amongst the local people when we boarded the bus. It was quite an old rickety contraption, very hot and noisy, and we were glad to arrive at our destination. Whilst in town we visited the House of Assembly of Papua and New Guinea, a modern building that was the Papuan Parliament. On the way back we decided to walk, but a white woman in a car stopped and gave us a lift back to Metoreia, apparently it wasn't usual for expats to walk either!

I'm not sure if the stress of leaving All Saints or the boat trip made me forgetful, but I mislaid my letter of introduction from LMS to Papua Ekalesia, but fortunately no one queried whether I was who I said I was! I also discovered that my allowance had not been paid into the local bank, and as I was completely without funds I had to go to the church office and ask the treasurer for a cash hand-out. It did not feel like a good beginning, but everyone was very good-natured about it all.

However, we did not exactly endear ourselves to our senior colleagues, as they had arranged a lunch party for us to meet some very respected retired members of the missionary community, Revd Percy Chatterton and his wife and Revd Sue Rankin. As we had the morning free we took the bus into town to buy some essentials for our forthcoming move to the country. The bus for the return journey had Hanuabada on the front, so we boarded it quite happily, and it was not until we had travelled several miles that we realised that it was going in the opposite direction. We asked the driver, who said we had to go to Tubusereia first, a village we had never heard of. There was nothing we could do but sit tight, and after a long bumpy ride we arrived at Tubusereia, where the bus waited for half an hour before the return journey. Eventually we arrived back at Metoreia, hot and dishevelled and over two-and-a-half hours late. The lunch was over and the guests were ready to depart. We just had time to mumble embarrassed apologies, and say hello and goodbye. As new recruits we had not made a very good impression on our host and hostess!

Apart from that incident we found our short time in Port Moresby useful. We were given the opportunity to go with two government nurses to an Infant Welfare clinic and we were also able to make a day trip to Gemo Island. This was a fascinating experience as we had already heard and read so much about the place made famous by Constance Fairhall. Gemo was leased to LMS for use as a Hospital for leprosy patients. Two LMS nursing Sisters, Joan Phillips from Wales, and Myra Kennedy from Scotland, were in charge and the Hospital was at the forefront of the work of combating leprosy, a disease that was endemic in the Territory.

Sally was to go to Kapuna in the west and I was on my way to Fife Bay in the east of the country. Neither of us were sure what awaited us and I felt a certain amount of trepidation at the prospect. It felt a bit like jumping out of a plane not knowing where I was going to land, or what awaited me.

CHAPTER 3: A WEEK OF FIRSTS

The first of August 1966 saw the arrival of the first baby to be born at Fife Bay since I had arrived. Thankfully it was a normal delivery of a bonny baby girl. I had had only had three months' experience of normal deliveries before and my midwifery textbooks had still to arrive so I was glad that there were no complications. We were really busy with inpatients, some of whom had to be housed in the Maternity ward. I was surprised by the high incidence of chest infections and pneumonia. We had two types of penicillin, a long-acting procaine penicillin and crystalline penicillin, which was used for more acute infections as it could be given six-hourly or more frequently, if necessary. Tropical ulcers were also prevalent. These were painful and debilitating for the patient and were slow to heal.

During that week I also pulled my first tooth. I had done an Emergency Dental Course whilst I was at the Selly Oak Colleges in Birmingham and surprisingly, Fife Bay was well-equipped with dental instruments. The accompanying course book explained which instrument was to be used for which tooth. There were no other dental facilities for local people who often had decayed teeth partly due to the habit of chewing betel nut, which I believe had a mild stimulating effect. I was as nervous, if not more so, as the patient who had a decayed and painful molar. He was a strong looking man about 30 years of age. As it was a back tooth and I was unable to do a nerve block, which was beyond my scope, I could only infiltrate the gum with local anaesthetic. I knew it would hurt and I explained this to the patient. He was however keen for me to stop dithering and get on with it. I asked Mary to support his head, as we had no proper dental chair, and he was a tall man. Praying that the crown would not break off from the roots I managed to remove the offending tooth although it was quite a struggle. I do not know which of us was more relieved when it was over. The extraction had been painful but the patient had made not a sound. I gave him some long-acting penicillin to combat infection and he went on his way quite cheerfully. I had to retire for a quick cup of tea!

Amputation of Toe

Also during that week I had to do my first piece of minor surgery. An elderly man hobbled in with a very smelly rag wrapped around his right foot. On examination I saw that his big toe was gangrenous. He said it had been like it for a while. I put him on a course of penicillin and finally persuaded him to give us a urine specimen to test for diabetes. He was reluctant to do this, as he was afraid his body fluids might be used for sorcery. Mary was invaluable, as she was able to negotiate with him. In the end we agreed to do the test in front of him and return the specimen to him. Fortunately the test was negative.

He was quite happy to have his toe removed and after boiling up the instruments I set about removing the toe under a local anaesthetic. As I had never done anything like this before I proceeded very carefully. It was not difficult to expose the joint but it was hard to find enough healthy skin to form a flap to cover the wound. The skin was very tough, almost like leather, as he had, like most local people, always walked barefoot. I removed two-thirds of the toe down to healthy tissue and somehow cobbled together what was left. I was right in thinking that he would not worry too much about the cosmetic result as long as he could walk without pain. He seemed pleased with the result, and I admitted him for bed rest to give the foot a chance to heal. Remarkably, he did well and was able to go home after a couple of weeks. I never discovered the cause of the gangrene but I assumed it was probably due to an injury to his unprotected foot. Fortunately there was no sign of the gangrene spreading into his foot or leg.

On Sunday I went to my first communion service at Isuleilei. Ravu led the service in a mixture of Suau and Motu, which was understood by most men. We all sat cross-legged on the floor, women on the left, men on the right, with children sitting facing us. The women wore white dresses and the men wore white shirts and ramis, the customary male attire made of a piece of cloth wrapped around the waist, reaching to the ankles. The people sung unaccompanied but in harmony. I recognised one or two tunes. They also sang perovetas or prophet songs, that had been introduced many years ago from the South Seas, mainly Rarotongan. The men began the tune and the women would join in singing the high notes. The communion wine was coconut milk and the bread was small pieces of hard biscuit, sold in the trade store, but it was entirely appropriate and I felt very much at home.

Samson

Later that afternoon I was called to the Hospital, as one of the pastors had brought his sick baby son in from a distant village. Samson was very ill with pneumonia. The family had walked five hours to reach the Hospital, and were quite desperate. I gave the baby penicillin but what he really needed was an oxygen tent, which of course we did not have. I managed to rig up a small device to attach to the oxygen cylinder, but it was not very effective. I knew that the next 48 hours would be critical, and Mary and I took it in turns to stay with the baby so that the parents could get some rest, but they were never far away. Samson's father prayed quietly, as I knew that Mary and I did too.

I began to realise what it was like to for people to live so far from any sort of medical help. The baby was dehydrated, as he was unable to feed and breathe at the same time. His mother fed him tiny amounts of a glucose mixture that I made up, from a pipette. His veins were too collapsed for me to put up any intravenous fluids. We spent a very worrying night, snatching a few hours sleep when we could. However, Samson proved to be as strong as his namesake, because in the morning we saw the first signs of improvement, although he remained very ill. By that evening he began to take small feeds from the breast and was breathing a little more easily. Mary and I felt we could both go to bed on the second night, as long as one of us could get up to give him his four-hourly penicillin injections. By Tuesday morning his temperature had returned to normal, and we all began to breathe more easily. After a few more days of treatment Samson made a full recovery, for which we were all thankful.

The MV Moturina pulled into the bay in the late afternoon, and next morning I was relieved to see my luggage arriving on a canoe. Eventually it was carried up to the Big House and I had great fun unpacking, especially as Andrew and the schoolgirls who boarded with Alan and Wendy wanted to help me. I was so pleased to be reunited with my medical books, particularly my *Textbook for Midwives* (1961) by Margaret Myles.

Also unloaded were drums of kerosene, essential for our lamps and fridges. The empty drums were floated out to the boat by schoolboys swimming across the bay, guiding drums in front of them. The full drums were pushed overboard and floated to shore in the same way (plate 9). These had to be rolled up the hill to our houses and Hospital. All vaccines were kept in the fridge so it was an important piece of equipment. However the fridges were notoriously temperamental and it took quite a lot of skill to ensure that they were fully operational. I had never seen a kerosene fridge before but soon learnt that it was necessary to keep the flame blue at all times, as a yellow flame spelt disaster. A tank underneath the fridge was filled with kerosene and the wick lit; if we were lucky the flame would stay blue and then all was well as long as we remembered to refill the tank when it was needed. Sometimes the fridge just stopped working and when all else failed it had to be heaved upside down for 24 hrs. For some reason this seemed to rejuvenate it and it would begin operating again.

Ablutions

Another item that required a bit of getting used to was the bucket shower! They seemed to be standard issue, but each one had its idiosyncrasies. The shower consisted of a zinc bucket fitted with a metal showerhead at the bottom. The bucket was attached to a piece of rope tied to the wall. The trick was to fill the bucket with water from a kettle or jug, making sure the water was at the right temperature, then haul on the rope to lift the bucket to the required height. With a bit of luck the water would cascade downwards on top of the, hopefully, already soaped recipient. The water then drained through a plughole, usually going under the house. I always inspected the rope to make sure it wasn't frayed, as if it broke the whole contraption would come down on the bather's head!

CHAPTER 4: LOCAL DISCOVERIES

On the way to have tea with Ravu and Lahui at Isuleilei, I passed the government Patrol Post where Geoff and his wife Kay lived. Geoff was the local government officer and was responsible for law and order in the Suau District. He had a police force of three, headed by a sergeant, and a jail, which was just an ordinary house with a locked door and no windows. Prisoners were only kept there for short periods and spent most of their time cutting the grass, which if left unattended grew very long. I had reason to be aware of this, as I was allergic to grass pollen and already spent a lot of time sneezing!

Ravu and Lahui

I was told that Geoff did a lot of patrolling and assisted the local government council with its affairs. Every two months the council met under its President, a local man, to discuss and augment ways of bringing improvement to the District. Each village elected one person to represent them on the Council, and each man and woman had to pay a council tax. The money was used in various ways, and at the time the council was saving up to buy a boat of its own. That would certainly have made a lot of difference to us at Hospital, as in a medical emergency it took six to eight hours to get a boat out from Samarai, depending on the weather, and the same for the return journey. My family and friends were bewildered by the place names I mentioned, when I wrote to them, so I drew them a map showing the location of the main landmarks (map 3).

Education

There were two primary schools in the area, one run by the government and one by the church. The government school was near the Patrol Post and was staffed by an Australian Head Teacher called Dan,

Schoolgirls at Isuleilei Church

who had Irish connections and striking red hair and a beard. Also on the staff were indigenous teachers, including a man called Nelson, who came from the Territory of New Guinea. He also taught at the church school that was situated at Lawes College, in the afternoon. The government school tended to take children from nearby villages, as it was a day school only. We had no full-time teacher, but

Wendy, who was a qualified primary school teacher, taught at the church school in the mornings whilst Bertha looked after Andrew. Nelson came over in the afternoons on a voluntary basis, as he was keen for children to have the same opportunities. All the teaching was in English as the teachers came from different language groups, and the textbooks, such as they were, were also in English. We hoped that a full time teacher for Lawes College School would join us later in the year. The two schools were in friendly competition but helped each other out when they could.

Many of the children at the church school came from distant villages and were boarders. The boys lived in small groups in a house on their own and the girls lived in staff houses. Some had to stay all term, but some were weekly boarders and were able to go home at weekends. This group was able to bring food back with them and so supplement their diet. We were only able to provide rice and tinned

Schoolboys with their catch of clams

fish called mackerel pike, which seemed to be a staple for adults and children alike, as we provided the same for Hospital patients. The children also had their own gardens to grow food. The staple diet in villages was sweet potato, taro, yams and sago usually cooked in coconut milk, which gave the meal added flavour.

When the children were old enough to go to secondary school, they either had to go to Sogeri High School in Port Moresby, or to Wesley High School, at Salamo on Fergusson Island in Milne Bay, which was run by the Methodist church. There was an entrance exam for each school, and only a few children went on to complete secondary education. The majority ended their school days at primary school level. Many children did not start school until they were eight or nine years old and were therefore in their teens before they left primary school.

Language Problems

The Territory was a linguist's paradise, as over 800 distinctive languages were spoken in the country. I was told that Suau was a relatively easy language to learn but I did not find it easy to find the time to study it. There were no books or written grammar, nor was there anyone to teach it, so I muddled along as best I could. Mary and the other nurses did their best to help me out, but we were kept busy most of the time, so had little time for formal study. They also wanted to improve their English and sometimes were nonplussed by my colloquial expressions. Mary asked me one day "What is this more-or-less that you keep talking about?" I did not find it easy to explain.

Lawes College students also spoke Motu, the main language of the Central District and Ravu's native tongue. There was also a trade language called Police Motu (or Hiri Motu), which was meant to be easier for people to understand. Alan and Wendy both spoke a little Motu, but I only managed a few words. Learning a language has never been easy for me and it was a real disadvantage not to be able to pick up a language quickly as some people can.

The first Suau word that any newcomer learnt was *agutoi*, which was a greeting used at any time of the day, and was also the word used for please and thank you. The school children learning English found our use of different greetings at different times of the day confusing, and often on their way home from school would call out, "Good morning, Sister." Likewise the indirect question that we are so fond of using. I would ask a patient, "You haven't any pain, have you?" To which he would reply, "Yes Sister," meaning, I haven't any pain. I would get confused by this conversation and quickly learnt to ask a direct question, "Do you have a pain?" to which he could only answer yes or no. The second word that I learnt was *aioni*, which means goodbye. It was said in a very musical way, and the sound could carry quite some distance.

There were long strings of vowels in the Suau language such as *taumaeamaeaem* and *woeawoeaedi* that were in the hymn book called the *Buka Wana*. When I looked into my Suau New Testament, *Riba Harihariuna*, I wondered how I would ever be able to pronounce any of the words correctly. The Suau word for a white person was *dim dim*, which I found rather expressive!

Repairs and Uninvited Inhabitants

Ravu was true to his word and sent over a very efficient man to supervise repairs to Middle House and Hospital. Gauleko was a local government councillor, and a man of some authority, which was a great help. In the General ward one room had been used as a kitchen, and I explained to Gauleko that we would like to use this room for patients to sleep in, if he could build the kitchen elsewhere.

It did not take long for the kitchen to go up outside, and although it looked like a corrugated iron shack, the patients seemed quite satisfied with it. The people seemed to need very little in the way of cooking

33

Patients outside their kitchen

facilities. As long as there was a shelf to put vegetables on, and a few big stones to balance the cooking pot on, all was well. Dishes were washed up in a bowl or in the sea where sand was readily available to use as a scourer for more stubborn stains. Gauleko added a lean-to that provided a place to keep firewood dry, and positioned the door away from the wind so that the fire would not go out. A hole was left in the roof for the smoke to go out, but in fine weather patients or their relatives would often light their fire and cook outside the kitchen area. Gauleko also set about repairing the wooden beds, and managed to make up a couple for patients to put their sleeping mats on. This made it easier for us to nurse people who were really ill, rather than their lying on the floor.

We went up to Middle House and I explained what needed to be done and before long the men were up there doing repairs. Alan ordered some paint that came on the boat, and Lawes College students painted the woodwork, which improved things greatly. I was keen to move in, if possible, before Mary went on patrol to the villages. She would be away for over a week and it was not the custom for schoolgirls and nurses to be left alone in the house for any length of time. Mary said she would postpone her patrol until I was in residence.

As I was looking round the house, I became aware of a few extra inhabitants. I saw some brilliant green lizards sparring on a window ledge, and equally green tree frogs lined up like taxi cabs on wooden beams. There were also a lot of ants and ever-present cockroaches.

The legs of food cupboards stood in old tins full of kerosene to deter entry, but I am not sure how successful they were, as there always seemed to be ants in the sugar! My favourites were the geckos; transparent lizard-like creatures, about two-and-a-half inches long, that came out at night and walked across the ceiling, darting about to catch insects for their supper with long forked tongues. Every now and then there was a plop, as one of them lost his grip on the ceiling and fell off onto the floor, but they appeared unharmed as they climbed up again quickly to resume their evening activities. Lahela, one of the schoolgirls showed me some gecko eggs hidden in the crevice of a door, and sometime later I saw a delicate baby gecko, about an inch long, scurrying across the ceiling in pursuit of some fleeing insect, of which there were many.

Communications and cooking

It had been very helpful to me to stay with Alan and Wendy at the beginning of my time at Fife Bay. I needed to talk about my experiences at Hospital and to offload some of my concerns about patients into the willing ears of my colleagues. Andrew was a delightful little boy and liked to come into my bedroom in the morning to play marbles. He had quite a good vocabulary and knew some Suau words, as the schoolgirls, who liked to play with him, enjoyed teaching him their language.

Every day we had a medical *sked*, a scheduled time to speak on the two-way radio. Our time was 12.30 PM, when, if I needed to, I could speak to Dr Peter Calvert at Kapuna Hospital for advice about patients. Our call sign was Delta Echo, Peter's was Bravo Victor, but the reception was often poor and I was only able to get through to him occasionally about serious cases. Often it was quite small things that I need to talk about, which is where Alan and Wendy came in. Alan also used the radio to contact Port Moresby about church or college matters. Without it we would all have felt more isolated as it was a lifeline to the outside world.

I could also contact the resident doctor at the government Hospital in Samarai, on the two-way radio, but it was such a hit-and-miss affair, that I was rarely able to use this facility, nor was it available on Sundays. However in the event of a medical emergency, I had to contact the doctor as only he could obtain permission from the local government authority to charter a boat to pick up a patient from Fife Bay, who needed to be transferred to the Hospital in Samarai. Patients could also travel on the regular fortnightly boat, with their fares paid by the government, provided I obtained the agreement of the doctor before hand.

Wendy had a kerosene stove, as well as a wood stove. The former was useful as it was necessary to make bread on most days. The flour was often full of weevils and had to be sieved first, but some always managed to slip through. We used Dribarm yeast and, as the weather was so hot, it didn't take long for the dough to rise. I had never made bread before and my first efforts were not very impressive but I improved with practise!

As there were no cows in Papua I had to get used to the taste of powdered milk, which we made up in jugs daily. Sometimes the milk we made up was lumpy or too thin but with practise we got it about right. People in villages used tins of condensed milk, available in the trade stores, but I found it too sweet for my taste. They mixed it in with tea in the teapot, so you had to drink it and after a while I got used to it.

Stocks of staples like flour and rice had to be ordered from Samarai or Port Moresby, together with other items, like soap or tinned meat and fish, but it was difficult to get the amount right. The two main stores were Steamships Trading Company and Burns Philp, who both sold a variety of goods. However, sometimes a really basic item like rice would come back marked "No stock Samarai" on the Bill of Lading, so we tried our best to keep some stores in reserve. Fresh meat was in short supply, but we got used to tinned goods, and I developed quite a liking for a tinned meat product called Mountain Maid Mince.

Living so near to the sea meant we were sometimes able to buy fresh fish if students or local men went fishing.

Wendy usually cooked in the evening, when it was cooler. There were plenty of vegetables, as Lawes College students had gardens, and fruit grew in abundance. It took me a while to get used to eating sweet potato, taro or yams, which formed the staple diet. These were all root vegetables, but there were very few green leafy vegetables, apart from silver beat that tasted a little like spinach. There was a large mango tree outside Middle House and numerous pawpaw trees, which bore wonderful fruit if we could get to it before the flying foxes did. Their other name was fruit bat; an apt description. They were furry little mammals with dog-like faces, and webbed feet, so they could fly. Another attractive little creature was the sugar glider, so named, I think, because of its sweet tooth. They were also partial to pawpaw and other fruit.

Less welcome visitors were mosquitoes, and for protection we had to sleep under mosquito nets each night. Europeans had no immunity against the malaria parasite carried by the female *Anopheles* mosquito, and we all had to take anti-malaria tablets regularly. Local people had built up immunity through being bitten over many years, but not before they had suffered considerably from malaria as children. Most people had enlarged spleens as a result of repeated attacks of malaria and some did not survive the more virulent form of the disease. A newcomer, such as I, had to cover every mosquito bite with a sticking plaster, to prevent scratching and subsequent infection, which could develop into a tropical ulcer. I had some insect repellent but this had a limited effect, so when I went outside it was sometimes better to keep my arms and legs covered, even if it was very hot. Most of the time I went around with purple spots all over my legs, as a dab with GV was quite effective in preventing infection. Most people were so used to it that they did not think that I suffered from some unpleasant skin disease!

CHAPTER 5: HECTIC TIMES!

After I had been here almost a month we were finally able to move patients back into the General ward, which made life easier. The local Women's Fellowship had woven some new mats for us from the *Pandanus* plant (the leaves of which are boiled, then dried and woven - see also plate 31 for the plant growing), so it all looked spick and span. I had to do monthly statistics for the Department of Health and since my arrival our numbers had increased to 30 inpatients and 96 outpatients.

Eye Glass

I had a rummage around and found some old spectacles. I was prompted to look for them because an elderly man came and asked for "eye glass" and Mary said we had some in a box somewhere. The man said that he could not see to read his Bible properly, which was the only book he had and his prize possession. I realised how little the people had of the things we take for granted like books and spectacles. I had not envisaged that I would have to be an optician as well as everything else and I wasn't sure how to go about it, but in the end it was quite simple. I took out the glasses and a Bible and the man tried various pairs of glasses on until he found a pair that improved his eyesight and he could read the words on the page. He polished them up and went off feeling quite delighted. I decided to try and get some more specs because I suspected that before long others would come along with a similar request.

Carrying Pandanus

Rolling Pandanus

Boiling Pandanus

39

Time To Say Goodbye

Liasa one of our assistant nurses, was planning to get married and we had arranged for her to go at the end of the month, but her father arrived with a boat and she wanted to leave with him the next day. As she had worked at the Hospital for five years I didn't want her leaving to go unmarked, so we hastily arranged a tea party for that afternoon, to wish her well. This event left us short of staff and Mary and I agreed that we would need to take on some new recruits as soon as we could. Suitable girls from the villages were not difficult to find, as paid work was scarce. I decided to ask Ravu if he knew anyone of in the right age group who would be interested.

An Unusual Student

One of the students at Lawes College, John Gwilliam, was an Australian, who wanted to undertake his ministerial training in Papua, as he felt called to work there. John began his training at Lawes College in 1964 and left at the end of 1966 to continue his studies at the Congregational College in Sydney, Australia. I only knew him for the first six months of my time at Fife Bay. However, I had met John's mother in Sydney and had looked forward to meeting him. Whilst at Lawes College, John taught in the school, which he enjoyed. He also worked with 'Dr' Lameka, a much respected local man, on the Suau Hymn book, the *Buka Wana* that also contained some traditional prayers. It was published by Stanmore Missionary Press and was very well received by local people.

After he was ordained John went on to work at Porebada, in Port Moresby, then Moru, in the Gulf District and finally Kwato, before being appointed chaplain to Port Moresby High School, fulfilling his life's ambition and calling. In 1971, John married Laka, a trained nurse who came from Hula (in the Central district). The couple had two children, Caroline and Steven. Many years later I met with Caroline when she was working in the UK.

First Feast

At the end of the month we had a feast, given by Lawes College students, including John, who had just completed their exams. They had spent the day fishing in preparation for it. The feast was held in the school hall and students' wives decorated it with palm branches and flowers, so it was very attractive. The food was arranged on a long strip of banana leaves, placed on the floor in the centre of the room. Great heaps of cooked bananas lay side-by-side with whole fish and bowls of rice. Dishes of taro and sweet potatoes, with loaves of bread and biscuits from the store, were spread out for people to help themselves. We all sat on mats on the floor, and mothers with babies and small children let them fall asleep where they were, amidst all the din and excitement. When all the food had been eaten and cleared away, it was time for the entertainment, and as it was my first feast in Papua, school children sang a special song of welcome. After that there were various items performed by different groups. The Boy Scouts were very active when it was their turn and there was a lot of slapstick. Everyone joined in the singing and dancing that went on until well after midnight.

A Problem Delivery

Mary and I were called out to a woman in labour before the feast was over. We were up for the rest of the night as it was a difficult case. It was the mother's first child and the baby was lying in the posterior position, which meant that the baby's back was lying next to the mother's spine rather than her abdomen and that made it difficult for the baby's head to enter the pelvis. The optimum position is anterior, so the young mother, Liani, had a prolonged and painful first stage of labour, and a very long second stage of two-and-a-half hours. I was

41

seriously worried, especcially as there were signs of both foetal and maternal distress.

I began to think that I would have to use forceps to assist delivery so I put them into boil, consulting my midwifery textbook as I did so. I had never used forceps but had only seen them used by an obstetrician. We had a vacuum extractor – an instrument to aid the delivery – but the baby's head was too high to get the suction cup to attach to the scalp. Before applying the forceps I decided to make one more effort and found that in the interim the baby's head had finally rotated into the anterior position and descended sufficiently for it to be delivered normally, although I had to perform an episiotomy (an incision in the mother's perineum) to assist delivery, because of the poor condition of the baby.

When she was born, the baby girl did not breathe or cry and she was very shocked and asphyxiated. Liani was also exhausted. Thankfully I was able to resuscitate the baby, while Mary delivered the placenta. When the baby was well enough to breathe on her own, I did the necessary suturing of Liani's perineum and made her as comfortable as I could. After cups of tea all round, we all felt a little better. The baby was too weak to suck but we were able to express a few drops of the mother's colostrum (the first milk that contains antibodies) and give it to the baby on a teaspoon, which she did swallow. We then left baby and mother to sleep.

It was around noon the next day before Mary and I were able to get to bed, after a quick check on the other patients. Although I was very tired, I found it difficult to sleep as I realised how close we had come to losing the baby, and perhaps also the mother. After that experience I realised that I was truly on my own as far as medical help was concerned and that I had better get used to it, as no doubt there would be more to come!

When I went down to the Hospital at about 6 PM, baby and mother were looking much better, and the baby had been able to take her first breast-feed. Papuan mothers have few, if any, problems with breast-feeding, as they have watched their own mothers and other village women breast-feeding their babies throughout their own childhood.

Call Out

That same evening we received a message from a village four hours' walk away, asking if someone could go out and see one of the pastors who was very ill. Alan had left on the boat that morning to go to Port Moresby, so I decided to ask Geoff to take me in his dinghy with an outboard motor, as it sounded urgent. I did not think that either Mary or I, who had each lost a lot of sleep the previous night, could go on an eight-hour hike there and back in the next 24 hours. Geoff agreed to take me at first light and Kay, his wife, said that she would like to come along for the ride. We left at dawn the next day and as this was my first trip outside the bay I felt quite excited. I didn't feel so happy in a small dinghy out in open sea, but after about two hours we arrived at the village of Silo Silo safe and sound.

We found the sick man, Pastor Nickolai, in his house, and when I examined him I realised he had pneumonia and that he was indeed very ill. I started him on a course of antibiotics by injection, and explained to him and his wife that he needed to come back to Hospital with us to continue the treatment. They readily agreed especially as we had the dinghy as transport.

When I came out of the house, I found nine other people lined up on the veranda, asking for treatment of one sort or another. Word had got around the village of our arrival. Fortunately I had bought a small medical kit with me, and was able to treat them all for their various ailments, none of which were serious. The pastor's wife brought us a meal of sweet potatoes and pumpkin cooked in coconut, and some tea without milk, as they did not have any.

43

Just as we were preparing to leave a man came running up and asked me to go with him to the next village, where his father lay dying. Geoff looked resigned and said he would take me in the dinghy and so we set off again. This time I found a very old man lying in a small hut, which had been built for him under the house. Geoff said it was because his family was expecting him to die. His wife, also very old, was there with him in the smoke filled room, and he seemed to have been well cared for. There was little I could do for him as he had pneumonia and was semi-conscious. It was very dark in the room and I could not see very well, but it seemed that he was unlikely to recover. He was certainly too ill to be moved. His eyes were badly infected and must have been painful, and the smoky atmosphere aggravated the condition. I was able to clean his eyes gently to make him more comfortable. He roused when I gave him an injection of long acting penicillin, to fight the eye infection, as I doubted that his chest infection would respond to antibiotics. His son said he was able to drink a little so I gave him the few penicillin tablets that I had, with instructions to give them to his father three times a day, at sunrise, when the sun was overhead, and at sunset, for this was a world without clocks and *chronos* time meant very little. The old man was also dehydrated, so I explained to his son the importance of giving him as much to drink as he could swallow. Before I left I said a prayer with the family in English, and I had a sense that they felt they had done what they could to ease his passing.

Geoff meanwhile was talking over some problem with the village councillor. When he had finished we left in the dinghy and travelled back to the first village to pick up Kay and our patient Pastor Nickolai. His wife had prepared all they needed for a Hospital stay and we all piled into the, by now, rather crowded dinghy. During the afternoon the wind had changed and it was a very rough trip home. Each time the small boat lifted up and smashed down on a wave it was like hitting concrete. Kay and I were both sea sick. I was worried about Nickolai, who was huddled in the stern with a blanket round him, as I felt

44

that such a journey wouldn't do him much good. But we had to go on and eventually we arrived back, soaked to the skin by spray and very glad to be on dry land again. I installed Nickolai in the General ward and we all had a hot cup of tea to help us recover.

Orphan Baby

By the evening I was feeling very tired so I decided to have an early night. I was just getting ready for bed when Olinda came to tell me that some patients had arrived at Hospital. I groaned inwardly, but went out onto the veranda for some fresh air. Never had I seen such a beautiful night sky. Except for the brilliant twinkling of millions of stars, it was absolutely pitch black. The Milky Way lay like a great swathe of honeycomb directly overhead. No artificial light intruded upon the scene, and as the night air was filled with the cicadas' orchestra tuning up, the whole effect was rather magnificent. I spent a few minutes taking it all in before going down to the Hospital.

A small group of adults were sitting on the Hospital veranda, with a young woman who had a bundle in her arms. Inside was a baby about six weeks old, looking like a wizened old man. The girl, whose name was Nina, told me that his mother had died in childbirth and the village people had kept him alive by feeding him on vegetable juice from a spoon. I marvelled that he was alive at all. Weighing only four pounds, he was a bag of skin and bones and was too weak even to cry. A few days before, Nina, who was the baby's sister, had come from Moresby, where she was married to a policeman. Learning of her mother's death she had come to take part in funeral rites. When she found her baby brother in such a pitiful state, she brought him down to Hospital, as she knew we would have supplies of milk. Because he had been given fluids, he was only mildly dehydrated but he was in effect starving and probably would not have lived for many more days.

The baby, whom Nina had named Gordon after a police sergeant, was so hungry and desperate that he was unable to suck from the bottle of weak milk we prepared for him. We tried him with a spoon and as he was used to this, he gulped it down. Mary said she would take him up to the house, so that he could be given a small amount of the weak mixture two-hourly. If he was able to tolerate this we would increase the strength and amount gradually to avoid a stomach upset. The last thing we wanted was for Gordon to succumb to diarrhoea. I finally got to bed about midnight, and there was no further disturbance that night. We continued to feed the baby every two-hours for the next 24 hours and fortunately he tolerated it well. We were then able to extend feeding time to three-hourly, as he was sleeping in-between feeds and was beginning to lose that terrible hollow-eyed look.

After four days, Nina explained that she needed to go back to the village, but that she would return once her mother's feast time was completed. Gordon now weighed five pounds, and had regained his sucking reflex so we were able to give him a bottle. Mary and I took it in turns to look after him at night. When it was my turn, I took him up to the Big House and Andrew thought it was a great joke to have a baby in the house!

Chief Cook and Bottle Washer

After Gordon had been with us for about six days, Wendy went down with a really bad attack of tonsillitis and had to retire to her bed. Alan was still away in Port Moresby, so I had more or less to run the household. Early on Sunday morning, just as I was giving the baby his 6 AM feed, I received a note from Hospital saying, "woman in labour, delivery any minute, please come." I put Gordon back in his cot, which was really a washing basket and called Eileen, one of the schoolgirls, to mind Andrew, and rushed down to Hospital. Mary had beaten me to it, but the baby had beaten us both and lay with his mother on the floor of the veranda where she had given birth. Fortunately both were well, so we moved them into the Maternity ward, and after checking them both, I left Mary and Olinda to clear up and went back to finish feeding Gordon, who by then was wailing for his breakfast.

The Lawes College church service was at 8 AM, and the schoolgirls had Sunday school, so after seeing them off, Andrew and I had our breakfast together. Then I took both Gordon and Andrew down to Hospital to continue the morning routine. I had to remove Andrew from the Labour ward bed several times, where he liked to play *I am the king of the castle*. I was concerned that he might fall off and hurt himself, as it was a high bed, so at about 10.30 AM I took him up to Samoa House to play with Miriam (plate 10). Bertha and Tavita were sitting on their veranda, and they were happy to keep an eye on Andrew, so I made Wendy and me a much needed cup of coffee.

Wendy was definitely improving, and was glad to come off her six-hourly penicillin injections. However, I put her on a course of oral penicillin to ensure that the infection did not return. She got up in the night to take her tablets and groped around in the dark for the bottle, tipped it up and smothered her hands and feet, the floor and just about everything else within reach with Gentian Violet. The bottles were similar in size and Wendy had GV for mouth ulcers, the only treatment we had for them. Fortunately, this GV was made up in water and not spirit, so was easier to wash off, but for a few days her feet and legs looked as if she had contracted some dreadful skin disease. But it was impossible not to laugh and Wendy found it as funny as I did.

Alan came back from Port Moresby late on August 23rd, which relieved the pressure a bit. He brought with him as a special treat, what had been a frozen chicken, now defrosted, as August 25th was their wedding anniversary. Wendy was not well enough to cook yet, so I did the honours, with Wendy giving me instructions when necessary. It was a very pleasant occasion, and although it was hot it was really good to have a roast dinner.

47

CHAPTER 6: MIDDLE HOUSE

Finally, at the beginning of September, I was able to move up to Middle House (plate 11). The men were putting up the last of the *kipa* walls as I moved in, but that did not matter. I was gradually able to unpack all my boxes, and rediscovered some of the things I had bought with me and, most important for me, my books.

Ravu had also helped Mary and me to recruit two more Nurse Aides, Sineleki and Ruta (Papuan form of Ruth), who both settled in quickly. As well as Mary and the other nurses, Middle House was home to three schoolgirls, Merin, Daionesi, and Lahela, all of whom had to be kept an eye on (plate 12). There was also a stray cat, who seemed very pleased to see me, and numerous other occupants of the insect variety. I was surprised to find a house martin's nest in the corner of the sitting room and expected baby birds to make an appearance soon. As there was an open veranda all around the house, the parent birds were able to fly in and out quite freely.

As dusk fell, I was amazed to see the same row of bright green frogs. They seemed to be permanent residents and proved to be very noisy during the wet season when they were mating. Under the house I was fascinated to watch hermit crabs scuttling about. As opportunists, they inhabited discarded shells as protection. By the side of the house we had a huge guava tree, full of ripe fruit. There was competition between flying foxes and schoolgirls as to who could reach them first, as the fruit was so delicious.

Schoolgirls in a guava tree

Kitchen and Bathroom Facilities

I had a separate bathroom that had a water tank on a stand with a tap, but no washbasin. Instead there was a bowl that could be filled up but not emptied, except by throwing the water down the drain (a hole in the floor) of the bucket shower nearby. I quickly got used to this system that on the whole was quite efficient. More of a surprise was the fact that under the house was a WC! The water from the cistern came from the water tank in my bathroom and was erratic at the best of times. I tried it out but discovered that the water tank leaked and was liable to deluge when one was enthroned. I am not sure if I could find a plumber, but if the tank was repaired I think that the toilet would still only be used on special occasions, perhaps if we had visitors. I was also unsure if the nearby septic tank was actually functioning, as no one had any recollection of it being installed or serviced. The usual pit toilet built a short distance from the house was the safest bet, unless the water table was very high.

49

The kitchen was more of a problem. The concrete posts supporting the old kitchen were still standing at the back of the house. The stove had been moved to a section of the veranda that was part of the nurses' and schoolgirls' quarters. It was an ancient wood stove, which was all we had to cook on. It needed a great deal of firewood to keep it going and this had to be collected from the bush. Consequently the stove was only lit twice a day when the girls had their breakfast and evening meal, usually rice and vegetables grown in their gardens.

My first attempts at making bread were pretty disastrous as I found it difficult to do my cooking while the stove was alight, because of my Hospital commitments. Even if I had succeeded in lighting the fire, I did not like to use the firewood collected by the nurses or schoolgirls. If the wood was damp it caused the stove to smoke and its inadequate chimney delivered smoke back into the room. I had a primus stove and I used that to make tea or to boil an egg, but I became increasingly frustrated. Until a solution could be found, I had my main meal with Alan and Wendy in the evening, and Wendy baked an extra loaf for me when she made her bread, for which I was very grateful. Fortunately there was plenty of fruit including bananas, so I did not go hungry. I felt rather uncomfortable about not being able to manage the wood stove and cooking arrangements and I wondered what my predecessor had done. It seemed that she also had had problems, as Lahela told me that most of the time she ate her meals with her compatriots, Bertha and Tavita.

I was looking forward to keeping a few chickens, but would first have to get someone to build me a hen house. There were so many other things that took priority and as the men had only just finished making the repairs to Middle House, I did not like to ask them to do more work. A solution to the problem of the kitchen still had to be found, as I couldn't continue enjoying the hospitality of the Big House indefinitely. It was a good thing that the kerosene fridge stood on the veranda as the whole household needed access to it. We kept all Hospital vaccines in a special compartment and also the antivenin used to counteract snakebite.

50

On September 12th I managed to have my first full day off since my arrival at Fife Bay in July. Until then we had only managed half-days, but as we had two extra nurses I made a rota of time off for us all. However, Mary and I took it in turns to be on call. The nurses were local enough to go home to their villages on their days' off, which gave them a break. I mostly caught up with letters in time to catch the boat, or went for a walk to Isuleilei, or to the local waterfall.

Church Membership

On my first Sunday in Middle House, I was received into Church Membership by transfer from my home church at Ingatestone (plate 13). This took place at the morning communion service, at Isuleilei. Ravu officiated, and I was made to feel very welcome. Unfortunately, I had been up from 11.30 PM the night before until 5 AM with a woman in premature labour, so felt rather bleary-eyed. The baby weighed three-and-a-half pounds but was fortunately quite strong. We had no incubators but the weather was so warm it wasn't difficult to maintain the babies' body temperature if they were well wrapped up. Church Membership of Papua Ekalesia meant that I was now part of the indigenous church and could participate in its life (plate 14). I would be eligible to vote at church meetings and would be under the pastoral care of Ravu, the District Minister.

Influenza Epidemic

During September, the District Council of the Church met at Suau Island. This event attracted a large number of people, but whilst there, there was an outbreak of influenza. On their way home most of them called in to Hospital. We had to admit several older people and the rest we treated as outpatients. Papuans seem to have little immunity against the virus, and some were very ill indeed and developed pneumonia and other complications. In all we treated over 300 people and were run off our feet. We almost ran out of aspirin but fortunate-

51

ly everyone survived, though some people took a while to recover. None of the Hospital staff caught the flu virus and for that we were all thankful.

I made little headway with the Suau language, which I was told was not difficult compared with the other Papuan languages. There were no textbooks and the medical needs of the patients always came first. Unfortunately, I had little aptitude for languages and was not good at picking it up. I should really have set some time aside each day to learn a few words, but there were so many other calls on my time that it didn't happen!

Teaching

Alan suggested that I might like to teach students' wives some basic midwifery skills on one afternoon a week. When appointed to their village pastorates, the people would turn to the pastor's wife for medical help if there was not an Aid Post in that village. I decided to start with normal pregnancy, as it was important for them to know what was normal and what was not. Lives might be saved if complications were dealt with in time. I didn't have much in the way of teaching materials but as most wives already had children it was not too difficult. Fortunately they all understood English, as my Motu was also pretty poor.

Meanwhile, baby Gordon continued to make good progress. He put on weight and was a lively little fellow. However, his sister Nina was becoming restless, as understandably she wanted to return to her husband in Port Moresby. I was not keen for Gordon to leave us until he was older, as bottle-fed babies did not usually do well, outside the supervision of the Hospital environment. Nina was a sensible young woman and it was also important to maintain the bond between the siblings, as Nina was going to raise Gordon as her own child. If she left him behind, the separation would not be helpful to either of them. After much discussion, it was agreed that they would leave as soon as Nina's husband came to fetch them, which was likely to be sometime next month. Nina knew how to sterilise Gordon's bottles and she promised that if he developed diarrhoea and/or vomiting, she would take him to Hospital at once. Nina and her husband were Gordon's best chance of a normal family life, and it would be wrong to deprive him of it.

Our newest baby arrived late one night with his mother and grandparents. They had walked all night to reach Hospital. The baby, a boy, was about 17 days old and weighed under six pounds. When I examined him I realised that he was very ill indeed, as he had broncho-pneumonia and cerebral irritation. He was cold and limp when he arrived, and was unable to feed, so we started antibiotics immediately and fed him expressed breast milk through a naso-gastric tube. I asked Mary to explain to the family that he might not recover, but that we would do our best to help him. The baby, who had not been named, kept having attacks of cyanosis and apnoea (blue colour and stopping breathing) although he maintained a weak pulse. Each time this happened he went quite limp, and his grandmother, thinking that he had died, started to wail in distress. We gave him continuous oxygen through a funnel, the only method we had, and resuscitated him each time. I think I used all methods of resuscitation that I knew. We could not use mouth-to-mouth resuscitation too often because his airways were blocked. He came in on a Friday, and one of us had to stay with him all the time to be on hand to resuscitate him. This continued over the weekend and in that time he stopped breathing at least twelve times. By Sunday evening the antibiotics were beginning to have some effect and his mother was able to breast-feed him for a short time. From Monday onwards the apnoea attacks stopped and we all heaved a huge sigh of relief. We were able to remove the naso-gastric tube later that week and against all the odds he began to thrive.

Third Stage Problems

A few nights later when I was just beginning to recover from nights up with the baby boy, Mary called me about midnight. She told me that a pregnant woman who had been staying in Hospital with her sick daughter was in advanced labour. I had not thought that she was at full term, but remembering that it was her seventh child, I quickly dressed and hurried to Hospital. It had been raining and in the dark I managed to slip and fall my full length. Fortunately only my dignity was hurt, but my uniform dress was wet and muddy. The baby arrived one minute after we did, weighing just under four pounds but was quite vigorous and a good colour.

Fifteen minutes later the placenta had not arrived and the mother began bleeding profusely. Postpartum haemorrhage (severe bleeding after the baby is born) is every midwife's nightmare and I was no exception. When I examined the mother I was horrified to see membranes and what looked like the cervix visible in her vagina. The bleeding showed no signs of stopping in spite of our giving her a second injection of ergometrine, a drug that helped the uterus to contract, and massaging her abdominal wall. Knowing that most mothers were anaemic and that we had no blood to give her, I asked Mary to put up a saline drip while I prepared to remove the placenta manually. I put on a clean gown over my wet and muddy uniform and explained the situation to the mother.

Normally this procedure would have been carried out by a doctor, under a light anaesthetic, and although I had never before carried out the procedure, I knew that if we did nothing she would die. I was afraid to sedate her in her weakened state but asked Mary to give her some penicillin in an attempt to prevent infection. We only had a hurricane lamp which gave a very poor light and that did not help matters. I had brought my torch and had to ask Ruta who was assisting us to hold it and direct the beam onto the Labour ward bed. Praying for guidance, I gingerly examined the mother as gently as I could and discovered that the placenta was partly separated. I managed to remove it manually, and examined it carefully to make sure that it was complete. The uterus contracted and the cervix was no longer visible, and in a few moments the bleeding stopped. The baby was crying and we put him to the breast because the baby suckling also helped the uterus to contract.

The mother was exhausted and my legs were like jelly. Leaving Mary and Ruta to make her comfortable, I went home to change and make a cup of tea. I resolved that I would buy two Tilley pressure lamps for the Hospital as soon as I could. They gave a much brighter light, so that we would not be so disadvantaged again. Before going back to bed I went back to the Maternity ward. The mother had been moved into the ward and although pale she was sleeping peacefully. The baby looked well and was also sleeping. I went home and fell asleep almost immediately, but went down again at first light to check on them both. Ruta had stayed close by for the rest of the night, so she went back to the house to have her breakfast and go to bed. We gave the mother a full course of penicillin and iron tablets but there were no further complications and after a week we were able to discharge them both, as the baby was gaining weight.

I discovered that there were no family planning facilities available for couples in Papua and many women had large numbers of children. With each pregnancy and sometimes no antenatal care, the risk to mother and baby increased. So when her husband came to take his wife and baby home I took it upon myself to advise the couple to delay further pregnancies if at all possible, as the mother needed time to recuperate. Following this event we had a spate of babies arriving; five in ten days. Four of them were born at night, but all were normal deliveries, thankfully. I was pleased that more mothers were coming in to have their babies, as it was safer than having them in the village.

After the influenza epidemic, a number of people came in from the villages with pneumonia. There was a radio broadcast from Port Moresby that mentioned the flu virus could result in a viral pneumonia and that had certainly been our experience. Fortunately I had remained very fit, in spite of the sleepless nights. I usually went to bed early, as the lighting wasn't conducive to doing much after dark.

The last mailbag that arrived brought me some bad news. My aunt Laura who lived in Oxford had cancer of the liver and was very ill. As a child I used to spend my summer holidays with my aunt and uncle Charles at their home in Dedham in Essex. My uncle, who was my mother's youngest brother, was a Congregational minister and had taken on the job of sending out my newsletters. I wrote immediately and sent Laura one or two pretty shells from our beach, but I did not know if the letter would reach them in time. This news was quite unexpected and accentuated the feeling of distance between my family members and me.

CHAPTER 7: MINOR SURGERY

On Sunday afternoons, I usually tried to get some letters written, as it was normally a quiet time. However one Sunday afternoon in September, Olinda called me and said that a boy had come into Hospital with a cut foot. Knowing what masters of understatement the girls were I hurried down to Hospital, where I found a boy of about 12 years old with his little toe hanging off. His mother had carried him on her back for three hours to reach Hospital, after he had sliced his toe with an axe, whilst chopping firewood. The cut extended for about three inches downward between his toes and was quite deep, but reasonably clean. Most people in Papua did not wear shoes and subsequently their feet were very hard especially the sole of the foot and this boy was no exception. I gave him some aspirin for pain and a penicillin injection before attempting to sew the toe back on. I was relieved to see that when repositioned the toe was quite a good colour and had obviously retained some of its blood supply. It was still attached to his foot at the back by a narrow piece of skin and tissue as his mother had wrapped it around quite tightly with leaves, which acted as a splint.

After giving him a local anaesthetic, I closed the wound between his toes and stitched the toe back on as best I could. It took 14 stitches altogether, and must have been painful. When I had finished we were both sweating, but the lad was very good and did not complain. I put a dressing on the boy's foot and commended his mother for bringing him in as quickly as she was able to. They were both in need of some food and a rest, so were admitted. I explained to the mother that her son would need to stay in Hospital until the stitches were ready to come out, as I needed to be sure that the wound would heal without infection and to prevent this he would need antibiotics. I managed to find him a pair of crutches to avoid weight bearing on the foot until the wound had healed. He was tickled pink with them and hopped around all over the place.

The next day the mother went back to her village to get food and other essentials for their stay in Hospital, as she had not been able to carry anything with her, other than her son. This meant a six-hour walk there and back, and once more I was impressed by the woman's stamina and her determination to do the best she could for her boy. She told me that she had been afraid that he would never be able to walk properly again and I was able to reassure her that although the toe was not as straight as before, it should not impede his walking. Although I did say I thought he should avoid playing barefoot football for a while! I also felt a sense of satisfaction at the outcome of my efforts.

A New Arrival and New Uniforms

A young man, Brian C, arrived in September on the MV Moturina. He was with VSO (Voluntary Service Overseas) and had come to help in Lawes College School as a teacher. This was really good news as we needed more school staff and he seemed very keen and energetic. He was also from England, Essex in fact, which was quite a coincidence, being my home county. Brian moved in with Alan and Wendy at the Big House, bringing the UK contingent up to four. The school children were really excited that Brian had arrived and he settled in well.

The new nurses were doing well but they needed new uniforms, so I was very pleased when the District Council gave me a grant to buy material. I went to the local trade store and bought a length of blue cotton material that was very suitable. Ruta and Sineleki got out the Hospital sewing machine, an ancient but prized possession, and ran up two dresses each. These girls were able to cut out and sew dresses without a pattern, which was impressive, and they looked very attractive. There was enough material over for Olinda to have two new dresses as well so that they all wore the same. As a qualified nurse, Mary had yellow uniform dresses and I bought white and blue uniforms with me, so we were now all kitted out.

A Wedding and a Funeral

Another event during that week was Liasa's wedding, which took place at Isuleilei. As she had been one of our nurses when I first arrived, I went along with some of the other girls. It was a white wedding, European style, and men wore suits. This surprised me but apparently this was what modern Papuan girls wanted. However there was nothing European about the feast that followed afterwards. We all sat on the ground and helped ourselves to piles of local food spread out on banana leaves. I hoped their marriage would be a happy one. The custom was that Liasa would go to live in her husband's village, but it was not too far away from where her family lived, which she was pleased about.

Nick Thomson, the doctor from Iruna, was to have paid us a visit that week but at the last minute he was unable to come. I was disappointed, as I had been looking forward to discussing various problems with him. We had our first death in Hospital that week; it was unexpected, although the woman, who was called Rosi, was quite ill with pneumonia. A couple of days after she was admitted she became jaundiced, and I was uncertain of the cause, which is why I would have been glad to see Nick. As it was I was left wondering what had caused Rosi's death, which made me very aware of the gaps in my medical knowledge and the absence of any diagnostic tests that might have helped us treat her.

Rosi was only about 38 and had five children. Her husband was naturally very upset when she died suddenly in her sleep at around 2

AM. I was awakened by his loud crying and wailing, the custom here when a person died. At first light I wrote a note to Ravu and Sinėleki took it across to Isuleilei for me. I thought that if anyone could comfort the family, Ravu would be able to. He came quickly and spent some time praying and talking with Rosi's family who had arrived and were all wailing and crying. I learnt from Mary that people expressed their grief very openly for the first 24 hours, and during the funeral, which was held as soon as possible because of the heat. Then they had a feast after the person was buried, and another a month later. This was followed by another feast on the first anniversary of the death. These were clearly defined rituals that everyone in the village took part in and I thought that it aided the grieving process in a way unknown in our western culture. Rosi's relatives took her body back to her village about 9 AM. I felt rather depressed after they had gone but I was relieved that the wailing had stopped, as it was very hard to listen to. I was afraid it would unsettle other patients, who might have thought that Hospital was not a good place to be. Having Ravu in the Hospital was a great help as he stayed for a while and talked with the other patients, and nobody left.

Although most of the people were Christians, I discovered that sometimes they also believed in *puri puri*, which was bad magic that made people ill. This was part of a very old belief system that existed when people had no knowledge of bacteria as a cause of disease. It was their way of understanding the world and why people become ill or died. *Puri puri* was a magical force that produced illness via the *puri puri* man who had the power to inflict disease that could lead to death. This was often linked to guilt over real or imagined wrongdoing, and was seen as an act of revenge on the part of the wronged person or community. People feared the *puri puri* man and his ability, as they saw it, to do them harm. They tried hard to find out who had caused them to become ill, and why. Therefore they were careful with nail parings or bodily fluids in case they fell into the wrong hands and were used to make magic against them.

Puri puri was also the term used when herbal remedies or other traditional methods were used to treat illness. One such practitioner was 'Dr' Lameka, an elderly man from a nearby village, who was a church member, and whom I had met. He was much respected by local people and was known as a healer. In the days before Europeans came with their medicines, he would treat people using herbal means. As I had experienced complications with women in labour and was interested to learn more about means to prevent these problems, I asked him what he would use to treat women with postpartum hae-morrhage but he would not tell me. He preferred to keep his remedies secret and on reflection I thought that he was probably right to do so.

Later that week the boat arrived with supplies and mail. As I half expected I had a letter from my uncle to tell me that my aunt Laura had died before my letter to her had arrived. She was able to remain at home as her sister Dorothy was there to care for her. By the time I received the news, they had, of course, had the funeral. I felt sad on two counts: that I was unable to be present at her funeral and to support my uncle Charles, who had also lost his first wife, Ruth, to cancer, when she was in her late twenties.

I reflected on the universal nature of grief and the finality of loss and although the circumstances may be different, and the cultural ex-pression very diverse, the feelings of the bereaved are much the same the world over. At the time I felt quite isolated, in that I was the only person affected by this particular loss, although my colleagues were sympathetic and supportive. I felt strangely out of sync because of the time lag between the event and my receiving the news, and because it was in such contrast to the shock of the death of Rosi with all its immediacy.

Village Visit

One morning when we were treating outpatients, a man arrived and asked me to accompany him to the nearby village of Sea Sea where his wife was very sick. Joseph had not been able to get enough men to help him carry her into Hospital, as they were all away making copra. About 11 AM I set off with my medical bag, accompanied by Sineleki. I had not been so far into the bush before and it was very hot. I had to ask Joseph not to walk so fast as I could not keep up. At one point we had to cross a river over which there was a single log bridge. Joseph ran over it in a matter of minutes, followed by Sineleki, while I stood nervously on the riverbank. I put one foot on the bridge but I couldn't pluck up courage to go any further. Joseph and Sineleki both came back, and with Joseph in front of me and Sineleki behind me, each holding a hand, I managed to make it over, feeling very silly. I wondered what their private thoughts were, but I did not enquire.

We arrived in the village not long after that, and Joseph took me into his house where his wife, Mele, lay. She was semiconscious and seemed very ill. I listened to her chest and it appeared that she had pneumonia, so I gave her the antibiotics I had bought with me and treated her for malaria. I did not think that the prognosis was good and I asked Sineleki to explain this to Joseph. When I gave Mele the injections she stirred and I was able to get her to drink a sip or two of water, and I encouraged Joseph to continue giving her fluid when he could, as she was dehydrated. I left Joseph some tablets for his wife if she was able to swallow, but there was little else I could do. Before we left, Joseph's sister came into the house and gave us some green coconut milk to drink, which was wonderfully refreshing (plate 15). She also gave Sineleki some sweet potatoes out of her garden to take home with us, which was very kind.

Joseph quite naturally wanted to stay with his wife, so he called a village boy to walk back with us, as I was not sure if we could find our way home. There was also the dreaded bridge to negotiate and when we reached it Sineleki organised the young lad to help me across, while she brought up the rear. Judging by the laughter and giggling going on as they chatted together in Suau it was the subject of much mirth. When we arrived back at about 3.30 PM, I gave the lad a packet of biscuits for his trouble, which more than pleased him. Before I made a cup of tea, I looked in the mirror and my face was as red as a beetroot and my hair was wet with sweat, so I had a cold shower and then lay on my bed for half an hour to recover.

I was surprised by the amount of chest infections I had encountered since I arrived. Bronchitis and pneumonia were by far the most common ailments, apart from malaria and obstetric complications. It was not something I expected to find in the tropics, but possibly the damp, humid climate had something to do with it. Skin diseases were also common, scabies often afflicted schoolchildren, and a condition called sipoma (*tinea imbricata*, or ringworm), which was a fungus causing rough scaly patches to appear on the skin, could affect anyone of any age. The treatment was to paint the skin with a green substance containing salicylic acid, but it was usually successful.

On the whole the people did not smoke, although some of the men rolled their own cigarettes, if they could buy tobacco. However, nearly all the adults chewed betel nut, which was mixed with lime (calcium hydroxide or slaked lime, not to be confused with the citrus fruit) and stained teeth and gums black. It produced a dark red juice, which was not swallowed but spat out. I believed it was used as a mild stimulant, but it did not do their teeth much good. The nuts grew on the Areca palm tree (not a true seed but a drupe or fruit of the palm) that was found in the bush and was much sought after.

CHAPTER 8: A PRAYING MANTIS IS TRYING TO STARE ME OUT

Fortunately, I do not mind insects, which is just as well, as a large fat grasshopper landed on my head as I was writing some letters. The light from the lamp attracted them. If a boat was due we would try and get the mail ready in time to catch the boat, and that meant writing in the evening by the light of the Tilley lamp. Writing letters home was important, as it was the only way to stay in touch, but as letters took so long to arrive, the news was often out of date by the time they were received.

Insect life was abundant, and creatures I had only vaguely heard of suddenly materialised in the flesh! I was particularly fascinated by the praying mantis, so brilliant was it at camouflaging itself, yet seemingly able to fix me with that large eye, until I felt quite uncomfortable! The feats of the grasshopper astonished me; it performed something very like a dance, and then washed one leg like a cat.

I often wondered why God created the mosquito, and what its place was in the evolutionary chain, as it caused such havoc. Although I usually hate killing any living thing, the mosquito proved to be an exception, especially when one or more got inside my mosquito net. Their buzzing was a sound impossible to ignore, so sleep was interrupted, but catching them was difficult and they usually proved too quick for someone befuddled with sleep. Once completely awake and standing up on the bed under the net, my gyrating usually met with success, and the number of small bloodstains bore witness to the fact that the offending insect had enjoyed a good meal before being dis-patched!

There were also masses of birds, including red and green parrots that screeched from trees, and numerous humming birds and others that I was unable to identify. Some built very flimsy nests that hung from branches of the kapok tree near our house (plate 11). The wind sometimes blew down nests and eggs or chicks were lost, but it did not deter the birds from building again.

Happy Birthday

It was Alan's birthday on Sunday, 9th October. We had a party to cel-ebrate it on the Saturday evening, at the Big House, which I enjoyed. There was a variety of food, and we each contributed to the entertain-ment. Brian played his clarinet and Wendy the recorder. As I don't have much musical ability, I demonstrated how to pull teeth!

I became aware – perhaps for the first time – of how isolated we were, as far as the more usual western cultural pastimes were con-cerned. When I lived in London I enjoyed going to art galleries and theatres but now that experience seemed a lifetime away, instead of only a few months. Twinges of homesickness tended to catch me out when I least expected them to. I realised that I had not yet become accustomed to the recreational activities of the local people, who en-joyed dancing, but who seldom had much leisure time to enjoy them-selves. Most of the time I was kept busy with medical matters, but I was glad that I had bought so many favourite books with me, even if I had had to paint them with a substance that protected them from termites.

Sick Child

Liani, one of the schoolgirls who boarded at Samoa House, was tak-en ill during the night with a raging fever and symptoms of cerebral irritation (headache and stiff neck). I gave her some aspirin but the next morning she was worse and was barely conscious. I was very worried and asked Tavita if he knew where her parents lived, but it transpired that they were away in Port Moresby visiting relatives. Liani was about twelve years old and had been at Lawes College School for around two years. Tavita sent a student to Liani's village to see if he could contact any of her relations, whilst I moved Liani up to Middle House into the spare bedroom next to mine. We had no staff available for night duty, so usually relatives who accompanied a patient looked after them during the night, unless they were very ill when Mary or I would stay up.

I put Liana on a course of anti-malarial drugs and at the same time I started her on six-hourly injections of crystalline penicillin. After I had spoken to Dr Peter Calvert on the radio, I increased the penicillin to four-hourly at his suggestion. It was impossible to know without laboratory tests or the benefit of a lumber puncture, if she had cerebral malaria or meningitis, so it was necessary to treat her for both conditions. She had an enlarged spleen, which pointed to malaria, but that was not so unusual in a child of that age. Every morning Liani was included in the school children's prayers and at the Hospital we also prayed for her recovery.

I felt very keenly the responsibility of such a sick child with no family nearby, and wondered if I should transfer her to the Hospital at Samarai, where at least they would be able to do a blood test and make a more accurate diagnosis. However, when I tried to get the doctor at Samarai Hospital on the radio to ask him to arrange a transfer, the radio reception was so bad he thought I was saying that Liani had diarrhoea and advised me to give her mist kaolin, which was very frustrating!

As a result of the high fever, and her semi-conscious state, Liani became dehydrated. I put up a saline drip with some difficulty, as we only had adult size needles. The paediatric needles that we had were only suitable for babies, but eventually I found a needle small enough

66

to use without causing her too much discomfort. Bertha came to sit with Liani during the afternoons, as she was restless and I did not like to leave her on her own for too long. By the fifth day Liani was beginning to show some signs of improvement and, to my great relief, her grandmother turned up to help look after her. She was surprised to find Liani in our house but she soon got used to it, and settled down on her mat on the floor next to the bed. As she became more alert, Liani was able to drink small amounts of *sipora* juice (a local citrus fruit, like lime), and her grandmother was a great help in seeing that she drank regularly.

After a week Liani was able to sit out on the veranda for short periods and I was able to reduce the number of injections of penicillin. She was still very weak but she began eating again and was now fully conscious, and enjoyed receiving visits from her school friends. The schoolgirls' usual diet needed to be supplemented for a convalescing twelve-year old, and I succeeded in coaxing her to drink milk (powdered) and to eat some of the scrambled egg that I made. Papuan children were not used to either of these. After ten days we agreed that Liani could return to Samoa House, but she still needed to rest and was not ready to return to school.

Later that week, Liani's uncle turned up in a canoe and we agreed she should return home with him, for the few weeks left of term. This seemed like a good solution, as she was not strong enough yet to walk the long distance to her village. Liani was a bright child and hopefully she would not take too long to catch up with her schoolwork. I was still not sure of her diagnosis, but I was thankful that she had recovered apparently without any permanent damage to her health.

Baptisms!

Once a year babies born to student pastors' wives were baptised in Lawes College Chapel. That year (1966) there were seven, five of whom I had delivered. When practising midwifery in the UK there is little or no opportunity to see babies growing up, so this service was rather special. It was scheduled for 8 AM but as Mary and I had been up in the night we overslept and nearly missed it. However we managed to arrive during the first hymn, sung in English rather than Motu, which was helpful from my point of view.

The student pastors and their wives looked very smart in their white clothes and Alan officiated. On the whole the babies were quite good having been amply fed by their mothers, but most shrieked their indignation when it was their turn to be baptised, although between them Alan and Tavita coped quite well. Later that morning we all had lunch together outside, under a shady tree. The pastors' wives had prepared food and I was relieved not to have to wrestle with the wood stove in Middle House. However, I was really tired and rather full. After we had eaten I had an awful job to stay awake, so slipped away to have a couple of hours of sleep before the evening work began.

United Nations Day 24th October 1966

I was surprised to find what a big event United Nations Day was in Papua, and it was celebrated at Fife Bay with gusto (plates 16-18). I have to admit that at home I had barely noticed it, but here it was a national holiday. People came to Fife Bay from all over the District including the District Commissioner who came with his retinue from Samarai. John Guise, who was the local up-and-coming politician and member of the House of Assembly, also attended. He later became first Governor-General of independent Papua New Guinea. The event was held at the government Patrol Post and Geoff and Kay acted as host and hostess.

We had sports most of the morning, soccer and basketball, during which there were a few wrenched ankles. Fortunately I had been advised to take a first aid kit, so we were able do on-the-spot repairs! In the afternoon there were dancing and choir competitions, first for school children and then for adults from different villages. Lawes College won both the sports shield and the singing competition. The District Commissioner with suitable ceremony presented the trophies.

In the evening we went over to Isuleilei for a feast prepared by village people that everyone seemed to enjoy enormously. I missed most of the singing that followed the feast because a boy was brought up from Isuleilei beach having been stung by a stonefish. They lurk in shallow water, and when people accidentally tread on their spines the fish injects a poison into the victim that is excruciatingly painful. Peri had been spear fishing with his father, who was carrying their catch. We took the child back to Hospital to get antivenin and pain relief. Fortunately Dad was able to carry him, as he was unable to walk because of the pain. He was crying and very distressed and frightened, needing reassurance as well as pain relief.

It was the first time I had had to deal with this type of emergency, but I had heard stories of such events. Mary said that an injection of local anaesthetic into the site of the sting sometimes helped, as I was loath to give morphine to a ten-year old. I gave antivenin first but found the injection into the Peri's foot difficult as the skin on the underside of the foot was like leather and I did not want to cause more pain. However I eventually managed it and it did help a little as his cries quietened. Peri's father was frightened of the consequences but made a good job of comforting his son. Fortunately the lad had only stepped on the side of the fish so had not received the full effects of spines and venom or it could have been fatal. The antivenin neutralises the poison that circulates around the body but we kept the boy in Hospital overnight and under observation. Mary volunteered to stay up to observe him. His Dad also stayed awake but Peri eventually fell asleep from pain and exhaustion.

The next morning he felt better but his foot was still sore, although the pain was diminishing. His mother arrived and scolded her husband for letting it happen! We kept the family for a couple more days until I was sure he was out of danger. I thought it would be a while before he went fishing at night again!

Picture Show

To round off United Nations weekend we had a film show. I don't think I had ever seen schoolchildren so excited. The battery-operated projector had been brought from Samarai, but there was no sound as the speaker was broken. I doubt we would have heard it above the noise the children made anyway. We saw a film of the Queen's visit to Australia in 1954, a short Western and a documentary about Papua. The projector broke down several times during the show but no one seemed to mind. It was such a change and we all enjoyed it.

Malaria

The last week in October was notable for the number of cases of malaria we treated. Mary said it was because we were nearing the end of the wet season, causing the mosquitoes to be more active. In the course of 24 hours we admitted a ten-month-old baby, with a temperature of 105.6°F, an unconscious four-year-old boy, and a fifteen-year-old girl with convulsions. They all responded quite dramatically to injections of chloroquine, which was the treatment of choice for malaria, especially if patients were caught early enough before there were too many parasites in the bloodstream.

CHAPTER 9: VENTURING FORTH

Fife Bay was very wet, situated as it was in an area of lowland rainforest and boasting a rainfall of 140 to 200 inches annually (*Atlas of Papua and New Guinea*, 1970). I had arrived during the wettest season, May to August, when the southeasterly or trade winds, as they were known, blew. The only footwear possible were flip-flops (thongs as Australians called them). Fortunately I had brought a pair with me, but had to get used to wearing them or go barefoot. During September to December the rain eased up a little, with the driest period between January and April. This was also the hottest, and a time when we could run short of water due to the lack of storage facilities.

Samarai

At the end of October, Wendy and I decided that we would make a trip to Samarai for a few days' break, as the weather was relatively good. I felt confident that Mary and the nurses would manage while I was away. We arranged to stay at Kwato, a small but very beautiful island a short boat ride away from Samarai. Kwato was part of Papua Ekalesia but had been in the hands of one family, the Abels, for at least two generations. My colleague, Sally Green, had told me that her aunt and uncle had worked at Kwato and Sally's cousin Oliver had been born there. The Abels had adopted a holistic approach and set up thriving sawmill and boat building businesses that employed local people. They were interested in the Moral Rearmament movement and taught the Papuans to play cricket. Kwato staff also had oversight of an Inland Mission in the Abau District.

We embarked on the Moturina, and as the sea was reasonably calm I was not seasick. The boat left in the morning and we reached Samarai by early evening, in time to catch the launch to Kwato, where we were warmly welcomed. The staff were used to having guests and looked after us very well. Kwato had a small Hospital, not dissimilar to Fife Bay, but much closer to the Hospital in Samarai. It was staffed by a Sister from Australia who had come to Kwato as a volunteer under the AVA scheme (Australian Volunteers Abroad). We found plenty to discuss and talk about. I had thought I might visit the Hospital on Samarai and make myself known to the doctor in charge, but in the end I did not find the time to do so.

Wendy and I spent the next day in Samarai. The island coastline was only four miles in circumference, but it was quite hilly. The Hospital and Governor's residence stood on top of the hill with the town below. After being deprived of shops for several months, Wendy and I enjoyed ourselves, as we shopped in both stores. Any heavy purchases could be sent to the boat, and smaller items carried with us. I stocked up on flip-flops, so that I would always have a dry pair. It was also useful to see what was available for the next time we had to order stores. During the Second World War, Samarai had been raised to the ground to prevent the Japanese from using it as a base, and it was hard to imagine what it must have been like to experience such devastation, as the small community there appeared to be thriving.

Toby

Just before we were due to catch the launch from Kwato to Samarai, a lad arrived with a puppy on a piece of string. He asked me if I would like to buy the dog, and in a rather quick transaction I paid him the A$3 he asked for. The person in charge told me that the puppy's grandmother was a pure bred Chow and that his mother was a half-breed Chow. He did resemble the breed with his thick coat and dark spots on his tongue, although no one knew who his father might be. He cried a little on the boat journey back to Fife Bay, but soon settled down. I called him Toby. We had no tinned dog food but I had managed to buy some dog biscuits. He had to be a Papuan dog and eat rice and tinned fish, but he thrived on this diet and had an enormous appetite.

I judged him to be about two-months-old but he was not house-trained and left little puddles everywhere. Nurses and schoolgirls were quick to pick him up and put him outside and were generally delighted by his antics. I had thought I would like to have a dog and this seemed the ideal opportunity to acquire one. He quickly became known as Sister's dog, as he followed me up and down to Hospital. If I did not watch him he would help himself to patients' food, which was often in dishes on the floor.

Cleaning Up

It was good to have a break away from Hospital work and when I returned I had more energy. I put it to good use as I had a major clean up in the house and Hospital. Two schoolgirls, Noami and Merin, offered to help me, but I think they regretted it as after a while they took off to the beach to escape.

One reason for the clean up was that the Medical Assistant from Samarai was due to pay us a visit to check up on our TB (tuberculosis) patients. He had chartered a special boat and was bringing a nursing Sister with him. I looked forward to the visit as Alan and Wendy were both away for a few days, Alan, with Ravu, at the Papuan Church Assembly and Wendy visiting Jan and Nick at Iruna. Brian was on patrol and Bertha and Tavita had taken some of our school children to compete in a school choir competition in Milne Bay. I waved them all off on their respective boats and felt quite lonely.

The visitors only stayed one night, and I decided to invite Geoff, the Patrol Officer and his wife Kay, plus Dan, the government Head Teacher, to dinner, as this was a government visit. I had to get the girls to help me cook because I still found it difficult to manage the wood stove. I scrounged a chicken from Dan, as our chook house still hadn't been built. The chicken was a bit tough and the food tasted distinctly smoky but apart from that it was passable. The visitors left at first light with as many of our TB patients as I could summon from villages. They wanted to X-ray them and check on their progress, which was good, as I had no way of knowing if they were improving or not.

Of Medical Matters

At the beginning of November we had a minor epidemic amongst the school children. Every morning and evening they lined up on the outpatients' veranda, complaining of sore eyes and runny noses. Most of them had a slight rash and I was worried that it might be measles as they were all thoroughly miserable. We treated them with aspirin and as they recovered after about five days, I decided it must be rubella. I made sure that they did not go anywhere near any mother in early pregnancy. We had several women awaiting delivery, but were not worried as they were in no danger from the rubella virus.

We had two babies born within 24 hours, both boys. The first baby was very shocked at birth, although labour was not overly long. He was difficult to resuscitate and did not breathe for 20 minutes or cry for six hours. His mother bled heavily after birth as her uterus failed to contract after the placenta was delivered. While I was dealing with the baby, giving mouth-to-mouth resuscitation, Mary was struggling to apply manual pressure to the mother's abdomen. As soon as the baby started to breathe on his own, I put a saline drip up on the mother. I remember wishing that we had some blood to give her, as she had lost copious amounts. Although she had had two doses of ergometrine by injection to help the uterus to contract, it had failed to do so, so I took a chance and put another dose into the drip so that it went directly into the blood stream. This seemed to make a difference and eventually, after what seemed like hours but was in fact only 25 minutes, the uterus contracted. The baby was too weak to put to the breast, which also aids uterine contractions, but his mother was able

74

to hold him and keep him warm. I found myself shaking afterwards, as there is nothing more frightening than an uncontrollable post-partum haemorrhage. I was also aware that if the delivery had taken place in the village both mother and baby would probably have died. As it was she was very anaemic, and even with iron tablets it would take a while to recover from such a heavy blood loss.

This was mother's fifth baby in as many years, although only two had survived. I explained to the mother and her husband that if she became pregnant again, she must come to Hospital for the delivery, but it would be preferable to avoid another pregnancy, for at least a year or two, if that was possible. The baby's father was very pleased to have a son, but was anxious about his wife's condition, so I hoped he would follow my advice – a difficult thing to do when there was no contraception available.

Mary told me that in the old days it was traditional for parents to wait two years before resuming marital relations, which ensured that babies were evenly spaced, and children were able to breast-feed for up to three years, giving them a better start in life and preventing protein deficiency which led to a disease called kwashiorkor. Small children were unable to eat large amounts of the mainly vegetable diet required to maintain an adequate protein intake. Mary volunteered to sleep in Hospital that night to keep an eye on both the baby and his mother, but fortunately there were no further complications.

A second mother delivered her son three hours after the first, but mercifully it was a normal delivery of a healthy infant. I went down to Hospital at first light and remarkably I found the sick baby sleeping peacefully and looking much better. He had had a feed and his mother, although pale, was rested and looking forward to food her husband was cooking for her. Later that day he went out in his canoe to catch some fish for his wife, that would be nutritious, and I was hopeful that both mother and baby would make a complete, if slow, recovery. Around lunchtime I examined the baby, and as far as I could tell, at that stage, he appeared not to have suffered any brain damage from his failure to breathe at birth. I explained to the father that I would like mother and baby to stay with us for longer than usual to give mother time to recover, and for me to monitor the baby's progress and he readily agreed to this.

CHAPTER 10: FIRST PATROL

Both Mary and I felt it was time that I went out on patrol. I needed to visit some of the villages and to see the extent of our District. We were roughly in the middle, so normally covered the areas to the east or the west alternately. This time it was the turn of the western half of the District that ended at Gadaisu. This area included Bona Bona Island that could only be reached by canoe, so quite a lot of organisation was required beforehand. I was quite excited about the trip but I was also apprehensive, as I knew I was not used to walking long distances, particularly in the heat. We planned the patrol to coincide with the MV Motorina's return journey down the coast from Gadaisu, so that we could get a lift back and would only have to walk one way.

We always hired local men to carry our medical equipment. I tried not to take too much, but we had to include enough medicines to treat any sick people, as well as vaccines for the babies, and iron and folic acid tablets for antenatal women. As we were to stay in houses of village pastors, we also took small gifts of tea or biscuits for them, plus our mosquito nets and sleeping mats as well as our personal items. In order to let village people know that we were coming, and in particular mothers and babies that we needed to see, we sent messages via Radio Samarai, in the hope that someone would hear the message on their radio and pass the word around. This was a bit hit and miss, but it was still the most effective way of communicating.

Day One

I had two girls to accompany me, Margariti, one of our Nurse Aides, and Eileen, a schoolgirl, who was the daughter of one of the pastors whose village we would be visiting (plate 19). Eileen was hoping to train as a nurse when she was old enough, and we thought it would be good for her to have some hands-on experience. We set off on a Saturday morning, after the rain stopped and walked for several hours until we came to our first village, Silo Silo, where we spent the night. I was not used to sleeping on the floor, but was tired so I managed a few hours.

Everyone was up at first light and the pastor's wife had kept some firewood aside to boil a kettle to make us tea that was very welcome. Women started to arrive and we held a clinic under a tree that afforded us some shade. Whilst we were working the pastor's wife went off to gather more firewood and fresh water to make our breakfast of vegetables cooked in coconut liquid. After we had eaten, we went to the village church for Sunday service. It was an opportunity to meet most village people which was good (plate 20), but I was anxious to move on, as I knew it was quite a long walk to the next village and we needed to arrive in daylight.

Day Two

The walk on the second day was much tougher as there were four big hills to cross. They felt like mountains to me and the paths were wet and slippery. I was puffing and blowing up the hills and was glad when we reached the edge of a lagoon. The carriers decided that the path around the edge would be too difficult for me and that I should cross by canoe. There was a small dugout canoe at the water's edge and I got into it with some trepidation, as one of the men suggested that I remove my watch before I set off. One man remained to paddle me across while the others, including the two girls, walked. The men said there was only room for one in the canoe, but I took the flask with vaccines in with me. I thought they would probably travel faster without me, although they were too polite to say so!

The sea was very rough and waves crashed over us, so that within minutes we were both soaked through. The man paddled hard but I had to bale out all the way with an empty tin. I could only do this with one hand, as I dare not let go of the vaccines, as they would have been lost overboard. The canoe was very low in the water but I kept reminding myself that the Papuan men were very skilled sailors and knew what they were doing. I was thankful that my mother didn't know about this journey, as she would have been extremely worried. However, we arrived safely, if wet, and my watch was returned to me with a knowing smile.

It was not far from there to the village of Kau Kau where we were to stay the night. I was glad of the bowl of hot water that I was given to wash with. Village houses had no bathrooms, as people generally washed in the river, but for visitors there was an empty room, a bowl of water and a cup to pour the water over yourself. The water was then tipped out of the bowl through gaps in the floor. I had brought a towel and was more comfortable when I had put on some dry clothes.

We had a meal and it was soon dark, so everyone went to bed. We used our own hurricane lamp and kerosene, so that we would not use up the pastor's supply. The girls and I were given a room to sleep in, but the men had disappeared and Eileen said they probably had relatives in the village to stay with. In spite of being really weary, I found it difficult to sleep on the floor, and there was a lot of activity in the roof thatch above our heads. Eileen said that this was the time the rats became active, and they sounded as if they had hobnail boots on.

From where I lay I could see out of the window at the most amazing night sky. I regretted not being able to identify the stars and thought of my friend Stella, aptly named, to whom I wrote regularly. She was interested in astronomy and would probably have recognised most of the constellations.

Day Three

The next morning, not surprisingly, I was quite stiff. After clinic, I took a couple of aspirins, as I knew we would be walking for a while. In fact we took a canoe part of the way. This time it was a bigger canoe with a sail and we made quite good progress. We arrived at the village of Dahuni, and were given green coconut milk to drink. It was refreshing and very healthy as it contained a lot of potassium, which was lost whilst sweating. We held a clinic at Dahuni, and treated a man who had a badly cut leg and a boy with malaria. We were given some sago mixed with coconut for lunch. It had little taste and was very chewy, but it filled a hole.

We had arranged to travel from Dahuni to Bona Bona Island and the men were ready with a decent sized canoe, as we were crossing open sea. Fortunately, the wind was in our favour, and we flew along, so I quite enjoyed it. When we arrived on Bona Bona, the people had not received the message that we were coming, and had gone to their gardens. A young lad was dispatched to fetch the mothers and eventually they arrived, all wearing their grass skirts. Whilst we were waiting, Margariti and I checked school children, all of whom thought it was a great joke and couldn't stop giggling. One or two of the babies had skin problems, probably scabies, which we treated, and we also examined some pregnant women. Although I advised them to come to Hospital for delivery, I knew it would be difficult for them to get to Fife Bay from such an isolated spot.

When we had finished, I expected to travel onto our next village, but the men said the sea was too rough to take us that afternoon. The wind had got up, but Margariti said it was really because they wanted to spend time with their *wontoks*. However this put people in a flap because they had not expected to provide hospitality for us, particularly me, being an expat. They were not used to entertaining Europeans, and were worried because they had no meat or biscuits to offer us. The village didn't have a pastor, so there was a great debate about where we should sleep. Eventually someone offered her house as it had a spare room. There was a flurry of activity behind the house and I gathered from a giggling Eileen that they were hastily constructing a toilet for me to use, as normally they went in the sea or in a designated area of bush. The toilet was a hole in the ground, screened off by some rather flimsy woven coconut walls. I appreciated their efforts but the local children could not resist peering through when I went inside and I had to station Eileen or Margariti outside to allow me a modicum of privacy.

Various women appeared with dishes of food for our evening meal, of vegetables and fish, which included the fish head, so nothing was wasted. I asked the girls to explain that I was very happy to eat their food and that I did not mind sitting or sleeping on the floor. We had some tea with us and one of the women made tea in the kettle and shared it around. I gathered it was quite a treat for them and was glad I could contribute something.

Day Four

At first light we were woken with tea and leftovers from the meal the evening before, as we had to make an early start to get to our next stop, Mariawatte Plantation. Children and some adults came down to the beach to see us off. It was certainly a beautiful island, if isolated, and I wondered how the people kept in touch with the rest of the world. Whilst at Bona Bona, it was hard to remember that the outside world even existed. The canoe dropped us on the mainland and to reach Mariawatte we had to walk through what seemed miles of coconut trees that formed part of the plantation. I thought we were lost and when a man on a tractor emerged from the trees, I asked him the way. He answered in the broadest Glaswegian accent I had ever heard, which came as quite a surprise.

When we arrived at the village, we held the clinic as usual and treated some people with minor injuries. I had lost count of the days

81

but Eileen said it was Wednesday. We had a long walk that day along the beach. It was very hot and there was no shade. In spite of wearing a hat and carrying an umbrella, I got quite sunburnt, and became very red in the face. The people at Mariawatte gave us a pineapple and at lunchtime, we sat down and Margariti expertly cut it into several sections and we all had a piece. It was absolutely lovely and a real change from the warmish water in our water bottles. The ice in the flask carrying the vaccines had long since melted, but we had no way of replenishing it, so just tried to keep it as cool as possible.

We spent the night at Mariawatte, after visiting the plantation for a cup of tea and treating one of the workers for pneumonia. We met the Papuan manager, who introduced us to his four wives. It was the first time that I had encountered that type of marriage and did not know quite what to make of it, so I confined myself to checking their health and that of their children.

Day Five

Our next port of call was Laimodo. This was the village where Eileen's father was pastor, and I knew we would receive a warm welcome there. At the end of a long walk from Mariawatte, we arrived at Mullins Harbour, which we had to cross by canoe. There was hardly any wind that day and the men had to paddle nearly all the way. It took us three-and-a-half hours altogether and I got even more sunburnt. We had some green coconuts with us, which we certainly needed, as it was so hot. Eventually we arrived at Laimodo and were greeted by Eileen's parents and her younger siblings. Her mother then produced tea and cakes that she had made, which was a lovely surprise. Eileen was excitedly chatting to her parents, so Margariti and I went for a walk around the village.

I wanted to visit the Aid Post and introduce myself to the medical orderly that worked there. We had visited the Aid Post at Silo Silo and I knew there was an Aid Post at Gadaisu also. The medical orderlies were young men trained by the church at Kapuna Hospital to provide basic medical care to the village people. The village built the Aid Post and provided the orderly with a house and some land for a garden but the church employed them. It was a system that worked well for general medical care. For cultural reasons the medical orderlies were not expected to attend women in labour unless it was an emergency. Villages with Aid Posts were fortunate in that they had access to some medical care. Other villages had no way of getting a couple of aspirins for a headache, or treatment for malaria, if they needed it. At Laimo-do, the orderly was running short of penicillin and I was able to give him some to tide him over until the next order arrived on the boat. That evening we had a meal followed by prayers, led by Eileen's father. The family's English was quite good and we talked for a while about various things, before going to sleep.

Day Six

We left the next morning for Gadaisu, where there was a plantation run by a European couple, although we planned to sleep in the village, in order to be ready to do the clinic in the morning. Eileen left carrying a large bunch of green cooking bananas on her head. These were to supplement her diet back at Lawes College. We were also given a bowl of cooked food to take with us for our lunch, and some sugar cane, which was very welcome as it was a long walk along the beach. Signs of erosion by the sea were everywhere, and coconut trees whose roots had lost the soil to hold them were strewn along the beach, bleached by the sun and wind.

When we arrived at Gadaisu in the early afternoon, we found a very ill man lying in a small lean-to outside his house. Margariti said this was because the family were expecting him to die. Sadly there was nothing I could do for him and he died the next morning. We set up the clinic straight away, as women were waiting and I also examined school children, many of whom had enlarged spleens because of repeated attacks of malaria. The examination included a basic sight test, which fortunately they all passed, as I had no idea what to do if I found a child who needed glasses.

Day Seven

The MV Moturina was due the next morning, Saturday, at 5 AM, so we were glad to go to bed early after the evening meal in the pastor's house. We were up at first light, and watched the boat come in. It had to load copra first, but we were away by 7.30 AM. Alan, the captain, remembered that I had travelled on the boat when I arrived in Papua in July. This time he did not need to give me his cabin and I sat on the deck with the local people and their various bundles plus a few hens and a piglet. Fortunately, the sea was not as rough as on my first trip and although we stopped several times to load and unload goods we arrived at Fife Bay about 3 PM. I had been away for a week and looked forward to a shower and my own bed, but I was pleased that my first patrol had been completed without any major hiccups.

1. LMS painted on Lawes College School roof in the rainy season, with Margaret under red umbrella

2. CWM logo

3. MAF plane in which Ruth flew to Mailu, refuelling at Popondetta, July 1966

4. Owen Stanley mountain range with village on ridge

5. General and Maternity wards - back view

6. Patient arriving on double hulled canoe

*7. Moving Maternity ward
water tank for repairs!*

*8. Fife Bay from Isuleilei
Point*

*9. MV Moturina delivering
oil drums to Fife Bay*

10. Bertha and Tavita, with Miriam and Andrew

11. Middle House with kapok tree in foreground

12. Middle House schoolgirls, one playing cat's cradle

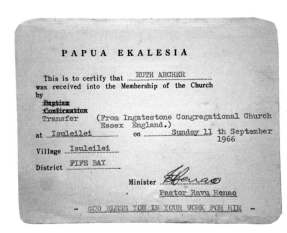

13. Ruth's certificate of Papua Ekalesia membership

14. Papua Ekalesia logo

15. Ruth enjoying coconut milk

16. United Nations Day celebration - schoolgirls dancing with Brian in foreground

17. Schoolchildren performing traditional dance in evening light

18. Tavita conducting Lawes College School choir on United Nations Day

19. Margariti, Ruth and Eileen (L to R) starting out on patrol

20. Ruth on patrol - Women's Fellowship group outside village church

21. "Sail Oh!" Boat in the bay

22. Waterfall frolics included Toby

23. Walo twirling kapok to remove seeds

24. Ruth washing her pilipo (smalls)

CHAPTER 11: SURGICAL EMERGENCY

After I returned from patrol I thought I would take a day off to recover, but my hopes were quickly dashed when a few hours later, a young woman was brought in on a stretcher. She had acute abdominal pain and vomiting and was already dehydrated. I recognised her as Misi, a lady we had delivered of a bouncing baby boy six weeks earlier. I remembered that although she was only about 25 years old, the new baby was her sixth child. Her husband, Jaki, told me that she had been unwell for two days already. When I examined her alarm bells started ringing, as her abdomen was as hard as a board and the pain was so severe I had to give her morphine. My fears were confirmed when she started vomiting offensive, foul-smelling brown fluid (faecal fluid), a classic symptom of an intestinal obstruction. I knew then that she needed an urgent operation, and that my job would be to care for her until that could be arranged.

I remembered from my days on a surgical ward that I would have to set up a regime known as drip and suck, to rehydrate her and to keep the stomach empty. I also knew that if she did not get to Hospital as quickly as possible she might not survive. After putting up a saline drip, I explained the situation to her husband. Most Papuans were not familiar with surgical operations, and were naturally frightened of this type of intervention. I was afraid that Misi's husband would not co-operate, but Mary helped me put the problem to him very clearly. As for Misi, she just wanted the pain to go away. When she was a little more settled, after the morphine began to take effect, I passed a naso-gastric tube with some difficulty, as it made her want to vomit. The tube was passed into her nostril and down into her stomach and I was able to aspirate a large quantity of faecal fluid. As the stomach and small bowel emptied Misi began to feel better and the pain lessened.

Meanwhile Misi's baby was bawling his head off, as he was hungry. Mary made him up a bottle but he did not take to it very readily and his screams were disturbing his mother who badly needed to rest. In the end we put him to the breast for a brief period to take the edge off his hunger, but I was worried about the effect of morphine on him. I did not know if the drug would be present in breast milk, and did not want to take a chance.

By now it was nearly 9 PM and I realised that we would have a long night ahead. I was really tired, but as Mary was unfamiliar with the drip and suck technique, I decided it would be best to move Misi to the spare room in the house, next to my bedroom. I needed to get some sleep, so I showed Mary how to aspirate the nasal tube, and watch the drip, and I knew she would call me if I were needed. Moving Misi up to the house underlined the seriousness of her condition. Her husband, slept on a mat on the floor by her bed. The nurses took baby Josep into their room. He was still indignant but hungry enough now to settle for the bottle without too much of a fight.

I had not had an evening meal but settled for a cup of tea and some bananas, which were always plentiful, before going to sleep. I was conscious of the weight of responsibility for this very sick woman and did not sleep well, partly because the sounds from the next room were disturbing, and partly because I was worried about how I would get Misi to Samarai. I knew none of the scheduled boats were due for a week or more as I had disembarked from the MV Moturina that afternoon. I got up at 1 AM to take over from Mary, and she relieved me again at 5 AM. Misi was much the same but the pain had lessened slightly. I did not want to repeat the morphine if I could avoid it, as she wanted to breast-feed her baby because her breasts were engorged with milk. We aspirated her naso-gastric tube every hour and maintained her IV fluids. Her blood pressure and pulse were steady and she had been able to sleep for short periods.

Chartering a Boat

As it was a Sunday, I could not use the normal daily radio sked, and had instead to find the emergency frequency. This seemed to take forever, but eventually I got through to the resident doctor at Samarai Hospital. I explained the problem and requested a boat to transfer Misi to the Hospital for surgery. Dr D had to contact the Samarai Harbour authorities and eventually said that the earliest they could get a boat out to Fife Bay was the next morning. I had to be content and was relieved that he had been able to authorise such a venture, the cost of which had to be met by the local government authority.

I explained to Misi's husband what was happening and he seemed relieved. Jaki would accompany Misi to Samarai but he wanted to go back to their village first to make arrangements for the care of his other children. He returned later that day with Misi's sister who would help them to care for baby Josep. At six-weeks he was too young to be separated from his mother.

We faced another night up, as Misi could not be left alone for long, so Mary and I snatched some sleep when we could, taking it in turns to keep up the drip and suck regime. Misi had no bowel sounds, which meant that her gut was not working at all, so it was vital that we kept her stomach as empty as possible. I worried as to what was causing the obstruction, praying that it was not a malignant tumour, as well as for strength for all of us to keep going until I could hand our patient over to the doctor at Samarai. Prayers were also said for Misi and her family at the Hospital and in Lawes College Chapel, for which I was profoundly grateful.

Thankfully Misi's condition did not deteriorate overnight, and there were no signs of infection, but neither did she improve, as we were still aspirating copious amounts of faecal fluid. Eventually at 3 PM on Monday afternoon, we head the cry of "Sail Oh!" and a small boat came chugging into the bay (plate 21). I decided to accompany

Misi into Samarai, as I wanted to give Dr D an up-to-date account of her condition. Four Lawes College students volunteered to carry the stretcher down to the beach and out to the boat. Fife Bay had no wharf and it meant that any vessel had to anchor in the bay. I had been keeping an eye on the sea all day and it was quite choppy.

Transfer by Boat

I don't think I will ever forget loading Misi onto the boat; it was such a nightmare. First we loaded the stretcher onto the dinghy with the outboard motor. The stretcher took up nearly all the space, and its handles stuck out over prow and stern. I was also on board the dingy, trying to hold the drip aloft in the tossing sea. The stretcher-bearers also clambered on board. Jaki and Misi's sister who had the baby, paddled out in a canoe. There was a big swell and every time the dinghy surged upward on a wave the men on the boat deck leaned down to make a grab for the stretcher. After several attempts we realised that this was impossible, so two of the men in the dinghy lifted Misi off the stretcher as best they could and at an opportune moment heaved her up onto the boat. Willing hands completed the task and eventually she was laid on deck. I had to relinquish my hold on the drip that mercifully stayed connected as it was laid beside Misi. Fortunately I had sedated her before we attempted the transfer, so she was not too distressed. In fact she remained calm through out the whole ordeal.

Then it was my turn to be hoisted on board. I felt rather like a sack of copra being hauled aboard, but could not worry about my dignity. I was just glad to reach the deck. Next it was baby Josep's turn. His aunty held him aloft and a seaman leant down and attempted to grab the bundle of sleeping baby. He succeeded at the third attempt and Josep was deposited in his father's arms. As I watched, my heart was in my mouth, as I had visions of Josep slipping from the seaman's grasp and falling into the sea. Aunty and Nancy, the nurse who was accompanying us, climbed quite nimbly onto the deck, and we were all aboard.

88

Misi was moved to a sheltered spot and the drip was attached to a convenient pole nearby. The doctor had sent a medical orderly out on the boat to help us, which was just as well, because as soon as the boat left the bay and headed into the open sea it pitched and rolled and I was very seasick. In the end I couldn't do much except lie on deck and try to keep an eye on Misi. She was also sick, as the naso-gastric tube had come out so we could not aspirate her stomach. The drip was swinging madly, but fortunately remained *in situ*, though I was not sure how. The Papuan orderly was very helpful as he had his sea legs but Nancy felt very queasy and, like me, was unable to do much to help. We were a sorry lot when the boat finally pulled into Samarai at about 9.30 PM after the six-and-half-hour journey. It was dark but I recall feeling relieved when I saw the outline of a wharf, with an ambulance pulled up alongside.

Hospitalisation

Dr D came on board and we exchanged pleasantries. I was sure that I looked really dishevelled, having lain on deck for the best part of the journey. I thought it was really good of him to come down to meet us, as I had not expected to see him until we got to Hospital. I took him to see Misi and he examined her briefly.

"She doesn't look too bad," he said, "its probably a bad case of gastritis." I could hardly believe my ears.

"No," I said, "she has been vomiting faecal material for over 56 hours. I have had her on drip and suck, which is why she isn't dehydrated; she is definitely obstructed."

"Have you a specimen of vomit?" I knew we had used a bowl when Misi was sick and hastened to find it, but Nancy, ever keen to clear up, had emptied it overboard, and carefully washed it out. I had not thought to ask her or the medical orderly to save it, and bitterly regretted my lack of foresight.

89

"I will admit her for observation," stated Dr D brushing aside my suggestion of immediate surgery.

Suddenly I felt extremely tired. Misi was loaded into the ambulance with the doctor. I was also given a lift, as I felt quite incapable of walking up the hill. Nancy went off to stay with her cousin-sister and we agreed to meet next morning in time to catch the MV Moturina that was due to sail at midday. I was thankful that I could relinquish responsibility, but I was also worried about the outcome, now that my diagnosis had been questioned. Dr D found a nurse to show me to a spare bedroom in the nurses' quarters, where I could stay the night. I was too exhausted to have a shower and fell into bed, weeping tears of weariness and frustration into the pillow. It was after midnight when I finally fell into a deep sleep, but I was awake at 5.30 AM thinking of Misi and all that had transpired. I got up about 7 AM, showered and went in search of some breakfast, after which I began to feel better.

Around 9.30 AM there was a tap on the door and when I opened it, there stood Dr D.

"I owe you an apology," he said, "for doubting what you told me."

Apparently, after Misi had been admitted to the ward, she had started to vomit faecal fluid, but the night orderly had not realised the significance of this event and had not notified Dr D. Misi had collapsed a couple of hours' later, and the day staff had called Dr D who had managed to resuscitate her. He had come to tell me that she was being prepared for theatre and that he would perform an exploratory operation shortly. I was vastly relieved and thankful that she was at last going to get the treatment that she needed. I could not bear the thought that after all our efforts she might have died during the night.

"I do know faecal vomit when I see it," was my somewhat tart comment.

Dr D explained that he was new to the Territory and was not used to having to rely on the judgement and diagnosis of nursing Sisters.

"I won't make that mistake again," he replied somewhat ruefully.

90

I explained that I had to catch the boat back at midday, so would not know what the outcome of Misi's operation was. Dr D promised to speak to me on the radio, in due course. I appreciated his coming to apologise and letting me know what had happened and felt that I was leaving Misi in good hands.

Nancy and I caught the boat back, and this time the sea was quite calm. We both managed to doze on the way, as I gathered she had stayed up most of the previous night talking to her relatives. The folk at Fife Bay were waiting for news, and after I had explained, Mary reminded everyone that Misi would still need our prayers. I slept much better that night, and fortunately there were no night calls. I spoke to Dr D on the radio sked on Tuesday and he told me that when he operated on Misi, he had removed several feet of gangrenous small intestine. It was unclear what had caused the gangrene but we were all thankful that the obstruction was not caused by a life-threatening tumour. She had come through the operation and in time he hoped she would make a full recovery. We continued to remember Misi and her family in our prayers.

CHAPTER 12: TESTING TIMES

It was already December and extremely hot. I often had to change my clothes a couple of times a day and we had to be careful not to use more water than necessary as the water tanks were low. To cool off, I sometimes visited the waterfall with off-duty nurses and school children (plate 22). The waterfall was about 20 minutes walk away, in the bush. A river flowed over a rocky outcrop into a deep pool which in turn cascaded into smaller pools. Boys jumped from the top of the waterfall, but I contented myself with swimming in the pool. It was absolutely lovely to be able to splash about in cool water, and it meant we could also save water by not showering after a visit to the pool.

Toby, the dog, was growing fast; he loved water, and always jumped into the waterfall on our visits. One day he swam out to sea for about 50 yards before turning back. He followed me after I had left him on the beach whilst I went out in a canoe to the Moturina, to check on a delivery of goods. Unfortunately, he was not an easy dog to train, possibly because I did not have a lot of spare time or expertise to devote to correcting his behaviour. He did not like to be left out of anything and followed me everywhere. He was a real escape artist and when I shut him in the house before I went to church, he nearly always managed to get out and join the congregation, with a big grin on his face! He had a habit of leaning on people and howling during the singing, much to my embarrassment, but the girls thought it was hilarious.

After I returned from Samarai, we had a fairly quiet period at the Hospital, which gave me a chance to sort out clinic cards for 600 or so village children, under-fives who we had on our books. The kapok tree near our house was bursting with pods that girls picked when they were ripe. They had a method of removing the black seeds, by emptying pods into a bathtub and twirling them with a stick until the seeds were dislodged (plate 23). I used the fresh white cotton-like material to make new mattresses for our newborn babies, which when well-stuffed were quite firm. The babies' cots were laundry baskets on wheels and were mainly used during the daytime. No self-respecting Papuan mother would leave her baby alone in a cot at night. Each infant slept next to their mother with skin-to-skin contact and within easy reach of the breast, should they need a night feed. I had never heard of a baby being smothered whilst sleeping with its mother.

A local woman came in with her left arm broken below the elbow. Apparently her husband had hit her with a stick of sugar cane. It was a simple fracture without too much displacement so I was able to put a plaster of Paris bandage on without too much difficulty, although I had not applied one before. I had to be sure to get the thickness right, so I kept her in overnight to check on the circulation of the limb. She was able to move her fingers easily in the morning and they were a good colour so I let her go home with her arm in a sling. Mary said that her husband would be hemarai (ashamed) of what he had done. I was unsure how common domestic violence was, but I had heard that in fights men often used axes as weapons and I did not like to think of the consequences of such violence.

Preparation for Christmas

I felt uncomfortable that my contribution to the life of the church was minimal, mainly because I was making little headway with the Suau language. I decided to start a Fellowship group for nurses on Sunday afternoons, as we were usually all free then, unless there was an emergency at the Hospital. I asked the girls first and they all seemed enthusiastic. As we were in the season of Advent, at the beginning of the western churches' Christian year, it seemed an appropriate time to start. We met for an hour on Sunday afternoons, and thought about the season and what it might mean to us. It seemed to go quite well and as we all spoke English, there was not a language problem. As Christmas was fast approaching it also gave us an opportunity to discuss what we would like to do at the Hospital. I suggested that we make a crib scene for the Maternity ward, as I had brought some Nativity pieces with me. The girls made a stable by weaving leaves from the Pandanus plant into a box shape and we placed the figures inside. As this was my first Christmas in the Territory and in a tropical climate, I wondered how I would feel about it. The contrast with a wintry December in the UK was so great; it hardly seemed to be the same time of year. I had already noticed that the commercial face of Christmas had no place here; our focus was on celebrating the birth of Christ and it was the central reason for the planned festivities. It was at the same time much simpler but also much more profound.

Alan's father, Sidney Dunstone, arrived for an extended visit and was delighted that he was able to spend time with his family especially his grandson. Andrew and he got on like a house on fire. We were also to have a visitor for Christmas, which I looked forward too. Dorothy S had arranged to arrive on the next boat from Iruna. Dorothy was an Australian volunteer nursing Sister, working with Nick at Iruna, while Avis Martin from England, who was the Sister there was on leave. I had met Dorothy on my way down to Fife Bay in July. She was keen to have a short break and to see something more of the southeast coast. We prepared the spare room in Middle House for our guest and I thought about Misi and hoped we would not need the room for a patient over the Christmas period.

Complicated Midwifery

I always kept my midwifery bible Margaret Myles' *Textbook for Midwives* (1961) to hand as so many women in labour had complicated deliveries. This was partly due to lack of antenatal care, and partly the distance that families had to travel to reach Hospital. Before Christmas we had three babies born, two of them on successive nights, which played havoc with my sleep patterns. The first mother, Sakaria, was expecting her tenth child. At first, the labour progressed normally, although the baby's head had not entered the pelvis. This was not uncommon in a mother in her tenth pregnancy, but we kept a close eye on her.

During the night she had not made much progress so I decided to check if all was well, by doing an internal examination. At first I had some difficulty in recognising the presenting part, which was certainly not the head or a foot. Then with some consternation I realised that it was a shoulder. Sakaria's abdominal muscles, stretched by multiple pregnancies, were too slack to maintain the baby in the correct position. When I examined her abdomen I felt the head on her left side with the feet on the right, which meant that the baby was lying in the transverse (or sideways) position with the shoulder impacted in the pelvis and in this position could not be delivered.

In a well-staffed and equipped Hospital an emergency caesarean section would have been performed. At Fife Bay this was not an option and I quickly consulted my Maggie Myles to look up deep transverse arrest (technical term for the complication). I knew that the lives of both mother and baby were in danger from obstructed labour. By this time, Sakaria's waters had broken and she was in the second stage of labour, but was unable to push the baby out. She was in a lot of pain but the baby was already distressed and I could not risk giving Sakaria any pain relief. I asked Mary to explain the position to her anxious husband, as I was uncertain that we would achieve a positive outcome.

I realised that the only thing I could do was to try and turn the baby, which would be a difficult manoeuvre without an anaesthetic, with the added complication of a ruptured uterus if I was not very careful. I felt very anxious to the point of feeling nauseated, as I had never seen this procedure performed. In most cases it would have been corrected before reaching this stage. I asked Mary to explain the procedure to Sakaria, as I knew it would be uncomfortable at the very least and I needed her cooperation. I scrubbed up as adequately as I could, given the shortage of water, and prayed for guidance, as I attempted manually to rotate the baby *in utero.* Mary talked the mother through the procedure and helped her to breathe through her mouth and resist the urge to push. Thankfully the baby was in the dorso-anterior position, where the baby's back was lying against the mother's abdomen. Sakaria's roomy pelvis and slack tummy muscles allowed me to insert my hand and eventually, with much trepidation, I pushed the shoulder up and managed to grasp and bring down a foot, once I was sure it was a foot and not a hand. It was not easy to tell the difference, but I made sure I could not feel a thumb, which can be abducted, or fingers, which are of unequal length and longer than toes. I then found a second foot and by gentle traction on feet and legs, managed with some difficulty, to rotate the baby's body until it was vertical and presenting as a breech.

A breach delivery was not without hazard, but I reasoned that this was a better option than no delivery at all. The cord then became visible and as it was pulsating faintly I knew that the baby was still alive, but only just. The buttocks then appeared and were wrapped in a towel to keep them warm and I saw that it was a boy. I rotated the baby's body to deliver the shoulders and then allowed him to hang for a few minutes to bring down the head. This was the most risky part of a breech delivery because of the possibility of brain damage if the head descended through the pelvis too quickly. I supported his body whilst Mary cleared his airways when his mouth and nose became visible. He was quite limp and covered in meconium (sticky substance excreted from the newborn's bowel), a sign of the trauma he had experienced. Finally, the baby's head was slowly and safely delivered.

I left Mary to attend to Sakaria whilst I resuscitated the baby, who was quite small and pale. He took a few minutes to breath, but eventually he gasped and cried and began to turn a healthier pink colour. Thankfully the placenta was delivered without too much blood loss. Sakaria had been wonderfully stoical and was so pleased to have a baby boy, even if it was her tenth child. The baby weighed less than five pounds, and needed to recover from his ordeal, as did Sakaria. I decided to rest the baby rather than bathe him straight away, so I wiped away as much of the meconium as I could and gave him to his mother to keep warm. I examined the baby's arms to see if there was any nerve damage but thankfully they appeared normal. His left shoulder was slightly swollen and bruised where it had been jammed in his mother's pelvis, but that would not cause any permanent injury. Sakaria squeezed some colostrum into her son's mouth, as much as he could swallow, and then he fell asleep. Mary gave Sakaria a big dose of penicillin to prevent any infection, following my intervention. We also gave a small dose to the baby in case he had inhaled any amniotic fluid during delivery.

It was now about 5.30 AM, and Sineleki came down from Middle House to see if she could assist us in any way. I asked her to make us all a cup of tea, to help us recover. I felt like a wet rag and Sakaria was very tired. Her husband came in to see his wife and new baby, and asked me if he could call the baby after me, which would have meant calling him Arker as the Suau people did not use the ch sound as in my surname Archer. I suggested they might like to call him George after my father, which they seemed very pleased to do, so George he became. It seemed a big name for such a small scrap of humanity but I hoped he would grow into it. The Suau people, in common with most people in Papua, did not have a family name as such, but always used their father's first name as a surname. The baby's father's name was Ioanni (Papuan form of John), so the new baby's name was George Ioanni.

I fell into bed but did not sleep all that well, so got up at lunchtime. Wendy and Alan suggested I joined them for lunch, which I was glad to do, especially as I had not had time to bake bread that day. It always tasted smoky anyway, after my efforts with the kitchen stove with which I had a love-hate relationship! After lunch I went to Hospital to see Sakaria and baby George. He was still sleepy but I bathed him and he certainly looked better afterwards. He was still quite weak

97

but had started to suck which was a good sign. Both parents were there and I spoke to them about the advisability of preventing further pregnancies if at all possible. We had no family planning methods available, so I could not really help them. Sakaria was probably in her mid-thirties with a good few childbearing years ahead of her. I also said that if she did become pregnant she should go into the Hospital at Samarai well ahead of time to prevent further complications. Both parents nodded but I was not sure how seriously they took my suggestions. I discovered that of the nine previous children only five had survived. Two had died soon after birth, one when he was four years old from malaria, and one aged eight from snakebite. I knew that local people favoured large families so that they would have adult children and grandchildren to care for them in their old age. The more children there were the more likely the parents were to manage when they were old or infirm.

Mary had slept most of the day, so that when a second woman went into labour around 8 PM, Mary said that she would look after her and would call me if she needed me. I was happy with this arrangement and after checking that all was well with the mother I went to bed early. I awoke at first light and peeped around Mary's bedroom door, to find her sleeping soundly, so all was well. I learnt later that the woman had given birth to a healthy little girl at 3.30 AM, thankfully without any complications.

However, when I went down to Hospital after breakfast, I found Sakaria nursing a sleepy baby George and looking miserable. Ioanni had gone back to the village and their two elder daughters had come and brought food. They were in their teens and looked at me with solemn expressions. When I looked at George, I saw he was jaundiced and that he had lost more weight than was usual after birth. He now weighed only four-and-a-half pounds. He was also dehydrated, as he was not feeding well from the breast. What a difference 24 hours could make in a fragile little life. Sakaria began to weep silently, and one of her daughters said that two babies who had died after birth had looked yellow and floppy like George, before they died. My heart sank but we had to give him a fighting chance. I explained to Sakaria that I would pass a tube into his stomach to feed him, if she would express her breast milk, which was better for him than the powdered baby milk we could make up. Mary helped me pass the naso-gastric tube, and we gave him his first feed, which he tolerated well. We had to feed him three-hourly to maintain adequate fluid and nutrition, but I suggested that Sakaria try him on the breast after the midnight feed and before the 6 AM feed so that we could get some sleep. She was an experienced mother and I knew she would do her very best for her infant son. If she could get him to suck even for a short time, it would stimulate the flow of breast milk that we needed to maintain at all costs. I asked Sakaria to drink as much as she could and offered her some of our powdered milk, which she declined as she did not like the taste, preferring instead to drink the coconut liquid that her vegetables were cooked in.

Meanwhile Dorothy had arrived by boat. It was good to see her. I showed her around Fife Bay and in the afternoon we went to the waterfall, to try to cool off as it was extremely hot and humid. Dorothy proved to be a great bread maker and made extra bread for the nurses, so she was very popular, as it was a real treat for them. There were so many weevils in the flour that it was impossible to pick them all out, but after a while we did get used to them. As someone said, "It's all extra protein." Dorothy also helped us with baby George's tube feeds, which we continued for another week. He regained his birth weight, and gradually the jaundice faded. As he began to gain strength, he was able to feed from the breast and Sakaria looked much happier. We still gave him top up feeds but as he became more vigorous he pulled his feeding tube out. I decided to see how he got on without it for a few days and as he did well we did not replace it. The family went home a few days later as Sakaria wanted to see her other children. They left me some yams, which made a change from the sweet potato and taro vegetables we usually ate. I knew we could follow-up George at the next clinic, but I asked Sakaria to return if she was at all concerned about him.

On December 20th, a young woman, Mimosa, came to Hospital; she was 38 weeks pregnant with her ninth child. She had severe anaemia and looked almost exsanguinated (bloodless). I was horrified and started her on iron tablets and iron injections of Imferon straight away. The latter were quite painful but it was necessary to try to improve her haemoglobin level before she went into labour, as she was at high risk of heavy bleeding. I asked her husband and mother who accompanied her to give her green leafy vegetables if they could find any. They did not understand what I was fussing about, but they managed to produce some Chinese cabbage. When I examined her I discovered she also had thrombophlebitis in her right leg, which was red and swollen. Mary put on a dressing of glycerine and ichthammol, which was a dark brown colour and rather messy, but it was very good for reducing inflammation and swelling.

Mimosa went into labour next day. I was worried because of her poor condition, but she had quite a short labour and delivered a healthy baby girl weighing six pounds. The placenta was delivered without too much blood loss, as I gave her intravenous ergometrine. We all breathed a sigh of relief, but she suddenly began to bleed and we had considerable difficulty in controlling the haemorrhage. There is nothing quite as frightening as a postpartum haemorrhage, especially if mother is anaemic. As I feared, she suddenly collapsed, and although I tried to put a drip up, I could not get into a vein. In desperation I resorted to an old fashioned method of giving fluids, and put up a rectal drip of two pints of warm plain water. Amazingly it worked and she began to recover, but remained very weak. I was then able to put an IV drip up, to restore her blood chemical balance. What she really needed was blood, but as we had none, we had to do what we could with diet and iron injections.

I asked Mimosa to stay at Hospital for about a month so that we could treat her anaemia. It would also give her chance to have a good rest over the Christmas period. Her husband was not to keen at first but Mary explained to him that his wife had very nearly died because her blood was so thin, which was why it was necessary, and he agreed.

Mimosa's mother stayed to look after her when he returned home to fetch food and their two youngest children. Other children were cared for by the extended family. Fortunately the baby thrived and to my surprise Mimosa was able to breast-feed her normally. Mimosa still looked very pale, so I gave her some tins of corned beef, as her diet was normally low in protein. I was not sure why Mimosa was so anaemic but it could have been a combination of repeated attacks of malaria and intestinal parasites, so I decided to treat her for both, after she had recovered from the birth. I doubted if she would be willing to travel to the Hospital in Samarai for further investigations. At least she had come to Hospital to have her baby, as she would most certainly have died if she had stayed in the village.

I pondered long and hard on the problem of the poor health of mothers who had too many pregnancies too close together, but I did not come up with any answers apart from trying to improve their antenatal care, which was not easy given the distances involved.

CHAPTER 13: CHRISTMAS IN THE TROPICS

I HAD BOUGHT SOME DRESS MATERIAL IN SAMARAI, with the intention of making up a new dress for Christmas, but I never found time, so had to make do with what I had brought with me from England, which already looked shabby because of frequent washing (plate 24). Clothes dried in the sun faded quickly, but I chose the least faded dress and Dorothy kindly ironed it for me. As we had no electricity we used an old flat iron that I had brought with me, which had belonged to my mother. The girls used a charcoal iron, which they filled with burning coconut husks to heat it up. This was the only time that I valued the wood stove as I could use it to heat my iron up, but it meant that we could only do any ironing when the stove was alight and hot enough.

It gave me a glimpse of how my mother had had to manage when my brother and I were growing up in a farm cottage without gas, electricity or running water. She had used a couple of flat irons then, to iron our school uniforms and everything else. Later when we moved to a council house that had electricity, we used those irons as doorstops. I had only brought one iron with me and that had been an afterthought but I had reason to be glad that I did as I found it difficult to use a charcoal iron because they either got too hot or went out altogether. They were also quite heavy as they had to be big enough to hold the charcoal or in our case the coconut husks, and the heat they produced was uneven.

It was really great having Dorothy to stay over Christmas, although she was due to leave on the first boat out after Christmas Day. She was a great help when it came to putting up some decorations on the morning of Christmas Eve – we had not got around to making anything earlier. We made a mobile by cutting out shapes of stars from coloured paper and the girls cut some branches off the Casuarina tree (type of evergreen fir), for the General ward and we put the crib in the Maternity ward. Then we turned our attention to the house and made another tree, and some paper chains, so it all looked festive. Toby got very excited and ran round and round chewing up anything he could find.

On the evening of Christmas Eve we had a feast prepared by Lawes College students and their families and we all sat on the floor to enjoy food laid out on banana leaves on the grass. This was followed by games and carol singing and ended with dancing. Most people wanted to stay up until midnight to welcome in Christmas Day, but Dorothy and I and most nurses decided to go to bed in case we were called up in the night. It was just as well that we did, as local villagers woke us up at 3 AM when they came around singing carols. Another group appeared about 4 AM, also carolling. It was a lovely sound and was apparently a tradition in the Suau District, although it took me a few minutes to realise what was happening. We stood on the veranda and listened as the sound faded into the distance.

The school children had all gone home for the holidays but after breakfast on Christmas morning I gave each nurse a present of a length of material to make up a dress or blouse. The sewing machine would be busy for a few days and Sineleki started cutting her dress out straight away. The girls never used a pattern but the dresses always seemed to turn out well. There were also a few odds and ends that had come in gift parcels from different churches in Australia and I distributed those as well; combs and note books, or soap, which was always popular. Dorothy and I also exchanged small gifts and then after a visit to Hospital to check on patients we went to morning service in Lawes College Chapel at 9.30 AM.

I had asked Ravu to come over and hold a short service for Hospital patients and he arrived about 11 AM. Afterwards I gave all General patients a tin of meat and a packet of tea each, to help them celebrate. They were all very pleased with their small gifts. In the Maternity ward we gave each mother a baby blanket and bar of soap, also from the gift parcels. I had bought some sweet biscuits for children from the store, so everyone was catered for.

Dorothy and I had invited nurses to lunch, which was quite a simple affair of tinned meat, bread and fruit, but we were relaxed and all enjoyed it. Alan had asked the Hospital staff to take the 4 PM service and I was a little apprehensive as I was leading it. We had decided to re-enact the Nativity story, as it was the simplest thing to do. Students came and Hospital patients were invited, as it was largely visual and in English. We borrowed one of the newborn babies as baby Jesus, but he started crying half way through and had to be rescued by his mother. However, it went off quite well considering it was the first time the nurses and I had done anything like that together.

On Christmas evening Wendy and Alan invited Dorothy and me to dinner, but we managed to have a dip in the sea before going up to the Big House. It was a novel experience for me to go swimming on Christmas day, but as Dorothy was Australian it was not something unusual for her. Fortunately, I was able to enjoy the meal, during which we reminisced about cold Christmases, without my being called away to Hospital.

Boxing Day

Boxing Day was given over to games and sports. Lawes College students played local village teams at soccer and a form of rugby. It got quite rough at one point and a local man was injured. He had a back tooth knocked clean out, as well as a bang on the head. I was unsure if his jaw was fractured as it was very swollen, but it was impossible to tell without an X-ray. I admitted him to Hospital for observation and pain relief. Fortunately, neither he nor his team bore a grudge and he was regarded as something of a hero, especially as that team won the game. It might have been a different story if they had lost, because the men took it all very seriously.

In the evening Wendy, Alan, and Brian came up to Middle House for supper and I played my LP records of Handel's Messiah. Bertha and Tavita also came but had to leave early. It seemed a good way to end the Christmas festivities.

Old Friends and New

Alan told me that an Australian teacher had been appointed for the start of the new term and that she would live with us at Middle House. Her name was Margaret Cole and she had been in the Territory for three years already, working in the Gulf of Papua, so she was experienced and would be a great asset.

Dorothy left the next day on the MV Moturina on its usual trip from Samarai to Port Moresby. I went down to the beach to see her off, and saw a little family paddling from boat to shore in a canoe. When they reached the beach, I recognised Misi and her husband with their baby. Misi looked thinner but well, she handed me a letter from Dr D that contained details of her postoperative progress. She had had an infection that had been treated with antibiotics but otherwise she had made good progress. The family had stayed with relatives for a few days after she had been discharged, whilst waiting for the boat. They were with us for a day or two before going home to their village. I was so glad to see them all and they greeted me like an old friend. It was good to see Misi walking around doing all the normal things, when the outcome might have been so different.

New Year 1967

I could hardly believe that I had been here for six months; time had passed so quickly. New Year was celebrated with gusto but I was totally unprepared for it. We were woken at first light by shrieks from nurses and yells from male voices that turned out to be local village lads. Apparently it was the custom for boys to carry or drag girls down to the sea and throw them in, having first thrown flour over them. As I emerged to investigate, someone a little bolder than the rest threw flour over me, but evidently decided that he would not try to manhandle me down to the beach! There was a great deal of laughter and shouts of Happy New Year, from all directions.

Overnight Patrol

I had been sorry to say goodbye to Dorothy, but another visitor arrived on the next boat that came from Port Moresby via Iruna. Daphne C was an Australian teacher serving at Iruna; she took advantage of the long school holiday to take a short break with us at Fife Bay. Daphne C was interested in the local flora and decided that she would accompany me on an overnight patrol to a village four hours' walk away, to collect flowers and plants. Savaia (plate 25) was the third village to the east and was the only village with a clinic and a resident nurse, Mauri. Part of my job was to supervise her work and make sure that all was going well. Mauri was married with four children of her own, so was well placed to look after local mothers and babies.

We left at 8 AM on Friday morning and arrived in the village around 2 PM. It was a relatively easy walk because there were few hills and we walked mainly along the beach. We crossed a very wide river by canoe that took nearly an hour and although we had sun hats and umbrellas both Daphne C and I got rather sunburnt. When we arrived I inspected the clinic and found everything spic and span, with up-to-date records. I saw a couple of sick patients and suggested some further treatment. We also made the acquaintance of Mauri's tame cassowary, that she kept in an enclosure. It was the first time I had seen one at such close quarters. It seemed healthy if a tad restricted for such a large bird. Apparently it had been injured and Mauri had cared for it. Given the shortage of meat it was surprising that it had not been eaten, but I learnt later that there was some form of taboo on eating cassowary.

It was really hot and sticky and Mauri suggested that we might like to bathe in the river. It was 20 minutes' walk away, and was shallow and shady. We left our change of clothes on the riverbank and waded in. Local children, who had shown us the way, were very interested in the proceedings and although we had brought soap and towels with us both Daphne C and I were disinclined to undress before such an observant audience. We both emerged dripping wet and with our clothes clinging to us, and realised that we might as well have taken them off initially. We put on our clean, dry clothes, without drying ourselves properly, under the watchful eyes of amused children. On the way back from the river Daphne C made some drawings of plants found in the bush. There was an abundance of tree orchids and other plants we could not put a name to. Mauri had a meal waiting for us and after evening prayers we went to bed. Mauri had moved her children into the family room so that Daphne C and I could have a room to ourselves, which was very thoughtful of her.

We left after breakfast the next morning, but made slow progress, as we had not slept very well because of the activities of rats in the thatch over our heads. It was still very hot and we were well loaded with bags as the people, whose villages and hamlets we passed through (plates 26 and 27), kindly gave us more pineapples than we could easily carry. We ate two on the way home as they were so refreshing and thirst-quenching. When we eventually arrived back at Middle House mid-afternoon, I felt as though I had completed a marathon. My face was luminous red and Daphne C was also sunburnt, so we smothered ourselves in calamine lotion, and went to bed for a couple of hours.

Next morning I had just about recovered when Brian appeared with a tiny ginger kitten. It had been found under the Big House, but there was no sign of the mother cat. Alan and Wendy did not want to keep it, so I agreed to, although it looked as if it was too young to have left its mother. I could not tell if it was male or female but we hoped it was the former. We called it by the not very original name of Ginger. It had a huge appetite for such a tiny creature, and a very loud purr. Toby was fascinated with it and to my horror picked it up in his mouth, but it did not seem to mind and emerged unscathed. They became firm friends and sometimes slept together.

The mailbag arrived on the next boat and I had five letters from children in Junior Church groups in Australia. They had all been asked to write to a missionary nurse as part of a project they were doing. I made an effort and answered them all. I normally tried to write to my parents and to my friend Stella on a regular basis, whenever the boat was due, as this was the only opportunity to get mail out. It meant that Christmas and birthday cards were a hit-and-miss affair, but most people understood. I drew a diagram for my mother who felt she received letters less frequently than other families, mainly because the majority of other missionaries had access to an airstrip and we had to rely on our irregular boats. The diagram described the circuitous route taken by a letter after leaving Fife Bay, on its way to the UK. (see overleaf)

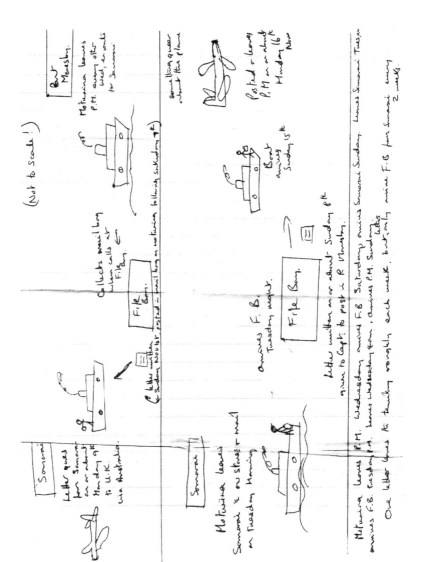

(Not to Scale!)

A Tale of Two Letters

109

CHAPTER 14: NEW FACES

We started the year with some phenomenal weather. It poured and poured with rain until paths ran like rivers, and I had to abandon any attempt at wearing shoes. The rain was accompanied by gale force winds that rattled shutters, which we kept closed, but the veranda was still awash with water. Our water tanks rapidly filled up and even overflowed, but we had no way of collecting surplus water. I had been told that sometimes up to ten inches of rain could fall in 24 hours, and it certainly felt like it. I got used to squelching through mud but it was the first time I had experienced a tropical storm, and the noise of rain falling on the corrugated iron roof was deafening. It was rough at sea, because even the Frigate birds came into the bay and were a sight to behold. They had a huge wing-span and swooped back and forth over the water. I did not envy Daphne C her return journey on the MV Moturina, which was sheltering in the bay.

Birthday Celebrations

Brian celebrated his 21st birthday early in January. Wendy made a birthday cake and we had a party in the evening. Lawes College staff were invited, also Kay and Geoff from the Patrol Post, and Ravu and Lahui. Most people arrived dripping wet and soon the Big House veranda was full of very damp people, but it did not stop our enjoyment of the evening. Alan's Dad stood on the veranda and got a cold shower down his back from a hole in the guttering, when he leaned too far backwards, and had to change his shirt. Andrew and Miriam had been allowed to stay up and thought this was extremely funny, which it was. We also welcomed Revd Riley Samson onto the staff of Lawes College, together with his wife and family. Riley was the first Papuan tutor to be appointed to a Theological College, so that was a great step forward. We also received a visit from Dr C Forman of Yale University who was touring Theological Colleges in the Pacific for WCC (World Council of Churches). We were all glad that he braved the travel difficulties to visit us. Students benefited from his visit and it was good to be reminded of the wider dimensions of the world outside our isolated corner of the globe, which it was all too easy to lose sight of.

Mary went on patrol, and just after she left we became really busy with five babies from the same village with gastroenteritis. It was difficult to locate the source of infection, but we were able to treat four of them with oral rehydration and antibiotics. The fifth baby who was about seven months' old was very ill and I thought we would lose him as he was severely dehydrated when admitted. He was too weak to take oral fluids but I managed to put a drip up, although the baby's parents were very worried by the procedure. At night I took him and his Mum up to the house so that I could manage the drip and give him six-hourly antibiotics. Fortunately he improved dramatically after 48 hours of rehydration therapy and I was able to remove the drip, much to his parents' relief and mine. We also had two women in labour and fortunately the first had a normal delivery. The second woman who had been admitted during the night, and was expecting twins, thought she was in labour but it turned out to be a false alarm.

Beetle *in situ*

At last the storms passed leaving everything with a well-washed look and several leaking roofs to be repaired. I wrote some reports by the light of the Tilley lamp, with its attendant insects drawn to the flame circling around it, when I felt something fly into my left ear. It was buzzing and so painful that my futile attempts to dislodge it only made matters worse. I ran to Hospital for the ear syringe and called

111

Olinda to come to my aid by syringing my ear with some warm fluid. The poor girl had never used an ear syringe before and was nervous that her first attempt had to be on me! Nothing happened except that I got quite wet, but the buzzing stopped and I wondered if the insect had drowned. Certainly the pain disappeared and when the creature could not be floated out I was resigned to having a dead insect in my ear until such time as it could be dislodged.

Welcome Visitor

I was looking forward to a visit from my friend Margaret Sharman who had come out to the Territory a year before me. Margaret S also came from Essex and we had been at missionary training college together at Selly Oak. Margaret S was stationed northwest of Port Moresby, in the Gulf District, at Orokolo, and decided to spend a few days visiting us on the southeast coast. Our coastline was well known for its bare outcrops of limestone, and bush-covered foothills, which came right down to the sea. Volcanic lava from a previous age gave the sandy beach its black appearance. The stretch of coast we covered in our patrols was approximately 70 miles long, which is why it took a week for us to cover the western side and up to ten days to visit all villages on the eastern side. Dotted between villages were hamlets of one to twelve houses, often situated near to a river, which people used as a water supply.

Night Call Out

At the beginning of February on a Friday evening, a man arrived from a distant village to say that a woman had been in labour since Wednesday and was "unable to give birth," and that "she was very bad." I suspected that labour was obstructed, and after consulting with Mary, who had only just returned from patrolling the eastern side, I decided to go to investigate. I packed an emergency bag and a change of clothes in case they were needed. The man was very vague about how far away the village was but on the way to Hospital he had alerted the Patrol Officer, who said he would send David, the young Australian cadet Patrol Officer, and a policeman with us, plus a boy to carry the light for David. I asked Olinda if she would accompany me and she agreed.

We set off about 7 PM and made a strange little procession, as we walked through the bush in the dark. Olinda carried our Tilley lamp and it showed a circle of light just wide enough to see where next to put our feet. It suddenly struck me that this was what the psalmist must have envisaged when he said "Your Word is a lamp to my feet, and a light to my path." I could not remember the reference, but made a mental note to look it up when I got back.

We walked for what seemed a very long time and when we reached a village we stopped for a rest. The policeman stretched out and went to sleep, and when we were ready to leave David tried to wake him but couldn't, so we left him there. The man who had brought the message and was our guide, led the way with a hurricane lamp, followed by Bono, the boy with the Coleman lamp, then David, Olinda, and, lastly, me. We had to walk in single file because the bush was so dense, and I found it difficult to keep up, so they slowed their pace a little. Twice we came to rivers too wide to cross and then David roused men from nearby houses to take us across in canoes. Our guide, whose name I had not grasped, explained why we were travelling in the middle of the night and the men seemed quite willing to ferry us across the river, but I think David probably paid them a small sum of money for their trouble.

About 3 AM we came to a village where they were having a feast, so we were given a cup of very sweet tea and some taro, which was very welcome. I began to worry that the woman we were travelling to help had either already given birth or died or both. I had no idea where we were and when I asked how much further it was to the woman's village, the reply was "little bit long, Sister" which made me even more apprehensive.

113

We set off again and the way was very rough. We all had soaking wet feet, as we had to wade through several streams, which made walking very uncomfortable. Just as I felt I could go no further we saw the first glimmer of dawn in the sky, and came into a clearing where there was a large village that had a church and a pastor. He showed no surprise at being roused from sleep by a bedraggled party, including two *dim dims*, and made us welcome. It was about 5.30 AM and we asked if we could stop to rest there, and his wife whisked Bono and Olinda off to another house, and showed David and me into an empty room with a couple of mats to sleep on. I had not expected to share a room with David, nor I suspected had he, but we were both too tired to comment. We took off our shoes and lay down on the floor, but I found it difficult to sleep though David was soon snoring. I must have dozed off because I was woken by a loud squawking and feared that some poor chicken was about to become our breakfast. This proved to be the case, as the pastor's wife brought us some water to wash with and announced that breakfast was ready. Tea was very welcome, but the scrawny bird rather tough. However I realised that to cook a chicken for our breakfast was a special honour. Olinda, Bono and Wita our guide, whose name I finally got right, joined us. They certainly enjoyed the repast.

David said he would return with Bono, now that it was daylight, and I thanked him for escorting us. I wondered if he would pick up the sleeping policeman on the way back. No doubt the policeman would be in trouble for not carrying out the duty assigned to him. Olinda and I continued walking with our guide for another four hours, but progress was slow, as I found the going difficult. Eventually we came to a wide bay and spent an hour on a canoe crossing to the village. It was 2 PM on Saturday, when we finally arrived at Navabu.

I was taken to visit the woman's house to find that the baby had been born that morning, but was premature and quite cold. The mother was bleeding heavily and had a fever, so I was able to treat her with antibiotics, anti-malarial tablets and drugs to control the bleeding. Fortunately the placenta had been delivered and seemed to be

114

intact. She was very young and frightened after what must have been quite an ordeal. I asked for some warm water and a bowl to bathe the baby. This warmed him up and he began to cry and later to suck at the breast, which was a good sign. It was the young mother's first baby and judging by the shape of his head and the bruises on his face he had been lying in the posterior position (where the baby's head doesn't flex and is born face towards the mother's abdomen) and that had caused the labour to be long and painful. I didn't have scales with me but judged him to weigh about four pounds.

The mother's husband, family and whole village were very pleased that we had come, and brought us gifts of food and fruit. Olinda and I were both really done in and she explained that we would need to spend the night there. When I was satisfied that all was well with mother and baby, we were taken to someone's house and, after being given some food and more tea, both fell asleep until 7 AM the next day. After breakfast, a small crowd of mothers and babies gathered and we did a quick clinic and treated a couple of adults who were sick. Fortunately I had enough medication with me for what was needed.

Wita appeared and told us that a boat had called into the bay to pick up copra and we could go back to Fife Bay on it. Rather than one of our regular boats, it was a K boat (where all the names began with K), the MV Kamonai and I was very pleased to see it, as I was not sure I could walk all the way back again. Judging by his face I guessed that Wita was also glad that he did not have to make the return journey. I checked on mother and baby before we left and all seemed to be well. I left mother some medication and then we set off at around 11 AM and arrived back at Fife Bay Sunday night. It was not an experience I wanted to repeat too often. I slept very well that night and, apart from feeling rather stiff, was none the worse for my 14-hour walk.

Much to my surprise Margaret S had already arrived on an earlier boat, together with Jan and Nick and their family from Iruna. They stayed with Alan and Wendy, while Margaret S stayed with us at Middle House, where Mary and the girls had already made her welcome.

It was good to meet up with Nick again especially as he syringed my ear with a practised hand and the beetle flew out without more ado. It was still intact and iridescent with a hard carapace, which no doubt accounted for the pain it caused me. The girls were most impressed when they saw it.

Margaret S decided she would like to walk to our two nearest villages, Avaroro and Isu Isu, as it was not a great distance to travel. I had some BCG vaccinations to do and over two days managed to vaccinate over 50 babies and children against tuberculosis, a disease that had taken such a toll on local people.

The next day I held an antenatal clinic at Hospital and discovered that we had six ladies-in-waiting. I prayed that they would all have normal deliveries, as it was complicated obstetrics that I found the most difficult to manage. Nick decided to go on patrol and Mary was happy go with him, as Margaret S was visiting me. We had a lovely afternoon picnic at the waterfall, with Jan and the children, who all enjoyed it. It certainly felt good to have a few hours off.

CHAPTER 15: REINFORCEMENTS

Our new primary school teacher, Margaret Cole, an Australian, arrived on the MV Moturina, a little later than expected, as she had been on leave. Everyone from the Lawes College School went down to the wharf to meet her; the schoolchildren were really excited and helped to carry Margaret's luggage up to Middle House. I hoped that Margaret's expertise would extend to the wood stove that I was still struggling with. I was glad to discover that she was a keen gardener as our small flowerbeds were sadly neglected. However, she was not fond of cats, though Toby made a good impression by licking her face vigorously. I had a great yearning for some chocolate, which we could not get in the Territory. Margaret brought some with her from Australia, which was a real treat.

Two new Papuan teachers arrived on the next boat, Mehere and Pison, who were accommodated at Isuleilei. Extra teachers meant that the school was able to increase its student numbers to 180 of which 117 were boarders. We took extra schoolgirls into our house and with nurses we now numbered 14, which made the squeeze in the kitchen even tighter.

Risky Childbirth

I did not see a lot of our new teacher during her first week, as I was really busy at the Hospital. Nick was still away on patrol, but Margaret Sharman helped me out, and although it was a bit of a busman's holiday for her, I was very glad of her midwifery and nursing skills. On Sunday night I was awoken at 11.30 PM by the Patrol Officer who had been on his way to a village to arrest someone, when he had met some people who came from a different village and were carrying a young women on a home made stretcher. Bonnie had had a miscarriage and had been bleeding heavily for 12 hours. When I asked why they had not brought her earlier I was told that they had tried traditional medicine "but it had not worked". At least they were honest, but once again I regretted that I was not able to give the severely anaemic young woman a blood transfusion. I gave Bonnie an injection of ergometrine to assist the uterus to contract and put up a drip; eventually she expelled the placenta and the bleeding stopped. I stayed up all night as I did not like to leave her alone, with the possibility of the haemorrhage reoccurring, but all was well, and Margaret S kept an eye on the Hospital for me so that I could get a few hours' sleep.

The next night I was called up again as one of our waiting mothers, Modesi, was in labour. She delivered a very large baby for a Papuan mother, as average birth weight was between six and seven pounds. This bouncing baby boy weighed in at ten pounds eight ounces. Having delivered its luggage, the uterus refused to contract and Modesi had a massive haemorrhage, which was very frightening, as her life-blood was literally draining away. The placenta was eventually delivered but bleeding still did not stop, in spite of my efforts. I asked Sineleki, who was working with me, to go up to the house to fetch Margaret S as I felt in need of some moral support, a second opinion, and another pair of hands. Margaret S came quickly and we put up a Pitocin drip to aid contraction of the uterus. This drug had only arrived on the boat that evening and was still to be unpacked, but eventually we succeeded in locating it and managed to run it in quickly. At the same time we gave Modesi a hot vaginal douche, an old fashioned remedy, to aid the blood vessels to contract. Fortunately Sineleki had boiled the kettle on the primus earlier and it had cooled sufficiently to use it, as we did not want to risk introducing infection into the uterus. At last bleeding stopped, but we were all quite exhausted. Sineleki made some tea and cleaned up the Labour ward, while Margaret S and I monitored Modesi, whose blood pressure had dropped to a dangerous level. We gave her some tea and then raised the foot of the bed on blocks to increase blood flow to her vital organs. The baby was bawling and we put him to the breast as this also helped the uterus contract.

Margaret S said she would keep watch and Sineleki went off to bed whilst I lay down on a mat on the floor, so as to be close at hand. Modesi's husband, who, with good reason, had been very alarmed, came in to sit with her. She was very pale and weak but alive, which was the main thing. He was very pleased with his son but sobered by the thought that his wife had nearly lost her life in the process of giving birth.

I realised how much I would miss Margaret S when she left on Tuesday, along with Nick and Jan. But at least Mary had returned from patrol. As Margaret S was passing through Port Moresby on her way back to Orokolo, I decided to order an up-to-date copy of Margaret Myles' *Textbook for Midwives*, from Australia. My copy was published in 1961, and as I had to deal with so many midwifery complications, I wanted to have the most recent textbook. Margaret would post my order in Port Moresby, which was much quicker than ordering one from the UK.

Margaret Cole settled in well and enjoyed teaching the children who were so keen to learn. She arranged for some of the older school-boys to build us a chicken house. It looked a bit rickety but I hoped it would stand up to the rigours of the weather. I had wanted to keep chickens (known as *kam kams*) for some time as eggs would be a great addition to our diet and we could also use them for malnour-ished children at Hospital. We ordered ten black hens and a rooster from Port Moresby, as the local hens were rather scrawny and did not lay well. They were probably the descendants of indigenous fowl.

February seemed to be a popular month for having babies, as after a couple of quiet days during which I was able to catch up on some sleep, we had four deliveries in as many days. Three were relatively straightforward but the fourth was Lydia, who was probably in her late thirties and expecting her tenth child. Only four of her previous babies had survived, which rang all sorts of warning bells in my head.

Forceps Delivery

Lydia was of small stature and build and I guessed that there would be some disproportion between the baby's head and the size of Lydia's pelvis, as at full term the head was not engaged. This was not unusual in a mother who had had multiple pregnancies, but when the first stage of labour was prolonged and lasted over three days I began to get worried. Eventually Lydia reached the second stage of labour but after three hours she had made no progress and both mother and baby showed signs of distress. I knew that the baby's life was in danger as the foetal heartbeat was weak and slow. I decided that I would have to do a forceps extraction, but as I had never performed such a procedure I felt really nervous. To make matters worse it was a dark night and it would have to be done by the light of one of our Tilley lamps. Olinda was helping me and I asked her to hold the lamp as close to the bed as possible. I sent for Mary and she came down and held my textbook open for me, shining a torch on the page. We had already sterilised the forceps but my hands were shaking as I tried to insert them. I knew it would be unpleasant for Lydia but I could not give her any sedation because of the poor condition of the baby. I had some difficulty getting the second forceps blade inserted, but eventually I managed it and I was then able to rotate and bring down the head. After about ten minutes of concerted effort a baby girl was born. She had to be resuscitated but thankfully she responded quite well. The baby had a bruised forehead which caused me some concern and her head was misshapen, but I knew that could not be avoided and in a few days it should return to normal. Lydia was so relieved that labour was over and she had a live baby that she was surprisingly perky considering her ordeal. We all had a cup of tea to recover, as there wasn't anything else we could do to restore our equilibrium. My legs felt like jelly, but I was relieved that we had a positive outcome and offered up a quick prayer of thanks.

Next morning both mother and baby were well. Baby was feeding from the breast and as far as I could see did not have any signs of cerebral irritation, which could be a complication of a forceps delivery. After a few days I asked Mary to explain to Lydia and her husband the danger of further pregnancies, although with no means of birth control, it would be difficult to avoid another such traumatic event. I felt the familiar sense of frustration that I was unable to help them and silently I hoped that Lydia would have an early menopause. I asked Lydia to stay at Hospital for a few days longer than normal so that I could keep an eye on the baby, but at ten days old she seemed to be thriving. The bruise had all but disappeared and her head was beginning to return to its normal shape, so they set off for home happily enough.

Psychotic Episode

The beginning of the month was very wet and windy. I made the mistake of leaving some sewing on the table when I went to bed and it was soaking wet when I got up, as the roof had leaked just on that spot.

Mary and I were called out to our nearest village Avaroro, at 1 AM as one of our TB patients was described as being "raving mad". Sarki was a dear old chap who must have been in his early seventies. He was usually very dignified and his disturbed behaviour was very uncharacteristic. We gave him an injection of a sedative, paraldehyde, which, being secreted through the skin, had a distinctive smell. It was all we had, but fortunately he settled down after an hour or two and fell asleep. I hoped that it was a one-off episode, as if it continued he might be difficult to contain.

We had a party at Samoa House the following evening, as it was Miriam's birthday. Bertha had prepared a large amount of food, and we played Squeak Piggy Squeak, which all the Papuan children thought very funny. I had to have three turns as I kept guessing wrongly and Ravu ran around squeaking for everyone, which added to the general confusion. It was enjoyable and gave me a chance to ask Ravu if we could apply for another trained nurse, as we had been so busy of late. The government paid for the nursing staff through a Grant Aid system, and it all took time, so I was pleased when he indicated he would support the application. Ravu also told me that he had ordered a new wood stove for Middle House as Margaret and I were finding the old one so difficult to cope with. That was a positive end to a pleasant evening.

Unfortunately, Sarki had two further episodes of disturbance during which he became very agitated and threw out all his daughter's cooking pots and pronounced himself 'king'. He refused to let anyone into his house, which made it difficult for us to treat him. I had not had much experience of psychosis but I was able to contact our Mission doctor on the radio, to discuss Sarki's delusional state. Dr Calvert suggested that we try him on Largactil, which meant twice-daily visits to the village to give him it by injection. It seemed likely that he would need long term treatment and it was fortunate that I was about to order our quarterly medical supplies. Largactil tablets were not usually supplied so I added a note of explanation as to why they were required.

Either Mary or I would visit Sarki morning and evening to give him an injection of Largactil, and when it was due, his TB treatment. I hated having to sedate him to that extent and I knew his family had consulted the *puri puri* man, as it was difficult to explain his mental condition to them. I was at a loss to know what had triggered the psychotic episodes, or how long he would need treatment. Because people thought he had been the target of an evil spirit or bad magic, I asked Ravu to visit the family to help them through the situation. Psychosis, although not unknown in Papua, was sufficiently rare to make it a rather frightening condition for both the patient and his family. Sarki's wife had died a few years ago and he lived with his daughter and her family. When the Largactil tablets arrived Sarki did not want to take them and accused us of trying to poison him. In the end I left them with his daughter, as she seemed able to coax him to take them but not as often as I would have liked. There was little more that we could do and I hoped that eventually he would settle down.

Our *kam kams* arrived on the Moturina. They looked rather bedraggled but soon perked up after a feed. We kept them shut in for a few days so they would roost in the hen house, as if let out too early they would roost in trees and would be difficult to catch. When they were finally released, Toby chased them around the house, until Margaret caught him and gave him a little lecture. I hoped he would get so used to them that he would ignore them or they would not lay any eggs. However next time he started to chase the hens, the rooster attacked him, and he backed off. The rooster was a fine fellow and quite fierce when aroused. He did a much better job protecting his hens than either Margaret or I.

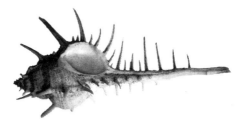

CHAPTER 16: ERIC'S STORY

At the beginning of March we had a baby boy born with a complete cleft palate and lip. It was a severe form with hardly any palate to separate his mouth from his nose. He was small and weighed just over five pounds, and I was concerned about how we would feed him. Fortunately, Mary was on hand when he was born to explain the situation to his mother in her own language. She was naturally very upset and her husband was very distressed indeed. Mary said it was because he suspected that his wife had been the victim of *puri puri*, and someone was making magic against his family. He seemed angry with his wife for giving him an imperfect child, and stormed off back to their village, leaving his wife in tears. It appeared that they both felt shamed and that was a difficult emotion to bear.

I thought at first that his parents would reject the baby as his father would not touch him and, although his mother cradled him, she could not breast feed him as milk ran out of his nose when he tried to suck. She found that difficult to cope with and turned her back on him. His parents did however give him the name Eka, the Papuan form of Eric, after a previous Principal of Lawes College, which I thought was a good sign.

Next day the husband returned and I asked Ravu if he would speak to him, as he was more likely to listen to him than to Mary or me. I asked Ravu to explain to him that when the baby was bigger he would need to go to Port Moresby Hospital for an operation to repair his palate and lip. Ravu was not familiar with the condition and I explained that it was a fault of foetal development not magic that had caused the problem and no one, least of all his mother, was to blame.

Ravu picked up Eka and gave him his blessing, which comforted his mother somewhat. It did not help that some of the other mothers were curious and would come and stare at the baby and make uncomplimentary comments. They thought he resembled a certain type of fish, and I thought what a difficult life this child would have, even if he survived and had his palate repaired. If he had been born in the village he probably would have died.

Meanwhile Mary and I fed Eka with a spoon. He could only swallow a small amount at a time, and we tried to give him expressed breast milk every three hours. We always sat with his mother so she could watch how it was done, as we wanted her to take over his feeding as soon as possible, but she was nervous as so much milk ran out of his mouth and nose. I radioed the Hospital at Port Moresby to ask them to send me some special teats used for feeding babies with cleft palates, as I hoped that this would be more effective, but it would be a while before they arrived on the boat so we persevered as best we could. I was worried that he would inhale some milk and develop a chest infection, but I did not want to give him antibiotics unnecessarily. He was hungry but it was difficult to give him sufficient milk so he did not sleep well. His mother often wept and I felt like it too, as he was such a pathetic little bundle.

Easter 1967

Alan had arranged for a short service to be held every evening during Holy Week and I took the Tuesday evening service. The theme for the week was *the Road to the Cross* and I led a meditation on the role of women in the Easter story. Fortunately I was able to complete the service without being called to Hospital. I found evening meetings during Holy Week really helpful in focusing my mind on the forthcoming festival of Easter. There were no Easter eggs to get in the way, and although I often had a hankering for chocolate, I had to make do with thinking about it.

Medical Problems

Maundy Thursday arrived and I was called out of the evening communion service by the arrival of a woman in labour. This was the
Nancy's sixth child and I did not anticipate any particular problems.
The baby, a little girl, was born about 2 AM. As usual we gave the
mother an injection of ergometrine intravenously, but after an hour
the placenta had still not appeared. She was not bleeding and we decided to wait and hope for a natural outcome. Nancy was quite comfortable and fed her baby, which should have helped the uterus to
contract. Mary sat up with her and I went to bed about 4 AM to try
and get a few hours sleep.

Next morning, Good Friday, Nancy started to bleed quite heavily. I
attempted to do a manual removal of the placenta but discovered that
Nancy had what I thought was an hourglass contraction of the uterus.
This is more usual during the first stage of labour, but it meant I was
unable to get my hand into the uterus to remove the placenta. We had
an ancient box of amyl nitrite that was used to relax muscle. I broke
open a capsule and asked her to inhale it. It was partially successful
as I then managed to get some of the placenta out, but most of it was
adhered to the front surface of the uterus and I could not remove it.
Poor Nancy was shocked and had suffered considerable blood loss.
I put up a saline drip and explained to her husband that she would
need to go into Samarai to have the placenta removed under a general
anaesthetic. As it was Good Friday, I could not get through to Samarai on the radio, but we had heard that there was a boat further up the
coast. I sent a runner to intercept it and to ask the captain if he could
come back to Fife Bay and pick up a medical emergency. I wrote a
note explaining the situation, and prayed it would not take too long
to arrive. I was afraid Nancy would die of blood loss as she was very
weak and pale.

That afternoon a man came in with a badly broken arm. He had
fallen out of a tree and bone was protruding through the skin. He was

126

in considerable pain and I gave him painkillers and antibiotics in an attempt to prevent infection. I knew he would need an anaesthetic to reduce the fracture but I put a dressing on and splinted it as best I could. He would also need to go into the Hospital in Samarai for treatment. The boat arrived in the afternoon but it was a very small yacht, and quite unsuitable for transporting a very ill woman in a rough sea. However I thanked the captain for the trouble he had taken to come back to see if he could help us.

Transport Needed!

On Saturday evening I finally got through on the radio to speak to the doctor in Samarai, after trying for two-and-a-half hours. By this time I was feeling desperate. Dr D said he would send a boat out at first light, and told me to continue with intravenous fluids. Mary and I were both really tired and Wendy, Bertha and Margaret took it in turns to sit with Nancy during Saturday night. Mary went to bed and I lay down on a spare bed in the Maternity ward so I could be called if necessary. Nancy continued to bleed on and off but she did get some sleep, which was important.

Easter Sunday came and went but no boat arrived, which meant we had to struggle through another night. I had a bout of diarrhoea and vomiting, which did not help and had to lie down. I assumed it was something I had picked up, as no one else was affected and we had more or less eaten the same food. Nancy was still bleeding and there was still no sign of the placenta. We kept her on the drip and antibiotics, but she was very weak and pale and drifted in and out of consciousness. I was afraid she would die before we could get her the help she needed, but she hung on, I think for the sake of the baby and her other children.

On Monday morning I did not feel very bright but went down to the office to speak to Dr D on the radio. He had sent a boat out on Sunday but it had run aground on a reef. They had had to wait for the tide to float it off before returning to Samarai with a hole in the hull. He was apologetic but would send another boat out that morning. I explained that I would accompany Nancy and also bring in the man with a compound fracture, and a new patient, a woman with a pelvic mass that was possibly a pelvic abscess, who I thought might also need surgery. We also had another women with an eye injury that was badly infected who needed more treatment than I could give her. The responsibility for these four people hung heavily upon me.

For some reason I had felt a little depressed before Easter, but the events of the last 48 hours had certainly shaken me out of it! On Monday evening a good-sized launch arrived in the bay. At first light on Tuesday morning we loaded Nancy and the woman with the pelvic mass on stretchers, plus the two walking patients, onto the boat. Dr D had sent a medical orderly along to help care for the patients, and two bottles of group O blood for Nancy, which I started to run in immediately. It would help her cope with the journey. Nancy's husband came along also and I carried the baby. It was a very rough trip and I was very seasick. The baby was fine and I lay on a spare bunk with her, most of the way. We arrived about 3 PM and were met by the ambulance. I saw Dr D briefly to hand over the patients, and he took Nancy straight to theatre. The others were admitted to the wards to be treated later.

I caught the boat to Kwato, where they expected me as I had sent them a radio message. I fell into bed after a quick meal and did not surface again until the next day. The following morning I went into Samarai to do some shopping. I had lunch with Dr D and his wife, which was very pleasant. He had had some difficulty in removing the placenta whilst Nancy was under anaesthetic and had come close to doing a hysterectomy, but fortunately this had been avoided. After four units of blood Nancy's blood count was only 50% what it should have been, which made me wonder how low it had been at Fife Bay. Dr D had also operated on the man with the fractured arm but decided to keep him and the other two patients in Hospital, along with Nancy for further treatment.

I discovered that the next boat left at 2 AM that night, so I went back to Kwato to collect my things, then spent the evening with Geoff and Kay, the Patrol Officer and his wife who had been at Fife Bay, but had recently moved to Samarai. I boarded the boat about 10.30 PM, and was lucky to get a bunk. The trip back took ten hours because it was so rough, but I took some seasickness tablets and slept most of the time. We arrived back at Fife Bay in the afternoon, a week and a day after it had all started with the birth of Nancy's daughter. Alan's Dad was leaving on the boat I got off, on his long journey back to England after his visit to Fife Bay. I just had the chance to say goodbye before the boat departed. We all missed him, especially Andrew, as he had been part of our lives for nearly three months.

CHAPTER 17: COMBINED PATROL

ONE USEFUL THING ABOUT MY TRIP TO SAMARAI was that I had the opportunity to talk to Dr D about Eric. When Eric weighed ten pounds he could be transferred to Port Moresby Hospital to see the paediatrician. The Ear, Nose and Throat surgeon visited every six months and Eric's name would be added to the list for surgery. The palate and lip would have to be repaired in stages, so it meant a lengthy stay for his parents in Port Moresby. His mother wanted to return to their village for a while but she agreed that Eric would stay with us whilst she was away, so that we could continue to feed him. The special teats had not been a great success but Olinda was especially good with him and had looked after him whilst we were engaged in looking after Nancy. Eric's mother still had ambivalent feelings toward her baby but agreed to take him into Port Moresby when the time came. Fortunately her husband had family there who they could stay with. The *wontok* system was definitely useful in such situations.

Wendy went into Port Moresby on the next boat and took Andrew with her. She was due to visit Hospital for some blood tests as she was pregnant. The baby was due in June and both Wendy and Alan decided they would like to have the baby at Fife Bay if I was in agreement and everything was normal. It was unusual but I thought that it was a something that could be arranged and it would be much more convenient for the family. Nick had suggested that Wendy went to Iruna for the delivery, but it would have meant that she had to go well before her due date and be away for sometime, so she opted to stay at Fife Bay.

Household and Health Matters

Ravu agreed that Margaret and I could have a new kitchen built on the back of our veranda where we had plenty of space. He arranged for some of the village men to build the walls and fit a new kitchen sink and plumb it in. The water ran in from a bathroom pipe, where there was a small water tank. We had Wendy's old kerosene stove as she now had a Calor gas appliance. Alan dismantled their stove and it was carried up piece by piece from the Big House by some students. Then Alan reassembled it in our new kitchen. It was a great improvement as previously there were 14 of us all using the same old kitchen and wood stove. The girls now had sole use of the recently installed new wood stove, which pleased them greatly. Their old wood stove went to the Hospital where it continued to belt out smoke but the patients did not appear to mind.

Just after the new kitchen was finished, Margaret and I managed to wreck our kerosene fridge! It had not been working properly so we decided to change the wick, which was never an easy job. After about an hour sweating and complaining we gave the mechanism a final heave with pliers and broke the metal wheel, that turns the wick up and down, right off. This event left us fridge-less. Fortunately the small fridge in the Hospital was functioning so we could use that, which meant storing our powdered milk there after we had made it up in liquid form. That was handy for cups of tea in the Hospital but not when we wanted to make one in the house. The old fridge was not very efficient so we were not sorry it was defunct and Ravu said we could have a new one. Margaret and I were aware that our needs were proving to be quite an expense on the District budget but it was agreed that these items were necessities.

Whilst Wendy was away we had Alan and Brian up for dinner one evening and cooked a curry using some tinned meat and fresh vegetables. The result was passable as the girls helped us by shredding the white meat of a coconut with a sharp implement, then squeezing it to

131

obtain the juice for us to cook the chopped up vegetables in, which certainly improved the flavour. Rice was a staple and we managed to cook that fairly well on our new stove. The hens had finally started to lay a few eggs, and we hard-boiled a couple of them to add to the curry, for a change. One hen had broken her leg and I tried to splint it but it stuck out at an odd angle. It didn't seem to impede her too much as she was still able to get around fairly well and continued laying.

The grass had grown very long around the house, and with all the rain the mosquitoes flourished. Margaret detailed some of the older schoolboys to cut the grass, which I felt uncomfortable about but we had no other means of keeping it short. I made some biscuits for them, which encouraged the boys, and they made a good job of it. This was a great improvement especially as I was allergic to the grass pollen. I had been sneezing and wheezing for some time and had to take an antihistamine tablet each night to keep the symptoms at bay. I was also a prime target for mosquitoes, as despite taking precautions my legs were covered in bites, some of which had become infected. The bites had to be dabbed with Gentian Violet so my legs had purple patches all over them. I hoped that eventually, I would develop immunity to mosquitoes but it took a year or so.

The Dog Toby

Toby, now an adolescent in dog years, had grown into a wily rascal. He was better fed and therefore larger than most village dogs, and his confidence was boundless. As few local people and certainly none of the children had watches, the system for keeping time was to ring a series of bells. A bell always announced time for church or school and Toby recognised these with great accuracy. For some reason he had developed a penchant for Sunday church services, that I found most embarrassing. He would arrive at church early and although there was always a man on the door to keep dogs out, he always managed to slip past him. Once inside, when the congregation was assembled, women on the left and men on the right, Toby would take up his position next to one of the women and lean on her, breathing heavily into her ear. As everyone sat crossed legged on the floor, it was difficult not to be pushed over by him. Attempts to dislodge him usually resulted in his moving to lean on someone else. When the singing started he would howl loudly, which caused great merriment amongst the children, who sat at the front of the church facing the congregation, where their elders could keep an eye on them.

In order to prevent this from happening, Margaret and I attempted to shut him into one or other room in Middle House, usually the bathroom, but he always managed to escape. We tried tethering him to the veranda rail with a length of rope but he simply chewed through it and arrived at church with a length of rope trailing and what I can only describe as a grin on his face.

Toby also joined every school assembly when he could get away with it. He followed Margaret to school when she left in the morning and positioned himself in the front row of children facing the teachers. Margaret would announce any changes in the timetable for the day and when she had finished he gave an approving "woof woof". When they sang the hymn his canine voice could also be heard: Margaret said he would sing high or low with the tune. After school assembly he would take himself off to look for alternative forms of entertainment.

Eastern Patrol

Ravu suggested that we did a joint patrol as I needed to go to the eastern side of the District and he needed to visit village churches. Brian would come along as well as he could visit local schools. It seemed a good idea to combine pastoral, medical and educational work in one patrol and we set off early in the morning, as the distance to cover was considerable. It was up to 10 days' walk from Fife Bay to the eastern edge of our District. Olinda came with me and we carried BCG vaccine to protect the children against tuberculosis, as well as the triple

133

vaccine to protect the babies against diphtheria, tetanus and pertussis (whooping cough).

Travelling with Ravu meant that large crowds turned out in each village we visited (plate 28). We spent a lot of time shaking hands with everyone, as all the men, women and children lined up for the occasion. When we had finished shaking hands, children sang a welcome song to us, under the watchful eye of village elders. We visited six large coastal villages and several hamlets. Two islands were included along the route (plates 29 and 30). Bonarua Island had its own boat, the MV Taiede, which roughly translated meant *That's Enough*. We had use of the boat to ferry us back and forth between Island and mainland. We also visited Suau Island and there I met a very old lady, probably in her eighties, who remembered one of the early missionaries, James Chalmers, living amongst the people there. He was known as *Tamate* and had been killed in 1901, by a group of people in the Delta region.

The church was thriving in these two islands and Ravu held services both morning and evening on the days we were there. Ravu carried out Baptisms and Confirmations with the help of village pastors. The clinics were well attended in all villages and we were kept busy treating a number of sick people. When he did not have a school to visit, Brian helped Olinda and me by weighing babies. In the nine days we were away we had nine chickens for our dinner, as in each village they killed a bird to mark this special occasion. On two nights, in true Papuan fashion, we all slept together in one room, on mats on the floor. I decided that it was easier just to sleep in my clothes. It is surprising what it is possible to get used to in a comparatively short time.

We travelled by large double-hulled sailing canoes most of the time and only did long walks on three days. On one occasion we were all very hot and decided to have a dip in the sea. We kept our clothes on and Olinda and I played about in the surf whilst Ravu and Brian swam out much further. Olinda and I sat on the beach to dry off when we saw the two men waving and shouting. We waved back as we thought

134

they were having fun, but when they finally emerged looking cold and grey, they said they had been caught in a rip tide and had been shouting for help. We realised that we would not have been able to do much, even if we had understood their predicament, but they would have liked us to understand what was happening. Fortunately they were both strong swimmers and had been able to get back safely, but we were all rather subdued as we trudged onto the next village, wet and covered with sand. We soon recovered after a hot meal but I did not like to dwell too much on what might have happened. When we returned to Fife Bay (plate 31) I felt as if I could sleep for a week and was glad to have a couple of days' respite without any emergencies.

CHAPTER 18: BIRTHDAYS AND BABIES

I CELEBRATED MY BIRTHDAY ON 1ST MAY in some style. Ten birthday cards had arrived on the latest boat, also a late Christmas card, which had been sent by surface mail. I went to the Hospital as usual and students' wives arrived with a hand-woven basket full of flowers and a tray made of the same material, Pandanus, as the basket. That was a surprise, as was the cotton bedspread given to me by Bertha. She had made it herself, with a Samoan design printed from a woodcut in black ink. Andrew came to Hospital with a card. We all laughed when he announced, "My Mummy has made you a happy birthday cake," as Wendy had intended it to be a surprise for dinner with Margaret at the Big House that evening.

A baby boy was born later that day, to a mother who was less than five feet tall, which was often an indication of a small pelvis. However, he was her tenth child, and, as far as I was aware, the other babies had been born normally, but this time she pushed much too early in spite of our efforts to stop her. The baby was pushed through the opening of the womb before it was fully dilated and when he was born he was very limp and shocked. I did mouth-to-mouth resuscitation, and gave him oxygen and lobeline, that stimulates respiration in the newborn. After seven minutes, just as I was thinking about giving up, he gave a feeble gasp and started breathing on his own, for which I was profoundly grateful. He slept for the rest of the day to recover but by the evening he was feeding normally. I was glad to have a baby born on my birthday and I was relieved that he survived his birth trauma.

The next baby to arrive was delivered on the floor, because his mother refused to stay on the Labour ward bed. It was her ninth child but he was in the posterior position, which meant a long and painful labour. Fortunately he appeared none the worse for his unorthodox arrival.

Twins

Immediately after we had put that mother and baby into bed, a man rushed up to say that a woman was having a baby on the beach. I gave the man our stretcher and he set off at a cracking pace. I grabbed my midwifery bag and followed him but met the stretcher coming up the hill carried by four sweating men. I recognised the woman as some-one I had seen on my last patrol and whom I had advised to go into Samarai Hospital, as I had anticipated complications from a multiple pregnancy. Ofeila had gone into labour and as there was not a boat going into Samarai, she had boarded the next boat to Fife Bay. My heart sank when I examined Ofeila, as her abdomen was huge and as tight as a drum. It was impossible to feel any foetal parts, and she was also jaundiced, with high blood pressure and swelling of her ankles.

We admitted her to the small single room on the Maternity ward, as she was not having any contractions. I gave her some mild seda-tion to help her to rest, and I hoped it would reduce her blood pres-sure. She settled down quite well and I think she was relieved to have reached Hospital. Ofeila's husband, Gudea, and mother accompanied her, and her little daughter was with them.

Margaret and I had invited Lahui and Ravu over for the evening meal. The girls had said they would help us prepare the food but they had all gone off to find shellfish that were visible at low tide, for their supper. It was quite late by the time we eventually served the food and sat down to eat and I had only had about three mouthfuls when Ofeila's mother came to call us as her daughter's waters had broken. Mary and I both ran down to Hospital and when I examined Ofeila, I found that the baby's head had not entered the pelvis but a large loop of umbilical cord had come down and was visible.

137

If Ofeila had been in Samarai Hospital she would have had an emergency caesarean section, but at Fife Bay we could do nothing but wait. I asked Mary to explain the problem to Ofeila and we put her in the bottoms-up position in the faint hope that by using gravity the cord would slide back inside her pelvis. Ofeila found it so uncomfortable that she could not sustain the position for more than a few minutes and such a lot of amniotic fluid was draining out that it carried the cord down with it. The bed was soaked several times over but as the fluid drained out, the baby's head entered the pelvis preceded by the cord. I knew that there could be only one outcome, so I explained the situation to Gudea and her mother. I decided not to tell Ofeila that her baby would be born dead until it happened, as there was a very slim chance that we would be able to resuscitate him.

During the second stage of labour the baby's head came down and compressed the cord cutting off the baby's oxygen supply. The baby's heartbeat became weaker and finally stopped altogether and although I did an episiotomy to hasten the delivery, the baby boy was born dead. It was heartbreaking, as he was a lovely baby, weighing six pounds twelve ounces. Ofeila's mother explained what had happened to her daughter, as she had seen the cord and understood that there was nothing we could have done. I had the most intense feelings of helplessness and frustration at the waste of a new life, while the family grieved the loss of such a healthy baby.

However, it soon became evident that there was another baby still to come, and I prayed for a happy outcome. Labour did not commence immediately and we all had a cup of tea whilst we waited for Ravu to come. I had sent for him, as we had to bury the first baby. I bathed him and dressed him in a white gown and Ofeila held her son for a short while before his grandmother carried him to the little grave hastily dug by his father. Mary stayed with Ofeila while I attended the short ceremony with his grandmother and father. Ravu said some prayers at the graveside, and then we went back to Hospital where he prayed with family and Hospital staff, which was a comfort to us all. Neonatal deaths were not unknown in Papua, especially in village births, and local people tended to accept their occurrence as part of life. As this child was a boy, Gudea was especially sad, as he was hoping for a son. Ofeila's mother treated the stillborn baby with a dignified reverence, whilst accepting the inevitable.

The second baby was not born for another eight hours, but we delivered a healthy boy weighing six pounds eight ounces and the family were delighted. Both babies were unusually large for twins, especially Papuan babies, which were often small. I was worried about the third stage of labour but one large placenta and membrane were delivered normally with average blood loss. Ofeila had been in labour for 48 hours, and was quite exhausted. Mary and I had been up for most of that time, and were also glad to be able to go to bed.

Hydramnios (excessive amniotic fluid) is sometimes associated with foetal abnormality or identical twins as in Ofeila's case. The swelling of Ofeila's legs and her jaundice gradually disappeared and her blood pressure returned to normal. The second baby thrived, which made the loss of his identical twin brother a little easier to bear.

Accidental Injury

One of our schoolboys, Rich, a boy of about 14, had a bad accident whilst out collecting coconuts. Carrying a sharp knife, he ran to catch up with his friends and fell, ripping open the back of his right leg from behind the knee to the ankle. The wound measured nine inches long and was four inches wide. Fortunately the Achilles' tendon was not damaged but the muscles and fascia (connective tissue that surrounds muscles) were exposed and there was considerable blood loss as a large artery and vein were severed and pumping blood. His friends half dragged, half carried him to Hospital, so the wound was dirty and had pieces of grass sticking to it. Our priority was to treat Rich for shock and to stop the bleeding. We lifted Rich onto the Labour ward bed as it was the firmest surface we had. He was faint from pain and blood loss, so we lowered his head slightly, and raised his legs to increase the blood flow to his heart and brain. I managed to identify and tie off the main artery and large vein that were pumping blood. Then we applied pressure by padding and bandaging the rest of the wound. Rich recovered quickly and was able to cooperate.

My first thought was to transfer Rich to Samarai Hospital where his leg could be properly sutured under a general anaesthetic. There were no boats in the bay and I left Mary to keep an eye on him while I radioed Dr D to send a boat out. Dr D said he couldn't do that and I should suture the wound myself. He told me to insert a drain, and indicated the size of sutures I should use for the muscle and the skin. I had no experience of suturing major wounds and felt very daunted by the prospect. I gave Rich 100 mg of pethidine to help sedate him and to ease the pain and then set to work. I asked Mary to scrub up to assist me, as it was difficult to stop the bleeding from smaller blood vessels even after I gave Rich local anaesthetic into the wound edges. It took me nearly two hours to complete the task but it was not a neat job. I sutured the muscle as best I could but I had difficulty in drawing the skin edges together as they were so ragged. When I had finished, after inserting 22 stitches, there were still pieces of tissue poking out between stitches. I thought he probably needed a skin graft, but that would not be possible. I was relieved to have finished the job, but felt worried about the outcome of my not very expert sewing.

Rich was amazing throughout the procedure, he did not make a sound or move the whole time. I had asked two of his school friends to run to his village, which was not too far away, to ask his parents to come, and when they arrived his father lifted him off the Labour ward bed and into a bed in the General ward. His Mum and Dad were glad to see that he was all right and I explained to them that he would need to stay in Hospital for a few weeks, until we could get him back on his feet. I gave him penicillin to prevent infection as the wound was dirty and had been exposed for sometime. He had a cup of tea before falling into an exhausted sleep. I found I also needed a cup of tea as I was shaking with the strain and tension of it all.

I dressed the wound daily and shortened the drain before removing it completely on the fourth day. Rich was a very good patient and never complained although the procedures must have been painful. The wound remained clean, despite some inflammation, and Rich managed to hobble around on an old pair of crutches that I found. I took the skin stitches out after six days, and then re-dressed the wound every three days. It still oozed small amounts of fluid but there was no pus and eventually after about three weeks, the wound was dry and healed enough for Rich to return to school. I suggested he wear a crepe bandage to support and protect the leg, as the scar was so extensive and the skin puckered in places. He still limped slightly, and was not ready to play football, but he was able to get around normally, which was the main thing. I saw him once a week to make sure the skin had not broken down, and when it was completely healed his mother rubbed coconut oil into the scar to help it remain supple. Surprisingly, he regained almost a full range of movement and six months after the accident he was back playing football (plate 32).

CHAPTER 19: RISING DAMP

I HAD BEEN AT FIFE BAY NEARLY A YEAR, but at no time had all our appliances functioned as they were meant to. I had to accept this as the *status quo*, although it was frustrating and time consuming. The latest thing to go wrong was the newly acquired kerosene stove which decided not to function. I felt like a true Papuan as I cooked lunch, squatting over a fire under the house, with the frying pan perched on three stones. I found it an easier method than going back to using the wood stove, especially as the firewood was often wet. The pump that siphoned water from the tank to the bathroom had also stopped working, so we had to carry the water up in buckets from the water tank.

We bought new blinds for the front veranda, in an attempt to keep the wind and the rain out, as the southeasterly wind blew straight in. The rain found more holes in the roof and we had to avoid the pots on the floor stationed to catch the drips. Tempers were a little frayed during the wet season, as it was difficult to keep anything dry and black mould grew on everything. Our cameras were kept in a sealed box filled with silica gel, to prevent mould growing on the lens. I had to send mine into Port Moresby to be cleaned and repaired and had to borrow Margaret's temporarily, ready for the arrival of Wendy's baby.

Middle House – A Maternity Ward

It would have been good to have everything dry and in working order, as we planned to deliver Wendy's baby in Middle House. We gave the house a thorough clean ready for the occasion and tidied up. I decided to give Wendy my bedroom, as I could sleep in the office next door where I would be on hand if needed after the baby was born. Wendy, Alan and I agreed that this was preferable to Wendy having the baby at the Big House, which was further from the Hospital. Fortunately Wendy had been well throughout her pregnancy and the whole family were looking forward to the new arrival. Andrew was especially excited, as it was his third birthday on 16th June.

Wendy organised a party for Andrew's birthday and invited 25 children from students' families and 20 schoolchildren for tea in the afternoon. We all crowded onto the veranda of the Big House and played games and enjoyed the feast. I could not stay long as we had two women in labour, one of whom had a normal delivery of a baby girl at 5 PM. The second woman had gone into labour prematurely and we needed to keep a close eye on her, especially as she had already been in labour for 36 hours and made only slow progress.

Wendy went into labour at 8 PM that evening. Andrew had fallen asleep about 7 PM, which was just as well. Brian stayed with him whilst Alan walked Wendy up to Middle House; Alan stayed for a while and then went back. Wendy had a straightforward labour but towards the end of the first stage the baby showed signs of foetal distress.

The second mother who was in labour had her baby in Hospital at 1.30 AM delivered by Mary, who sent for me as the baby failed to breathe. I just had time to resuscitate him and run back up to the house in time to deliver Wendy's baby girl at 1.40 AM. She gave a lusty cry so all was well, and one of the nurses went up to the Big House to give Alan the news that he had a daughter. The baby, Claire Wendy, weighed seven pounds twelve ounces, and for one fleeting moment, resembled her grandfather, Alan's Dad. I did not bathe her straight away, although she needed it as her skin was stained with meconium because there was a delay in the third stage of labour. For some reason the placenta failed to separate and inevitably Wendy suffered some heavy bleeding. It was a stressful time and I tried to remain calm, so as not to alarm Wendy, whose blood pressure began to drop because of blood loss. I put up a drip as a treatment for shock and to replace fluid. I have never prayed so hard in my life to see a placenta. I was really worried and thought I should let Alan know about the situation. After welcoming his new daughter he had gone back to the Big House to be with Andrew. One of the girls went to call him and he arrived very out of breath as he had run all the way. He stayed with Wendy for a while then Mary made him a cup of tea and then went into the office next door to wait for news. Finally after three-and-a-half hours the placenta separated and I delivered it with some difficulty around 5 AM. Thankfully the uterus contracted and there was no further bleeding. We were all vastly relieved. Alan sat with Wendy for a while and then went home to tell Andrew he had a baby sister.

Meanwhile Mary had bathed Claire who was crying loudly by this time and Wendy was then able to feed her, although she was not feeling too well. I gave Wendy an injection of Imferon, to boost her blood count and after a few hours sleep she felt better and was able to eat some breakfast. About 9 AM Alan brought Andrew up to see his baby sister (plate 33). He was rather quiet, and was probably over-awed at finding his mother in my bed with a new baby, but he gave Claire a kiss and then retreated to Daddy. Claire was born on 17th June. Because of the time difference, it was 4 PM in the UK on 16th June, Andrew's third birthday. If Claire had been born in the UK, their birthdays would have been on the same day.

The baby boy born ten minutes before Claire was called Dunstone, in recognition of the occasion. Local women were impressed that Wendy had had her baby at Fife Bay, as most Europeans went into Port Moresby to have their babies. Claire was a source of interest to the girls and local women who had not seen a white baby at such a young age. I kept thinking about the problems we had encountered, and Wendy told me later that although outwardly I had appeared very calm, she could tell by my eyes how worried I had been. I was able to take the drip down later that day and I took Claire into the office with me that night so that Wendy could sleep and recover her strength. I made up a bottle for Claire who was a hungry baby, and needed a lot of filling up. This trend continued and I looked after Claire for the next few nights. She needed both breast and supplementary bottle-feeds during the day as well. Mary brought baby Dunstone up to see Wendy, and Mary and I had our photographs taken holding the babies. I held Dunstone and Mary held Claire (plate 34).

Alan and Andrew came every day and sometimes Andrew came with one of the schoolgirls to play for a while. The girls were delighted and it was no trouble to keep him occupied. Brian, who helped look after Andrew, also visited, as did Bertha, Tavita, Ravu and Lahui. I was able to monitor visitors to ensure that Wendy had adequate rest and time to spend with her new baby and Andrew, who was keen to watch Claire's antics. She had a large appetite, but slept for most of the night, which was a bonus.

Party Time

Two days before Wendy left Middle House, Margaret and I decided to have a party. We had planned to have one in May but had not found the time. Now we had a number of things to celebrate: the first anniversary of my arrival at Fife Bay, various birthdays and new baby, Claire, a new chicken house, and new kitchen. We invited all European and Papuan staff, about 22 people in all. Ravu gave us two roosters, already killed and plucked, and we had two tins of ham and some tins of corned beef. We cooked rice and masses of sweet potatoes, yams and taro. It was rather hectic in the kitchen, as we had to use the wood stove and half way through the preparations I had to go to the Hospital to sew up a gash in a man's leg. Fortunately it was not too difficult and it did not take too long. Everyone enjoyed themselves, we played some games and sang songs but most of the time was spent chatting and eating. There was no alcohol but we had plenty of *sipora* juice, and we made tea and coffee as well. Not a scrap of food was left except some boiled rice, as everyone had very good appetites, especially the men.

145

I missed Wendy and the baby after they had gone home on 26th June but life at Middle House soon returned to normal. Claire continued to thrive and Wendy was well although she had to take a small dose of iron tablets for the next two months to boost her blood count. Some months later, as in 1966, there was a service of Baptism for all babies born to student pastors' wives in Lawes College Chapel, during which Claire was baptised by her father, Alan (plates 35 and 36).

CHAPTER 20: LEECHES AND MUD

For some time I had been putting off visiting a remote inland village, that was part of our District and therefore our responsibility, because of the terrain. Leileiafa had an Aid Post but no medical orderly, and was situated on a mountain plateau 2000 feet above sea level (plates 37 and 38). It meant travelling between four and six hours over slippery rocks and waterfalls following a river to its source, high in the hills behind Fife Bay. However, it was school holidays and much quieter than usual, and Brian said he would accompany me. Margaret was away visiting some of the teachers from the village schools, and had asked Brian to check on the school at Leileiafa.

We sent a message on the local radio station to alert the pastor as we would have to stay overnight, and we needed the people to be ready for the clinic. We left early in the morning by canoe across Sea Sea bay to the starting point of the overland trek. Margariti, one of our Nurse Aides, came with me and we hired two men to carry our medical box and personal bags. It was very hard going and before long we had our first encounter with leeches. Margariti started squealing and, when I investigated, several fat leeches were attached to everyone's legs – Brian's, Margariti's and mine. I had been warned about this and carried some *siporas* that we had rubbed on our legs as a deterrent. It had not been very effective but we applied them again directly to the leeches and eventually they dropped off. We were told by one of the men that we should not pull them off, as it would leave the head embedded under the skin. We had to repeat this exercise several times during the five-hour journey. Each leech left an opening

147

in the skin that oozed blood, which attracted mosquitoes, so we were well and truly bitten by the time we arrived at the village.

We had also been warned about snakes in the undergrowth. Two carriers went ahead of us and cleared the path, but we did see a Papuan black snake on one occasion. Its bite was lethal and was best avoided. Another common poisonous snake, the Papuan taipan, did not put in an appearance but we proceeded very carefully just in case. It was a very difficult walk, through bush and over boulders, which were slippery and difficult to negotiate.

When we arrived at the village, it was early afternoon and most people were away working in their gardens some distance away. These gardens were like large allotments; men cleared the bush and women planted, weeded and harvested the crops. The pastor and his wife were at home and she made us a welcome cup of tea. I was very glad to sit down after the long climb, but the view from the top of the ridge was spectacular. Miles and miles of tropical rain forest covered the mountainous terrain and the trees were full of birds. The pastor had a tame cockatoo that sat on his veranda and said "Hello Cocky," in English! The pastor said it liked to eat soap but I did not offer it any, as I wasn't sure it was good for it.

Brian and I walked through the village and located the teacher. He told us that the school was doing well even though the number of children was small. Adult literacy was a problem as few adults had been to school and therefore were unable to read or write, relying on their children when it was necessary. They had no books apart from the Suau Bible (*Riba Harihariuna*, 1962) which was common to all villages, but the pastor read the Bible to them, and older children read to their families as well. Brian had brought a few schoolbooks, written in English and the teacher was glad to have them. He was a Suau man but came from a different village, and was due to leave for home the next day, so we were lucky to see him before he left.

The village was so isolated that they had few visitors and after we had had the evening meal the pastor called people for evening prayers. More people than usual turned up to take a look at us but it was a good opportunity to remind women to bring their babies and pre-school children to clinic the next morning. We went to bed after prayers and found that Brian and I were to sleep in the same room, where there were two platforms that served as beds. Margariti slept in another room with the family. It was bright moonlight and we did not get a lot of sleep. We had not brought mosquito nets, and that night local mosquitoes had a real feast. I was fascinated by two large stick insects that made their way up the wall beside my bed. I got up in the night and looked out of the window. At first I wondered what the spectacle of light was and then I realised that the bushes were covered with fireflies. It was an amazing scene and one that I would not have wanted to miss.

Clinic

Early next morning, we held the clinic against a backdrop of bird-calls. Most mothers came and brought their babies and older children. There was a level of malnutrition among under-fives, mainly caused by a lack of protein in the diet. The staple food was vegetables grown in the gardens, but being an inland village, there was little fish and next to no meat. The adults consumed several pounds of vegetables each day, but the small children could only eat a fraction of that amount, which meant that their protein intake was very low. Babies were breast-fed for as long as possible, but if another baby was born the toddler came off the breast and as a consequence became quite severely malnourished. There was a cultural taboo against giving small children eggs, which I did not fully understand, but it would have given them a more balanced diet. The people preferred to keep the few eggs they had to grow into chickens, which were only occasionally killed for food. Pigs, which were a sign of wealth and prestige, were only eaten on special occasions, such as large feasts held for weddings or funerals. Older children all had enlarged spleens due to repeated attacks of malaria. Many also had the scaly skin condition, sipoma (ringworm), but they were quite delighted to be painted with Gentian Violet, which was all we had with us.

I was told that two young women had died in childbirth during the past few months, and neither of their babies had survived. Several young children had also died "from fever," which was probably malaria or pneumonia. This was generally accepted as inevitable, but it made me realise how important it was to get a medical orderly into the Aid Post, which also needed a lot of repairs. The men said that if they knew an orderly had been assigned to the village they would repair the Aid Post and build him a house as well. He would also need land to make a garden to feed himself, his wife and family if he had one, so it was quite a tall order. Most young men who were trained at the Hospitals at Iruna and Kapuna were not keen to live in such an isolated spot. I gave the pastor some basic medical supplies: aspirin, bandages and Gentian Violet, as well as iron tablets for three pregnant women that I had seen, and some chloroquine tablets for malaria. I wrote down the doses carefully to minimise mistakes, but the pastor had had basic training in First Aid and seemed competent.

Homeward Bound

We had breakfast after clinic and left late morning. For some reason we returned by a different route that was more difficult than the journey we had made the previous day. We had to cross what seemed to me to be a very high mountain but the carriers bounded ahead like mountain goats leaving Margariti, Brian and me to follow. At one point we lost the track completely, as we were walking through tropical rain forest. In the end the men came back for us and cut a path through the thick bush to make it a little easier. I think they were in a hurry to get home. I could tell by their voices and facial expressions that they felt hampered by our slow progress and they probably thought that we were a couple of useless *dim dims*. Margariti came from a coastal village and had never travelled far inland so preferred to walk with us at a slower pace.

It started to pour with rain and we were soon wet through, and our feet squelching with mud. We had no option but to carry on, and deal with leeches as we journeyed. At last we came to a river that cascaded down the mountainside over boulders, and was shallow but very fast flowing. There was no path so we walked down the riverbed. Several times I had to hang onto Brian to avoid slipping over. Margariti struggled on in front of us and managed to remain upright. Eventually we reached the foothills and then arrived at the beach, where there was no canoe available so we walked along the beach until we reached Fife Bay. I paid the carriers and gave them a little extra money as I felt they had earned it. They quickly disappeared and we were able to shower and get into dry clothes. It had taken us over five hours to complete the journey through very difficult terrain. I was glad I had made the trip to Leileiafa but did not think I would be able to visit the village very often.

Later in the month Ravu sent some village men to repair Middle House roof, which Margaret and I were glad about, as the rains were as heavy as ever. The new sheets of corrugated iron that they put up to replace the old leaky ones guaranteed us a dry house for one season at least. The medical store under our house also had to be repaired as the rats were able to get into it and they drank the intravenous fluids. They must have been given a health boost but we could not afford to waste such a valuable resource.

In addition the Hospital bathroom fell down under the onslaught of white ants (termites,

Men repairing the medical store

151

Isoptera spp, were called 'white ants' and often confused with true ants) that had appeared overnight and eaten through the timber, so that was added to the list of repairs. All the able-bodied people staying at Hospital voluntarily dug channels around Hospital buildings for water to drain away, after a particularly heavy downpour. It felt to me like it was one of the wettest places on earth, especially during the southwest monsoon season. It certainly took some getting used to.

The schoolchildren returned from their holidays and Margaret started to teach the older ones country dancing, which they really enjoyed. Our nurses wanted to learn a dance and I tried to teach them the Shoemaker's dance, the only one I could remember. We had great fun and couldn't stop laughing at our own antics. Toby ran around barking just to add to the confusion. I think he thought we had all gone mad but we needed some distraction from never-ending downpours.

School Medicals

I did a short patrol to two of our villages on the eastern side, Sagaaho and Savaia, to conduct school medicals (plate 39). I had notified Reggie the schoolteacher and arranged for Sineleki and me to stay with him and his wife. We left early in the morning when it was dry and bright but before we were halfway there it started pouring with rain and before long we were soaked to the skin. When we arrived at Sagaaho after the three-and-a-half hour walk we discovered that my overnight bag had been left behind and I had no dry clothes to change into. Fortunately Reggie's wife lent me a blouse and skirt that just about fitted me. I wore them whilst my clothes dried in front of their kitchen fire.

After lunch, schoolchildren lined up and we examined each child and treated them for any minor ailments. We also did a rudimentary eyesight test, by holding up a sight card and asking them to read graded letters with each eye, closing the other in turn. I asked Reggie to allow a couple of boys to sit at the front of the class, as they appeared to be slightly short-sighted. He said that to the best of his knowledge none of the children were deaf, which was encouraging. As most children understood English, I gave them a short talk on cleaning their teeth regularly but found very little dental caries (tooth decay) presumably because their diets were more or less sugar-free. As there were no toothbrushes or toothpaste available in rural areas, teeth were cleaned by chewing the end of a particular short stick, which was very effective.

We stayed the night with Reggie and at first light we walked on to Savaia where we held a clinic and did the school medicals. It was late afternoon when we returned to Sagaaho where we spent a second night enjoying the hospitality of Reggie and his wife before squelching our way back to Fife Bay the next day.

CHAPTER 21: A SHORTAGE OF UMBRELLAS AND BOOKS

In July we had 28 inches of rain in 21 days and the only creatures to enjoy it appeared to be frogs that croaked loudly all night.
There were not enough umbrellas to go around and each morning a
procession of banana leaves filed past the Hospital in the direction of
the Government primary school. Only a pair of small brown legs was
visible under each leaf-umbrella, giving the impression of an army of
brown ants carrying off some extra large trophies.

A favourite occupation of schoolchildren after school was to look
at some of my books and magazines. The most popular was a large
hardback book full of coloured pictures of birds around the world
and there was much oo-ing and aah-ing. Young and old alike were
starved of books and, as in most newly-literate countries, the printed
word carried great authority. Local people read my magazines of every variety, sent out from the UK and Australia, from cover to cover,
although some advertisements looked very odd in this setting. Any
magazine that found its way to Hospital quickly disappeared to the
villages where it was passed around, and usually ended up adorning
the walls of houses.

Robin

At the beginning of the month a one-week-old baby boy was brought
into Hospital from a distant inland village. His mother had died two
days after he was born and his young sister had fed him on vegetable
juice, as there was no other woman available to breast-feed him. He

weighed under four pounds and was covered in the ashes of the fire he had been laid in to keep him warm, but he was very weak and cold by the time he arrived at Hospital. The adults who brought him in said they could not stay at Hospital as they had his mother's burial rites to attend to. They said we could give him a name, so we called him Robin. I explained that we would need a relative to look after him once he had grown stronger, and I was told that his older sister would come back and look after him. As she was expecting her first baby in two months, I wasn't sure how this would work out but it seemed the best that they could do.

Robin was extremely hungry, but had to be fed small amounts at first, little and often, to give him time to digest milk he had been denied up until then. When the nurses left Hospital in the evening we brought him up to the house to look after him and the schoolgirls were delighted to have a baby in the house. His hungry yells during the night kept most of us awake but no one complained. After a few days he began to put on weight and looked much better.

Waiwai

One afternoon when I was feeding Robin, a small elderly lady came to the house to sell pineapples. Olinda brought her into the sitting room and I bought a couple of lovely big ripe fruit. Waiwai had a good look around and was fascinated by photographs of family and friends that I had on the shelves. She wanted to know who everyone was and when I had finished feeding Robin I made us both a cup of tea. She was delighted and we both enjoyed looking at my photograph album. Before she left I asked Margaret to take a photograph of Waiwai and me under the mango tree (plate 40). I had a feeling that she would visit again and sure enough she did. Eventually I got the photograph developed and she was thrilled when I gave her a copy. I felt as if I had made a new friend and although her English was as minimal as my Suau we managed to communicate.

Mimisina

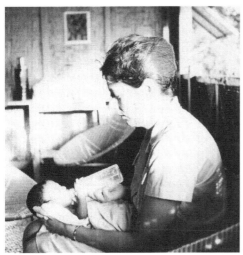

Ruth with baby Robin

A week after Robin's arrival, one of the village pastors brought in another premature baby, this time with her mother. The baby, Mimisina, was a most pathetic little bundle weighing only two-and-a-half pounds at twelve days old. Both her eyes were badly infected and oozed pus. She was like a little bird that had fallen out of the nest before it had any feathers. I doubted whether she would survive but we treated her eyes, and wrapped her up in a warm blanket. Without an incubator for premature babies we had to do the best we could. Fortunately her mother was able to care for her, but Mimisina was too weak to suck and had to be fed with a spoon every two hours. Our lives seemed to revolve around feeds and nappies. Her eyes gradually improved but the treatment must have been very painful. Still she hung onto life and was kept warm by sleeping next to her mother who was very devoted to her daughter.

In the middle of the baby feeding and nappy routine, Mehea, one of our teachers had a very bad attack of asthma that lasted for four days. I tried every treatment in the book including oxygen and he gradually came out of it. Apparently he suffered regular asthma attacks and I was not sure if the dampness of Fife Bay was the best place for him.

Mimisina was a little fighter and by the time she was four months old she weighed seven pounds and was fully breast-fed. Both her eyes had some scarring but we thought she probably had partial sight. At

156

a later date she would need to be seen by an ophthalmic surgeon, if it could be arranged.

Traditional Tattoos

Mimisina's mother, Mari, had the most amazing tattoos that covered every inch of her body, as did some of the other women. Apparently tattooing started when they were quite small girls but the custom was dying out, as most young women had very few, if any, tattoos. Although none of the men was tattooed, traditionally, girls had to be completely tattooed before they could get married. The dye used was powdered charcoal made from burnt wood. It was mixed with water and using a flexible piece of soft wood, patterns were drawn on the body. Then using a sharp thorn attached to a piece of wood from a special bush plant the skin was pricked to draw out blood, following the patterns drawn on the body. Another piece of wood was used to tap the thorn through the skin, altogether a very painful process!

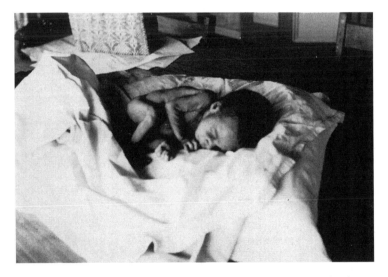

Baby Mimisina

157

New Nurse and Distinguished Guest

We had applied again to the Department of Health for an additional Staff Nurse and this time our request was granted. Walo I from Hula in the Central District was appointed to Fife Bay and she arrived at the beginning of August. I was so glad to have another trained nurse on our staff as it meant that Mary and I could have a regular day off each week. Walo was trained at our Papua Ekalesia Hospital at Kapuna in the Gulf area and was therefore familiar with the church set up. I was due for some local leave but did not like to leave Mary for too long when we were so busy.

The Revd Norman Cocks arrived on the same boat as Walo. He was the CCWM representative in Sydney, Australia and as such was responsible for all overseas staff under the LMS/CCWM umbrella. This was his first visit to Fife Bay but he kept in contact with each of us by regular letters that were very supportive. I had met him in Sydney and really looked forward to our renewed contact. Norman arrived later than expected as he had been held up at Kwato. This meant we had to fit the programme arranged for him into a shorter period of time, as he was booked out on a plane from Baibara airstrip which was outside our District. Whilst he was with us, Norman held a Quiet Day for all staff, which we appreciated as he was a man of great insight and wisdom. We very much enjoyed his visit but it was over all too soon. However, Ravu suggested that I accompany them to the airstrip to see Norman off, and then he and I could continue on to visit an inland village, as he had hired the Bonarua boat for the occasion and the village could only be reached by river.

We set off at first light and visited three villages on the way so that Norman could meet some local people (plates 41 and 42). Each village had prepared a feast and entertainment and villagers were all dressed in their best. Norman was presented with gifts and garlands and there were many speeches of welcome and great excitement all round. Consequently, by the time the celebrations were over, we were

158

very late arriving at the village where we should have spent the night. We could not land because the tide was out and our boat had no dinghy to take us ashore. We anchored in a sheltered bay, and prepared to spend the night on board what was a very small boat for the eight of us to sleep on. I was the only woman present and there were no toilet facilities so I spent a very uncomfortable night, wishing that I had not drunk so many cups of tea.

Early next morning when the tide was in we were able to land and we all sped off into the bush to deal with the calls of nature. We had to hurry to get to Baibara airstrip that was a five-mile walk away. First, we had to scale a small cliff, and then it was long trek over a hot sandy beach. There was little shade and both Norman and I got really sunburnt. We eventually arrived at the airstrip about ten minutes before the plane appeared, and said a fond farewell to Norman. Ravu was visibly relieved to have seen his distinguished visitor safely on his way and we made for the nearest village for some breakfast. People were quite surprised to see us, but Ravu was well-known and before long we were served coconut milk and biscuits, followed by tea and some fish and vegetables.

Boroai

As we still had the boat, Ravu thought it would be an opportunity for both of us to visit the village of Boroai, which was inland and only accessible by river. We had a medical orderly, Lohia, stationed there and I was keen to see how he and his family were coping in a rather lonely and isolated spot. We walked back to where we had left the boat and then travelled up a wide river surrounded on each side by mangrove swamps. The twisted roots of mangrove were home to a number of creatures some of which could be seen swimming through the murky water. An amphibian that lurked in the mud particularly fascinated me. It had gills like a fish but also legs to scuttle along, and was known as a mud hopper but I never found out its scientific name. We did not see any crocodiles but I was told that some of them lived in the area. The river soon narrowed and became too shallow for the boat to navigate safely. It was moored by the bank and we transferred to a large dugout canoe for the rest of the journey.

On both the way into the village and on the way back it was low tide and the river bed was emptied of water revealing the underlying mire. The men, including Ravu, jumped out of the canoe and proceeded to push it for about a mile. They were up to their thighs in thick, black, smelly mud. I sat on the canoe platform, with our bags and the precious cargo of betel nut. The men remained very cheerful and called encouragement to one another when they reached difficult places. We finally arrived and were greeted warmly, as visitors were something of a rarity in that part of the world. Women brought water for the men to wash the mud off their legs and when they were cleaned up, they served the food that had been prepared, including hornbill, a large bird that lives in the rainforest. It has a raucous cry that was easy to identify, and was shot by hunters using traditional bows and arrows. I was a little dubious about eating something that clearly wasn't a chicken, but Ravu encouraged me and as I did not wish to cause offence I ate a small amount with some cooked bananas and found it palatable enough.

Ravu and I stayed with Lohia's family that night, and the next day, after morning prayers, Lohia showed me around the Aid Post where all was in good order. He seemed quite content to work in the village but said his wife missed her family and *wontoks*. They came from a different language group, which was not easy, as it was as hard for Papuans to leave their village as it was for Europeans to leave their country. However the Boroai people were grateful to Lohia for providing them with some medical care. We left after a breakfast of cold vegetables and hornbill, and travelled back to Fife Bay, stopping one night in a village on the way. It was a very worthwhile if tiring trip, but I was pleased to be home.

I called into the Hospital and to my surprise found a piglet tied up under a bed in the General ward. Apparently its owner had been given it as a gift and as pigs are highly prized in Papuan society, he did not let a small thing like Hospital admission stop him from accepting it. During the day it stayed outside near the patient's kitchen, closely guarded by his relatives in case any one made off with it!

CHAPTER 22: THWARTED TRAVEL PLANS

W ALO SETTLED IN WELL. I had intended to take her on a short patrol to introduce her to local people but the boat we had planned to catch did not arrive when expected so we had to postpone the trip. It made a lot of difference having another trained nurse on the station as it meant that Mary and I had a little more free time. I began to make plans to take some local leave, probably in Port Moresby. Depending on the availability of transport I also wanted to visit Margaret Sharman in Orokolo.

Fife Bay Hospital nurses - from left to right,
back row Walo, Ruth, Mary; front row, Ruta, Nancy, Margariti

A coating of shellfish!

A favourite delicacy that helped to add protein to the girls diet was shellfish. They were in sea shallows in abundance during September and our nurses and schoolgirls could be found on the beach at low tide harvesting them from the sand. They were live and were fine if eaten quickly but if left they rotted and smelt foul. After school one afternoon Margaret found some shellfish in a bowl of water, under the house. They were absolutely reeking and she tipped them out onto the grass and then forgot about them. Later on Toby found the mess and rolled in it. He came upstairs as we were having dinner covered in foul smelling slimy stuff. The stench was too much for Margaret who abandoned her food. I continued but as Toby was wafting the smell all over the house, I decided that I had to do something about it. Donning my plastic raincoat, I hauled the reluctant dog off to have a bath. I put

Toby and staff and - from left to right Walo, Ruth, Mary, Margaret

him under the tap of our water tank, as we didn't have a suitable receptacle. He hated being bathed, but I persevered and did get rid of the odour.

We acquired another resident for Middle House when Brian turned up with a small creature, locally called a *sela sela*, not much bigger than a mouse with a soft grey coat and a prehensile tale. We were not sure if it was a type of flying squirrel or if it was related to a possum. We put it in a box on top of our fridge, out of reach of the cat, and fed

163

it on green leaves and coconut. It was nocturnal and made a noise at night like an engine revving up. It grew quite rapidly and when we thought it was strong enough we released it into the bush one night after dark. It bounded off into the night and I hoped it would survive.

The occupants of Middle House had an unpleasant weekend when we all went down with a gastric bug. Fortunately it only lasted 24 hours and we were soon back on our feet again. I developed mild bronchitis after that and an infected mosquito bite on my leg developed into something resembling a large boil. I had to stay in the house for a couple of days in order to recover from these minor ailments and spent the time planning my trip to Port Moresby.

District Church Council

We had a number of antenatal mothers waiting to have their babies and a very sick child with meningitis who I did not want to leave until he was better, so I delayed going to the District Church Council which was held towards the end of the month at Savaia village. The council was an opportunity for each village to send their pastors and deacons to discuss local affairs. Overseas staff were usually invited and Alan was there representing Lawes College. I had to give a report on the medical work on day two, but felt I could miss the opening proceedings. In the event we had a difficult breech birth and I was unable to get away. Mary went instead and read my report for me. We also requested some extra funds for Hospital maintenance work, which was granted, so all was well.

Breech Delivery

One of our antenatal mothers who was expecting her sixth child, went into labour with very weak contractions, during the night. The baby presented as a breech but had not entered the pelvis and I attempted unsuccessfully to turn the baby. About midday, Matilda's membranes ruptured and when I examined her I discovered that the baby's foot

164

had prolapsed into the birth canal. A footling breech presentation is rare and I had no experience of managing such a delivery. Unfortunately Matilda then went out of labour and I had difficulty hearing the foetal heart beat. Matilda naturally became very restless, as she felt so uncomfortable. I gave her penicillin to prevent infection and waited. Eventually after three days she had a few weak contractions and was finally ready to give birth. It was a very difficult delivery that took one-and-a-half hours to complete as the baby came feet first with his arms extended on either side of his head, which made them very difficult to extract. Sadly, but hardly surprisingly, the baby boy was stillborn. Fortunately Matilda came through her ordeal in quite good shape. I had warned her and her husband that the baby might not survive, so they were prepared but they were of course very sad to lose their son.

I was quite exhausted and was glad to hand over to Walo, while I went to have a shower and catch up on some sleep, all thoughts of the District Church Council gone from my head. Instead I reflected, not for the first time, on the absence of family planning facilities for the village people and how helpful it would have been to be able to offer birth control to those who wanted it. I also realised that had it been possible for Matilda to have a caesarean section, her child might have survived.

Cancelled Visit

My long awaited visit to Port Moresby failed to materialise, as the boat I should have travelled out on did not arrive. It came a few days later with our mail and went up the coast to pick up copra. It was meant to stop on the return trip to pick me up, together with the local agricultural officer who had been visiting Fife Bay, but it sailed straight past. It was extremely frustrating as I had had my bags packed and ready for several days and I had booked the plane to fly from Samarai to Port Moresby which had to be cancelled by telegram sent over the radio. I was disappointed, as I had looked forward to shopping in Port

Moresby for a few small gifts to send home as Christmas presents. Instead I arranged to go into Samarai on the next boat (plate 43) and to stay at Kwato for a few days, which was usually restful, and I felt I needed a break.

One of our long-term patients had died a few days before from heart failure. She was only in her forties and may have had a heart defect. When I told her husband that we could not do anything more for her he sent for her father and they took her home to die in the village, which they much preferred. It was always upsetting to lose a patient, even when we had done all we could and I felt that a few days away would set me up for the next round of events.

I boarded the MV Laurabada, which had replaced the MV Moturina, and was seasick all the way to Samarai. I had to spend the night on board after we arrived, as we were unable to dock at the wharf owing to lack of space. It was pleasant sleeping on deck under a starlit sky, but after dark the most enormous cockroaches came out on deck and crawled all over us. As the toilet arrangements were fairly primitive I was glad to get off in the morning and catch the launch to Kwato where I spent a relaxing three days.

New Doctor

I travelled into Samarai to do some shopping on the second day and decided to visit the Hospital. Dr D had left and I had yet to meet the new medical officer, Dr Michael P. He invited me to lunch with him and his wife, and I mentioned the problem I was having with back pain after he had noticed me limping. We went into the Hospital and he examined me and pronounced that I had sacroiliac strain (pelvic joint) which was something of an occupational hazard for nurses. Sleeping on the hard but uneven deck of the Laurabada had not helped it. I had been treated for it a few years previously whilst in London. However I had not bargained for Mike P's rather rapid treatment. He asked me to lie on my front, and then with one hand on my

166

lower back he grabbed my left leg and gave it a terrific jerk upwards to an angle of 90°. Beaming with satisfaction he asked me if I had heard the ligaments click back into place. I had certainly heard something but I was too startled to know what it was. I got off the bed rather gingerly but there seemed to be no harm done, and after a few days I noticed some improvement.

Bad News

I returned in time for United Nations Day on 24th October, Mary came to meet me off the boat, looking very sad. I had only been away four days but in that time two babies had been born, both fortunately normal deliveries. Jainona, one of the students, had been injured playing football and had broken his leg in two places. It was a bad fracture of the tibia and fibula, which were both displaced. Mary had splinted the leg but was waiting for me to return to decide what to do next. But the worst news of all was that baby Robin had become ill with a meningitis-type illness and pneumonia and had died within 24 hours, in spite of Mary and Walo's best efforts. They had stayed up all night with him to no avail and were naturally very upset. I was shocked and saddened that his little life should have ended so abruptly. His relatives had taken him back to the village for burial next to his mother's grave.

I examined Jainona who was in a lot of pain and decided he would need surgery to realign the bones of his leg, if he were to walk again. As a boat was due next day I radioed Mike P to say I was sending him into Samarai for treatment, which he agreed.

United Nations Day came and went with the usual singing and dancing competitions. Our schoolchildren sang well and came second in the District. We were kept busy at Hospital as a lot of people came in from villages to get some of their ailments treated. It was a fine dry day and that encouraged more people than usual to enjoy a day out.

CHAPTER 23: HIGH AND DRY

W<small>E HAD VERY LITTLE RAIN IN</small> O<small>CTOBER</small> and were now well into the hot, dry season and our greatest need was to conserve water. More babies had been delivered in the Maternity ward in 1967 than in any of the previous eight years, including 15 in three weeks, which was hard work but very encouraging (plate 44). However, washing bed linen after a delivery took a lot of water and I thought it prudent to ask the girls to use water as sparingly as possible. At least it was not a problem to get the washing dry, we just threw sheets over bushes and they dried and bleached in the sun.

Our only source of water for drinking and washing came from our water tanks that we had to lock to avoid overuse. We all enjoyed going for a swim in the waterfall and on those days we did not need to shower. After so much rain it seemed incongruous to be short of water but we needed more water tanks and corrugated iron roofs to drain rainwater. Most corrugated roofs could only support one tank,

New mother carrying her baby home in a basket

so at the Hospital we had three, one for each ward and the other at Middle House. Roofs made from local materials such as coconut palm, just absorbed water and most of it was lost. The only occupant

168

of Middle House to be pleased about this situation was Toby, as we could not spare any water to bath him!

Surprise Surprise!

This was a month of surprises as one afternoon a very smart yacht sailed into the bay. We were mystified as to why it had anchored but when the dinghy beached, I discovered that one of the three-man crew had an injured arm. Apparently their map had identified our station as having a Hospital and they called in hoping for treatment. Some very excited schoolboys led the men up to Middle House where I was resting. They were rather shocked at what passed for a Hospital but I was able to dress the wound in the man's arm and give him some painkillers and antibiotics to avoid infection, for which he was suitably appreciative. Margaret meanwhile laid on afternoon tea in the house, which we all enjoyed. They were touring the coast in what was a very expensive vessel and agreed to show some local men over their craft before setting sail at first light next day. Normally tourists did not call in at Fife Bay so this was a first for us.

A few days later I was awoken about 5.45 AM by the sound of heavy footsteps on our stairs and a booming voice calling out "Wake up Ruth, there's a doctor in the house." I staggered out of bed to be confronted by Dr Mike P standing in the middle of our sitting room. We quickly made some tea and he told us how he came to be in Fife Bay. Apparently he had been called out the day before to Gadaisu, the furthest point of our District, to a woman who had a retained placenta. Mike P found that the village women had attempted to remove the placenta and had pulled too long and hard. The placenta was adhered to the uterus and this had inverted and been pulled down into the birth canal. It was visible on the sand and the poor patient was in considerable pain. Fortunately Mike P was able to give her a light anaesthetic, clean and return the uterus to the pelvic cavity and manually remove the placenta. The patient was on the way back to Samarai Hospital under heavy sedation and antibiotic cover. Infection was inevitable and Mike P thought that a hysterectomy might be necessary. I was really thankful that I had not had that situation to deal with. Mike P had a quick breakfast with us and agreed to look at a few of our patients before returning to the boat, which was very helpful to me.

The other surprise was less pleasant. Two of the nurses had boyfriends. One was a Lawes College student who often popped up to Middle House to see his girlfriend. The other nurse's friend also called in when he could and they sometimes went off to the waterfall together. I thought little of it at the time. One afternoon after the District Church Council I received a delegation from a small group of deacons from the local churches. I invited them in for tea, wondering what this rather formal visit was about. The deacons told me that they were not happy about my allowing boyfriends to visit the two nurses without being chaperoned. Apparently local culture did not allow young men and women to mix freely before marriage as in our western model, especially so within the local church.

I felt very embarrassed that I had not realised this before although I did have a vague idea of this sanction being applied in the village. I thought that it did not apply in the more sophisticated confines of the Lawes College station. The girls and their two boyfriends must have known, but probably thought it was all right, as I did not object. I agreed to take this sanction more seriously in future and think that I was excused because of my ignorance. When I spoke to the nurses later they were quite shocked and not a little shamefaced and we agreed an arrangement where there would always be someone else in the vicinity when the young men called. Visits alone to the waterfall were taboo! I recalled the experience we had on patrol of men and women sleeping in the same room. This did not seem to quite add up but maybe the feeling was that there was safety in numbers.

Brian and two students decided to go out to look for crocodiles two nights in November when the moon was full. I was very relieved when they failed to find any, as I envisaged having to treat crocodile bites. We had some wonderful moonlight nights, so I could understand the need to venture abroad into a world transformed by moonlight and a canopy of stars.

Snake Pit

For some time we had wondered why there was a square concrete pit at the back of Middle House. It was quite deep but was unsuitable for rubbish so we agreed that was unlikely. The lid was broken but we kept it covered as best we could to avoid a child or animal falling into it. Margaret was in a nearby village one day, in conversation with a village elder. He told her that a missionary who had lived at Middle House "many moons ago" had an interest in snakes. Local people had procured them for him for a small payment and he had made the pit to keep them in, until such times as they could be shipped off to a zoo in Australia. Presumably he was paid for providing the zoo with snakes and so would have been able to supplement his income. The villager could not recall the missionary's name, and when I mentioned it to Ravu he had never heard the story, although he did not discount it.

Another unusual article hidden behind the house was a grindstone. No one knew where it had come from but it was still used and was handy for sharpening knives. It required two people to operate, one to turn the stone and the other to hold the knife or axe. One day Margaret heard an unusual sound coming from the direction of the stone. She went to investigate and found a schoolgirl trying to sharpen a teaspoon. By the time Margaret intervened, the spoon, instead of tapering in an oval shape, had a straight square end. On discovering that it was one of her spoons Margaret confiscated it and as far as I know she still had the spoon many years later.

We sweltered through some very hot days and found it difficult to sleep at night because of the heat. Sand flies appeared at dusk and tormented us; although very small, their bites were an irritant and it was

171

difficult not to scratch them. The insect population always seemed to be getting one over on us. The cockroaches ate labels off medicine bottles and the sugar was always full of ants. I began to worry that I had suddenly become deaf and wondered if this was a side effect of the anti-malarial pills that we all took. That was until I discovered that a mud wasp had built a nest in both earpieces of my stethoscope!

Baby Peri

One restless night we were woken about 2 AM by the sound of voices and footsteps on the veranda. In the torchlight we saw a small group of men and a woman waiting expectantly for us to appear. I recognised them as people from a distant inland village and wondered what had brought them down the side of the mountain in the middle of the night. One man had a cloth tied across his chest, which he thrust at me. Inside was a tiny premature newborn baby; he was cold and covered in ashes. Mary had appeared by now, and speaking in Motu he told Mary that the baby's mother had died, and they had put him into the ashes of the fireplace to see if "it was worth trying to save him." They had left at first light and were very tired after walking down steep tracks and a shallow creek bed. They had never been to the Hospital before but had been told that we might be able to help.

I took the little bundle of fragile human life and wrapped him in a soft towel. Mary found a bonnet in a pile of clean washing that we put on his head. I was sure he was hypothermic and as we had no cot prepared I put him into the warm spot in my bed that I had just vacated. The man who was the baby's uncle was only too glad to relinquish his charge. After making them some tea and biscuits, Mary took the little group down to the Hospital and showed them where they could sleep for the remainder of the night.

After giving the infant some boiled water on a teaspoon I laid down next to the child to keep him warm but did not sleep much for fear of rolling onto him. At first light I went down to the Hospital to prepare a cot and a feed, leaving him in my bed. Margaret was also up early and she took schoolgirls who were curious about the night's activities into my room to see the baby. She said they thought he was a doll until he whimpered and then they realised that he was real. "Their faces were a picture," Margaret told me later. The baby weighed under three pounds, but he was very hungry, and had to be fed small amounts every three hours. After he had been bathed and dressed he looked much more presentable. Another premature baby, in addition to Mimisina, taxed our limited resources somewhat, but the baby's uncle and his wife stayed to help us look after him, when the other people returned home to their village. Apparently they had no children of their own and would adopt the child if he lived. I was relieved as this increased his chances of survival.

Uncle and aunty, as we used to call them, were very grateful for our care of baby Peri and were a great help around the Hospital. We needed to grow more food to supplement our diet of rice, and they lived too far away for relatives to bring them food. We had established a Hospital garden and had planted several banana trees as well as sweet potatoes and taro. We rarely found time to give the garden much attention and during the wet season the weeds had flourished. Weeding was woman's work and aunty set to work with a will whilst uncle cleared more land and planted a few coconut trees and more bananas.

Surprisingly, baby Peri gained weight and did very well. The weather was hot and dry which made it easier to keep him warm. His aunt and uncle were devoted to him but along side Mimisina he would need to stay at the Hospital for at least a year, so that we could provide him with the milk he needed to thrive.

I tried to keep a stock of rice and flour in our store, both for us and to supplement patients' diets, if they or their families ran out of food. As a fallback position we kept a stock of hard biscuits known as navy biscuits. I think sailors on long voyages had used them in the past. They were approximately four inches square, and were very hard to bite into. I learnt to bang them hard on the table first to knock out any weevils. They had little taste but we sometimes took them on patrol, as they were easy to carry. The patients seemed to like them although I feared they had little nutritional value but they filled a hole if someone was hungry.

Hurricane Annie

Our usual boat failed to turn up due to a hurricane in the Milne Bay area, which was the furthermost point east of us. We had received a warning over the radio but only caught the tail end of Hurricane Annie. Others were not so lucky; when the cyclone hit Milne Bay a fair sized boat was lost plus two sailing cutters. Most people were rescued but some were missing believed drowned. There were no lifeboat or coastguard services and any rescue had to be organised by local government or local fishermen.

25. Maternal and Child Health clinic at Savaia - April patrol

26. Isolated hamlet visited on patrol

27. A quiet corner of a village, in early morning

28. Villagers welcome Ravu and colleagues on combined patrol

29. Pastor's house on Bonarua Island

30. Bonarua ladies with hibiscus flowers in their hair

31. The long walk home - trees with interesting roots on right (probably Pandanus)

32. Boys enjoying picnic on coral island in the bay, playing football with Tavita

33. Dunstone family after Claire's birth in Ruth's bedroom at Middle House

*34. Mary with baby Claire and Ruth
holding baby Dunstone*

35. Alan and Wendy, Andrew and Claire

*36. Lawes College students and Dunstone family after baptism of
babies born in 1967*

37. Leileiafa village

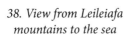
38. View from Leileiafa mountains to the sea

39. Ruth and schoolchildren crossing Sagaaho river on patrol

40. *Waiwai and Ruth under Middle House mango tree*

41. *Norman Cocks and Ravu with village friends, pastor and sea scouts*

42. *Early morning start with Ravu, Norman Cocks and Tavita on the way to Baibara airstrip, July 1967*

43. *Approaching Samarai by boat*

44. *"I'm proud of my sister, who is one day old"*

45. *Logo of the United Church in Papua, New Guinea and the Solomon Islands*

46. *Checking her weight - Lebohai on the scales*

47. *Sunset over Fife Bay*

48. *Bird of Paradise, from the cover of Ashton, 1975, emblem of Papua New Guinea and adopted on flag (see map 4), stamps and currency notes of Papua New Guinea, and on House of Assembly building (1964 to Independence), thereafter the National Parliament of Papua New Guinea*

CHAPTER 24: BIG DECISIONS

Papua Ekalesia held its General Assembly annually, towards the end of November, and following the 1967 meeting, we received news that affected us all. The good news was that the decision was made for Papua Ekalesia to join with the Methodist Church in Papua to become the United Church in Papua, New Guinea and the Solomon Islands (plate 45).

There had been preliminary talks for a year or two and the time had finally come to put the deliberations into practice. As they did not have a long church history, Papuan people did not understand the denominationalism that we brought to their shores along with the Gospel message. This was a step in the right direction even though other denominations would continue to function alongside the United Church. The Anglican Church worked in northern Papua and the Roman Catholic Church was active in the Gulf and the Highlands. We all got on well together but the theological differences were too great to achieve further union.

The not-such-good news for me was that it had also been decided to move Lawes College to Rabaul in New Britain to join the Methodist Theological College at Raronga. This was the cost of Church Union. It was also scheduled for January 1968, a year earlier than expected. I could understand the reasons for the move because men needed experience of urban life that they would gain in Rabaul. They would also have contact with a much wider community than was possible at Fife Bay. The move meant that Alan and Wendy would be transferred with the College and this coincided with Brian's term of work coming to an end. Bertha and Tavita were also nearing the end of their

175

six-year term and would leave on the next boat. Many students had already left for the long summer break and although they would need to return to collect their things, we would not see them again, as they would go directly to Rabaul.

Ravu had also been promoted to become the first chairman of the newly established Mainland Region of the United Church, and he was later appointed as its first indigenous Bishop. Ravu's contribution to the development of the church was recognised and honoured in 1976 when he was awarded the OBE. This was followed by a Knighthood in 1982, and later by an Honorary Doctorate from the University of Papua New Guinea. A new District Minister would be appointed in due course to take Ravu's place but I knew I would miss his wise counsel. However Lahui, Ravu's wife was pregnant with their sixth child and it was agreed that she would stay at Fife Bay until after the baby was born, although Ravu would have to go into Moresby to take up his new post.

I did not want to lose any of the people I had come to rely on and valued for their colleagueship, humour and support. I felt bereft. Brian, Bertha and Tavita left before Christmas, and Wendy, Alan and Ravu were to go in the New Year. Brian's replacement, another young man called Chris E, arrived and found us all in sombre mood. The Dunstones were busy packing as were the remaining students, whilst Margaret and I consoled each other that much at Middle House would remain unchanged. In spite of that it was difficult not to feel abandoned, although of course we had to carry on Hospital work no matter what happened around us. When the news of the Lawes College move to Rabaul filtered through to local villages, there was a real sense of unhappiness. The village people were proud of the College and felt the loss of prestige that the Suau area had gained over the years.

We had some wonderful moonlight nights, which were cool and to be enjoyed after the heat of the day, when the temperature sometimes reached 100°F. It also got light very early at about 4.30 AM and many

176

people got up then to get their work done before it was too hot. The afternoon siesta became a must, if we were to get through the day. Even Toby looked for shade and lay panting under the house.

Casualties of Malaria

The very hot weather brought with it a rise in the incidence of a particularly virulent type of malaria. All ages were affected with people going down like ninepins. Patients responded to treatment much more slowly and were left feeling very weak for quite a few days after their fever had abated. Mary and Walo both succumbed and were off sick for over a week. We took extra care that our mosquito nets were free from holes and covered us properly at night.

Nelson

Margaret and I decided to have a party for all those who were leaving us. We prepared food and were just ready to serve it too our waiting guests, when a couple appeared at the foot of Middle House stairs carrying a two-year-old boy, who was having a convulsion. I recognised Otubo, who had done some carpentry work for us, as he held his little son Nelson in his arms. He was their firstborn and the apple of his father's eye. Nelson's mother was breast-feeding their baby girl who was about five months old. I recalled seeing both of them at clinic the previous week, when they had both been well.

I put down my serving spoon and went with the family down to the Hospital. Both wards were full and we went into the Labour ward, which was not in use. I laid Nelson down in the big cot that we kept for our newborn babies. He was convulsing violently and I gave him two injections, an anti-malarial drug and a sedative, but they had little effect. When I took his temperature it was 106°F, and it confirmed what I had suspected, that he was very ill with cerebral malaria. I washed him in cold water to lower his temperature but it only fell by a small amount. In cerebral malaria the parasites multiply in the brain

177

causing congestion and inflammation. It is especially dangerous in young children. After a couple of hours Nelson lapsed into unconsciousness and his breathing became very laboured. I tried my best to keep his airways clear but we did not have a child or adult aspirator, only the very small type that we used for clearing the airways of newborn babies and that was not very effective.

One of the girls brought a plate of cold food down from Middle House that I shared with Nelson's parents. I heard the party goers pass the Hospital on there way home, and realised that I had left Margaret with all the clearing up, but I had little option. Nelson's condition worsened, I was unable to control the convulsions and I suspected that he also had pneumonia. I gave him oxygen via a funnel and antibiotics but nothing I did improved the situation. Otubo prayed and Nelson's mother wept, as did I, when I realised that in spite of all my efforts his condition was deteriorating.

Nelson's sister was asleep on a mat, mercifully oblivious to all that was going on. At 2.30 AM I lifted Nelson out of the cot and put him in his mother's arms. Otubo placed his hand on his son's head and there we sat on the floor, in the light of the Tilley lamp, awaiting the inevitable. Nelson died at 3 AM, less than twelve hours after he had been taken ill. His parents prepared to return to their village, and they left quietly, Otubo carrying the body of his son and Nelson's mother walking behind with their baby girl. As they reached the end of the path their voices rose in the terrible heart-rending wail that announced a death. As they neared their village, the couple's relatives would add their voices to those of Nelson's parents in grief for the lost child.

As I walked up to Middle House, I felt quite alone and was devastated that I had not been able to help the little boy. I fell into bed and longed for sleep that did not come until about 6 AM when I fell into a troubled doze. The following day I wrote a letter to a group of friends in a church in Sydney, who had offered their support. I asked them to purchase a foot-operated aspirator, and send it to me as soon as possible. I vowed that never again would I have to try and save a child's life without adequate equipment. Strictly speaking what I did was against the rules as it was felt that overseas staff, who had contacts in Australia and could obtain goods, had an unfair advantage over indigenous staff. I agreed with this, but on this occasion, I had no qualms about taking that course of action.

Exactly a month later, a man arrived from Otubo's village with a huge bunch of bananas. Otubo had sent me a gift from the feast that marked a month since Nelson's death. I felt that he had understood my distress and while grieving for his son he had included me in their traditional mourning ritual. I was very touched and grateful.

Wisdom Tooth

I had become more practised in extracting teeth, although each time I had to consult my little book on Emergency Dentistry in order to select the correct instrument. However, when a man in his forties asked me to take out his wisdom tooth because it was giving him pain, I was not at all keen. Instead I gave him some oil of cloves and aspirin but after a few days he returned asking me again to remove it. Part of my reluctance was because I would not be able to anaesthetise fully the area around the tooth. I explained all this but he still insisted. As we did not have a dental chair he sat on an ordinary chair and I asked Walo to support his head. I felt much more nervous than he appeared as I was afraid the crown of the tooth would break off leaving the roots *in situ*. It was quite difficult but the whole tooth came out intact and the patient did not make a sound although it must have been painful.

A Premature Ending

Unfortunately, I had to send one of our Nurse Aides home to her village after she was missing all night. I did not know that she had a boy friend so it was an unexpected occurrence. I felt quite upset, as she was a good nurse and full of life and bounce. After the incident

179

with the deacons, I could not afford to be lax and the rules were clear. I would have liked to give her a second chance in the New Year but I would have to consult Ravu over the appropriateness of that course of action.

Helicopter Visit

One Sunday afternoon when we were having an after-dinner nap, we heard a tremendous noise and to our amazement a large helicopter appeared from nowhere and landed on our sports field. Margaret and I went to investigate, but the school boarders who had never seen a helicopter before were all terrified and fled into the surrounding bush. We discovered that the men on board were conducting a geological survey and two of them were being dropped off to visit a couple of our nearby rivers to look for copper and gold. They did not stay long and did not tell us what, if anything, they found. That was the first and last time we heard or saw anything of them!

CHAPTER 25: GOOD NEWS!

Alan went into Moresby for a consultation with church leaders and came back with some good news. Chalmers College, that had been situated at Veiru in the Delta, was to move into the Lawes College premises. Chalmers College was for men who felt they had a vocation to train as pastors in the church, but who did not have the academic qualifications required for entry into Lawes College. Chalmers College was opened in 1958 by Revds Sue and Bob Rankin and the teaching was all in Motu. Margaret and I were very pleased to hear that we would not be left on our own. Revd Geoffrey W was the Principal of Chalmers College and he and his wife Shirley W would arrive with the students. They had a little boy about Andrew's age and were most welcome, as it was already very quiet because all except two of the students had left.

Most school children had also left for their holidays, but before he went one boy brought me a baby bird to look after. It was quite large with stripes and I had no idea what it was. We had difficulty finding anything it liked to eat so in the end I released it into the bush as I thought it would have a better chance of survival there. It could fly so should have been able to fend for itself. One of our chickens that had disappeared came out of the bush followed by six fluffy chicks. When Toby went to investigate the mother hen promptly saw him off. The hens became broody very quickly and hid away to incubate their eggs, re-emerging when the chicks were hatched. It was a good way to increase our stock, although we had little control over any of it. The hens followed their instincts as nature intended. The cat also produced three kittens, which was a surprise, as we had never seen a tomcat hanging around. So we had plenty of young life to celebrate and enjoy.

Water Problems

It was so hot and dry that I decided to cut my hair, in an attempt to cool down. It had been long for several years, so I decided it was time for a change. I persuaded Wendy to wield the scissors, although she was reluctant to do so. I liked the end result and it was much easier to manage especially as we were already short of water. Our water tanks were completely empty by the beginning of the month, which meant carrying drinking water from a spring about twenty minutes walk away. I was excused this duty but the girls went in early morning with various receptacles to fill and we tried to make the water last until the next morning.

We all had to walk to the waterfall pool for our baths wearing as little as possible, as it meant going into the water fully clothed. I usually wore an old blouse and skirt over underwear, and then went behind a bush to change into dry clothes. After bundling up the damp clothes we brought them back and laid them out to dry, which they did very quickly. More difficult was managing Hospital washing, especially after a delivery, when we had to deal with blood-stained sheets and soiled nappies. We had bars of yellow washing soap but they were limited in their effectiveness. Carrying back wet washing was heavy work and sometimes if we were not too busy the girls would wait for the washing to be nearly dry before returning.

We often ran short of bed linen and kind people in Australian churches would send us good quality second hand sheets and pillowcases. Unfortunately, they were often held up by customs as they had to be fumigated and sometimes they disappeared altogether. We repaired sheets we had, patching and turning sides to middle as they wore thin very quickly with frequent washing. We needed more water tanks but they were expensive to buy and erect and maintain. I decided I would try and save some money from our monthly budget to put towards an additional tank for the Hospital, as we had to rely on patients' relatives to fetch water that was needed for drinking and cooking. I sometimes thought of people at home in the UK who proclaimed a drought when a hosepipe ban was put in place, but who continued to flush toilets with abandon or waste water with impunity. I felt that this experience would alter my attitude to using water for ever.

Board Games

As the schoolgirls living in our house went on their holidays before Christmas, Margaret and I decided to give them their Christmas gifts before they left. Whilst in Samarai I had bought them two board games, Ludo, and Snakes and Ladders. They were thrilled and excited once Margaret showed them how to play, and spent every spare moment playing one or other game. In fact they were late for school and played games at lunchtime, even letting their food get cold. In the end Margaret had to confiscate the games on school days and allowed them to play in the evenings. I had not expected the games to be so popular, but I suppose they had never had seen or played board games before. They were reluctant to leave them behind when they went home but we said we would keep them safe until they returned, by which time the novelty had worn off!

Unusual Diagnosis

Generally speaking, if most children survived childhood they remained fairly well during their teenage years. However, we had a young girl of about 18 admitted with severe abdominal pain. She had collapsed in the village and her worried parents carried her in on a homemade stretcher. Madi was anaemic and her spleen enlarged, which was not uncommon due to repeated attacks of malaria that afflicted most Papuans. Madi's spleen was very tender to touch and

183

obviously the source of her pain. I thought that she might have a ruptured spleen but she had not sustained any injury and so it was unlikely. I gave her painkillers and made her comfortable before hot-footing it to the radio to speak to Dr Peter Calvert. He said that she was most likely suffering from perisplenitis, a condition I had never heard of. Peter said that small tears appeared in the spleen substance whilst the outer capsule remained intact. It was caused by inflammation following repeated bouts of malaria. The treatment was bed rest and pain relief, plus iron tablets and a course of anti-malarial drugs, all of which we were able to provide. After a few days Madi's pain lessened and by the end of the week she was able to go home.

Down But Not Out

Unfortunately I was the next person to become ill. I started by feeling unwell with nausea and loss of appetite. I thought I might have contracted hepatitis, which was endemic in Papua, but within a few days I had developed a high temperature, headache and stiff neck and had to take to my bed. In fact I was told later that I became delirious and semi-conscious although I could only recall seeing fried eggs on the ceiling! Mary was on holiday leaving Walo to cope with the Hospital on her own. Margaret, Wendy and Alan were very worried and called upon Dr Peter Calvert for advice.

Unbeknown to me the battery for the radio was flat and they were unable to get a signal. Margaret ran to the government Patrol Post to borrow a battery from them. Two prisoners from the local jail were enlisted to carry the battery back to the Big House, suspended on a pole carried between them. Margaret chivvied them along and Toby ran along side thinking it all great fun. The battery arrived in time to catch the medical sked, and Peter was consulted. I gather there was some discussion about transferring me to Samarai but it was decided that it was not a practical solution. Instead Peter prescribed six-hourly injections of penicillin and sulphadimidine tablets (similar to an antibiotic, used to treat some infections) which was really all we had.

However, he arranged for a more powerful antibiotic, chloramphen-icol to be flown from Port Moresby to Iruna and then sent down by boat. He thought I might have contracted a type of meningitis as the symptoms suggested this, although without tests this could not be confirmed. Which is why the treatment had to be given blind. I was used to this but it was still scary and I was concerned as to whether I might be left with residual problems from such a serious illness. Walo did not relish giving me penicillin injections that were painful, but we managed one way or another.

My being in bed for nearly two weeks made extra work for Marga-ret, as I had to have my sheets changed more frequently than usual, as they were often wet with perspiration. Taking them to the river and back was no easy task. Our schoolgirls who would have helped were away on their holidays and the nurses were struggling to deal with the Hospital bed linen. Somehow or other they managed, but every-one was glad to see me back on my feet again. My being ill over the Christmas period also upset most of our plans as Margaret and I had been invited to the Big House for dinner on Christmas day. However, I was not able to walk that far, but I was well enough to get up and eat some of the meal that Wendy brought up to Middle House.

This was my second Christmas at Fife Bay, but it passed by very quickly. I was not well enough to go to any of the Christmas services and we were all rather subdued, as we knew it was Alan and Wendy's last Christmas with us. Chris did his best to cheer us up and we tried to put a brave face on it, but I could not help feeling rather miserable. Baby Clare was six months old and able to take notice, and Andrew enjoyed himself opening his presents. The carol singers came even earlier that year, at 2.30 AM; I stayed in bed but some of the girls got up to greet them. I was left feeling quite washed out and it was three weeks before I was well enough to resume normal routine. I enjoyed reading paperback books I had received in a Christmas parcel from home as I missed having easy access to a library or bookshop.

Once I was well enough Walo often consulted me about patients she was worried about. Our two premature babies Peri and Mimisina continued to thrive, but it was hard work for the nurses who were left at the Hospital, as we were short staffed. We also heard that the nurse I had sent home had decided to marry her boyfriend, so would not be returning. Olinda also wanted to leave to get married, so I hoped that we would be able to recruit at least one nurse in the New Year to replace them.

CHAPTER 26: COMINGS AND GOINGS

I HAD INTENDED TO PATROL THE EASTERN SIDE of the District before Christmas but I was prevented from doing so by my illness. Mary
returned from her holiday at New Year so Walo did that patrol as
soon as Mary returned, in order to catch up with our schedule of infant vaccinations. I still needed to rest in the afternoons so felt unable
to tackle long walks through the bush in the hot sun that the patrol
entailed. The District Church Council was also held at Isuleilei during
the first week in January and I went over for some of the meetings. It
was a time when some of the pastors and teachers were relocated to a
different village to fill a vacancy. Some were reluctant to move but in
the end Ravu managed to sort them all out. We also recruited a new
nurse, Nancy, as Olinda and Sineleki had left to get married.

Farewell

On 6th January, the Feast of the Epiphany, (exactly two years since I left
the UK) we held a farewell feast for Alan and Wendy and Ravu and
Lahui. The local government officers came, as well as the remaining
staff. It was a good occasion to say thank you to our colleagues who
were due to depart on the next boat. True to form I had to leave early.
Some village people had carried a woman on an improvised stretcher
for five hours from their village to Hospital. Milli was bleeding heavily following an incomplete miscarriage, but fortunately I was able to
give her an injection of ergometrine to complete the process and stop
the bleeding. I also gave Milli an injection of Imferon because she
looked very anaemic. This was her first pregnancy and I suggested

she attend the antenatal clinic when we visited the village should she become pregnant again. I gave her some iron tablets to take home with her when she was well enough to leave.

Alan, Wendy and the children, together with Ravu, left on the MV Laurabada. I was very sad to see them go but put on a brave face for the occasion. However, I couldn't prevent some tears escaping as we waved them off. It seemed very strange without them in the days that followed. Ironically, we did not get a mailbag off the boat when it unloaded because the postal workers in Australia had gone on strike. Not getting news from home greatly increased our sense of isolation. We had Chris up for the evening meal most nights as he was rattling around on his own at the Big House, and was not used to cooking for himself.

Our new colleagues, the Ws, and Chalmers College students and their families were not due to arrive at Fife Bay until February. Apparently, there were 19 families with about 30 children between them, so our baby clinics would be busy. The Revd Kwalahu M had been appointed to take up the District Minister's post vacated by Ravu, but we had not heard when he and his family would arrive.

New Arrivals

Margaret and I spent one Saturday, soon after the Dunstones had left, tidying up the Big House, which was just as well because the Ws turned up unexpectedly on the following Monday, on a government boat which was passing through. They had flown from Port Moresby to Samarai and had only a couple of suitcases with them. Understandably Geoff W had wanted to arrive ahead of the students. Shirley W was pregnant but explained that she intended to have the baby in Samarai which was a relief to me. Their little boy, John, was glad to get off the boat and was soon exploring the house.

The family were pleased to be at Fife Bay after their stay at Veiru as the terrain was very different. The southeast coast was very beautiful, if isolated, and there was an amazing view of the bay from the Big House. We in turn were very pleased that our colleagues had arrived. Margaret and I invited the new family up to Middle House for the main meal on a couple of evenings until they were settled. The rest of their luggage arrived on the next boat but there was still no mailbag. We hoped that the Australian postal strike would soon be over.

An Historic Moment

January 19th 1968 was a great day in the history of the Church in Papua and New Guinea, as on that day the Methodist Church joined with Papua Ekalesia to become the United Church in Papua, New Guinea and the Solomon Islands. In a service of Union in Port Moresby, led by Ravu and attended by thousands of people, the Deed of Union was signed and traditional gifts exchanged. This historic moment was broadcast live on local radio, so that as many people as possible could share in this important event. We listened on our radio to the very moving ceremony that promised to bridge the historical gulf between Papuans and New Guineans in the name of Christ.

A Surfeit of Babies

During the last week of January, a number of babies chose to arrive. In all we had ten babies born in under seven days, most of them during the night. We ran out of nappies and had to resort to tearing up old sheets and pillowcases. One baby was stillborn, an event we had expected, as there was no foetal heart sounds when the woman was admitted, which was sad. The baby's mother went on to have a retained placenta and a postpartum haemorrhage after a long and difficult labour of 48 hours, which gave us a few nasty moments. She then developed malaria and had a high temperature of 106°F. Fortunately with appropriate medication she made a slow but complete recovery.

The second baby to arrive was Lahui's. She went into labour at Isuleilei and there was no time for her to travel to Hospital. I ran over as

189

soon as the message arrived and was just in time to deliver a lovely eight-pound baby girl. I telegrammed Ravu as soon as I could and he sent a message back to say that the baby was to be called Ruta Gloria (Ruth, after me). I felt very chuffed and was amused when Ravu also sent me a message of congratulations on the safe arrival of his daughter.

Ruta Gloria, Ravu's daughter, and Ruth

New Students

Although they were not due to arrive until February, 19 students and their families came on the next boat. Unfortunately, many of them had been seasick, so they were very keen to set foot on dry land. Travelling with them was their Papuan tutor, Kala. As a single woman she would stay with Shirley and Geoff W in the Big House. It took a while to sort out all the families and find them their accommodation in various student houses. There seemed to be hoards of children, who, when released from the confines of the boat ran around all over the place.

I was part of the welcoming group but left the chaotic scene as soon as I could, as a sick child was carried in. The parents were on the veranda of Middle House when I arrived, with their five-year-old son, who had a high temperature and was having convulsions. I gave him anti-malarial drugs but sadly he died before they could take effect, which was very upsetting and in contrast to the scene I had just left of healthy children enjoying themselves. It was a searing experience to lose another child to cerebral malaria, for which I could do nothing. I felt very sad as the weeping parents carried their little boy back to the village. He had only been ill for three hours.

Billi

Two babies presented us with particular problems that made them rather special. The first was a week-old baby boy who had been born in the nearby village. His tearful mother carried him in and said nothing but pointed to his left foot. I could see immediately what was wrong, as he had been born with *talipes equinovarus* or clubfoot. The foot turned downwards and inwards, which meant that without treatment he would be unable to walk. I told Susi, his mother, that we could treat the condition but that I would need to consult with the doctor first. I wanted to check with Peter that the treatment I thought was needed was appropriate.

I suggested that Susi go home and bring the baby back in two days' time, which she did. I explained that we would hold the baby's foot as near as we could to the correct position and then apply plaster of Paris to keep the foot as straight as possible. As he grew he would need to have the plaster changed and his foot manipulated each time. It would be uncomfortable but not painful and eventually the foot would straighten and remain that way, so that he would be able to walk. Susi was vastly relieved and agreed immediately to the treat-

191

ment. We applied the first plaster there and then. The baby, who had not been named, bawled his head off during the procedure. I was anxious about applying the plaster too tightly and thus impeding circulation, but eventually I succeeded and they went home.

Ten days later they were back. Susi carried the baby on her back, but in her hand was the complete plaster cast. I could hardly believe it. Apparently the baby, now called Billi, had banged his heel repeatedly on the ground, until the entire plaster cast had slipped off. This was not in the treatment plan! However this pattern was repeated several times over the next few months and we began to anticipate it. We used up a large amount of plaster of Paris, but gradually his foot straightened, until by the time Billi was 14 months old, we substituted a crepe bandage for plaster of Paris and he took a few faltering steps. His parents were delighted and brought me a gift of some yams from their garden. I said we would keep a close eye on him at the under-fives' clinic, as he might need to wear corrective boots. Susi never missed an appointment and managed his condition very well. He was a bonnie little boy who continued to thrive.

Billi and his Mum

Lebohai

The second baby was Lebohai who was brought to Hospital from a distant village. She was carried in a sling tied around her foster father's chest and when I pulled the cloth back to take a look, two big brown eyes peeped out and regarded me solemnly. I lifted her out and was appalled to see how malnourished she was, with a big tummy, stick-thin arms and legs and very sparse hair. The man explained that she was the daughter of his cousin-sister who had died in childbirth "three moons ago." His wife had a baby who was a month older, as well as two other children, and she had tried to feed Lebohai but had not had enough milk. He asked if we could look after her "until she could eat food," when they would be willing to take her into their family. There was no mention of the baby's father but I assumed that he had agreed to this arrangement.

When I examined the baby girl I found that she weighed only seven pounds, the weight of a newborn baby, but she was clean and surprisingly alert. It was clear that the family had done their best for her, and that bringing her to us was the best thing they could have done. It meant another baby for us to look after at night, but I said we would do all we could for her. She quickly endeared herself to the nurses and took the first bottle of half-strength milk in great gulps, as she was so hungry. There were no facilities for bottle-feeding babies in villages, which was why we needed to admit motherless babies to Hospital where we could sterilise bottles and make up feeds accurately.

Mary told me that Lebohai was an old Suau word that meant *to save* or *to lift up* which seemed entirely appropriate. Apparently, it was also the name that local people gave the Hospital. Lebohai spent her days at Hospital whilst the nurses were working there, and at night we took it in turns to look after her. Ideally one person should have cared for baby of her age, but we could not do that, and she did not seem to mind being passed from one to another. At first we had to feed her small amounts every three hours, day and night, but as time went on we were able to feed her more or less on demand, and as she became less hungry, she slept for most of the night.

After about a month her foster father and his family visited and were surprised to see how much weight she had put on (plate 46). By this time we had introduced her to solid food, which she seemed to enjoy, as well as regular bottles of milk. We all became very attached to Lebohai; she was a lovely baby, who wanted lots of attention, as she grew older. The nurses sewed little dresses for her from scraps of material and as her hair grew she became quite pretty. She was with us for the long haul but she certainly repaid all the attention she was given.

CHAPTER 27: STORMY WEATHER

Fᴇʙʀᴜᴀʀʏ ʙᴇɢᴀɴ ᴡɪᴛʜ ᴀ ᴛʀᴇᴍᴇɴᴅᴏᴜs sᴛᴏʀᴍ that caused us to batten down the hatches. We had to close all the shutters at the Hospital and Middle House, and move any furniture off the veranda into the house, as the wind was blowing a gale. It was dark inside both buildings with the shutters down and we had to light the lamps, which blew out if we did not move them out of the drafts. The cat ran around like a mad creature and Toby howled in competition with the wind! Several of our banana trees were blown down as they had shallow roots, and coconuts rained down from coconut palms. Fortunately no one was hurt and the rain was much needed. We ran outside with any receptacle we could find to collect extra water.

The following day all was quiet and a boat came in with our mail. I knew that my mother would have been worried when she did not have a letter from me but I had no way of letting her know about the postal strike in Australia. Lahui and baby Ruta, and her youngest son, Kingsley aged four, were leaving on that boat and Lahui agreed to post my letters in Port Moresby. We were sad to see Lahui go, but knew that she needed to join Ravu and her other children.

Girl Guide!

One consequence of Lahui leaving was that I was asked to become Girl Guide Commissioner for the Suau District. Lahui had previously held that post, but I had never been a Girl Guide and thought that that would disqualify me. However the Chief Commissioner in Port Moresby said that would be fine provided that I learnt the Tenderfoot

Test (the Guide Law and Promise for the novice,) and was enrolled. Legend has it that the use of the word Tenderfoot came from Robert Baden-Powell, the founder of the Scout and Guide movements. Its origins were as follows (Maynard, 1946): "When very 'green' young men went to the backwoods, instead of travelling by train or car, they had to walk for hours at a time carrying everything they needed. The first part to suffer was their feet; they were often chaffed by 'the old timers' and called 'tenderfeet'. This was thought to refer to newcomers to the American ranching or mining districts, as early as 1881, and first recorded by Baden Powell in 1908.

Two Guide trainers arrived on the next boat with a uniform and book of instructions for me to study. I certainly felt like a novice. We held a rally of local Brownies, Guides and Rangers. There were 28 Brownies in little brown skirts, 45 Guides divided into two companies, wearing ties without blouses that looked rather fetching, and 12 Rangers. Despite my protests I was enrolled as a Guide. The trainers said they would return to enrol me as Guide Commissioner. Chris was asked to take over Ravu's position of Scout Leader. He had been a Boy Scout and was fairly comfortable, whereas I had very little idea what I was doing. Fortunately, the local Guide Captains carried on with their Guide Company activities as usual and I was not required to do more than occasionally preside over meetings of senior Guides and trainers or provide a listening ear if needed.

Training Opportunities

Margaret and I were both pleased when one of our older schoolboys was accepted for training as a medical orderly at the United Church Hospital at Kapuna. Two of our schoolgirls had also reached the required educational standard and had been accepted for training as Maternal and Child Health nurses. I had spoken to Dr Peter Calvert on the radio and had been able to facilitate their acceptance, as the paperwork was held up by the postal strike. We all had quite a lot of written work that piled up from time to time, especially in the District

Minister's office. Eileen Jellico was a bright girl who had completed standard six, the last year of primary school. Her father, Jellico, was a respected church pastor, and he and his wife were keen for Eileen to find something to occupy her time. As I owned a typewriter and a book on learning to type I was asked to teach Eileen typing skills. As I could only type with two fingers I was not sure if this was a good idea, but as no one else could type, I landed the job. Eileen was a quick learner and my typing skills improved as well! She went on to learn to use the duplicator and some rudimentary bookkeeping from one of the local government staff, and in time was able to assist anyone needing office skills.

New Faces and a Small Survivor

Shirley and Geoff W settled in well and, as all the new students had arrived, the Chalmers College term began, although a little later than usual. Revd Kwalahu M, his wife Lesai and their six children arrived and moved into the District Minister's house at Isuleilei. Kwalahu was a quiet, gentle man and when I went over to meet the family, his wife was busy sorting out their belongings. I did not stay long, which was just as well, as when I returned to the Hospital the quiet of the afternoon was shattered by the spine-chilling crescendo of a death wail, coming from the Hospital veranda.

I found a father tearing his clothes in grief as he witnessed what he thought was the convulsive death of his three-year-old daughter, Matti. My heart sank as I recognised yet another child close to dying from cerebral malaria. I carried the inert form of the little girl over to the cot in the Labour ward where the equipment was and where we could have some privacy. Matti's father stood by his unconscious child and prayed for her recovery. Matti's mother wept quietly in the corner, as if she could not bear to watch her daughter's deterioration.

Matti's temperature was 106°F and Mary sponged her with cool water whilst I gave her anti-malarial and sedative drugs. We both

197

prayed silently that this child might recover. Mary said she would stay up with the sick child and her parents, whilst I went to bed. At first light we changed places. There was little change in Matti's condition, she was still unconscious, but had not had any more convulsions. Her temperature was still high and she was dehydrated. I explained to her father that she needed fluids and I would try to put a drip up. However, her veins were collapsed and I could not insert the needle, so I gave her half a litre of fluid into the abdominal cavity. This was a slower but effective method.

Ruta came down to sit with the child while I had some lunch and a rest, and then Mary returned in the evening. A second night passed without incident and the next morning Matti opened her eyes in brief recognition of her father, then fell asleep. We hardly dared hope and I was concerned about brain damage, but that evening she woke again and swallowed a few mouthfuls of coconut water, which is high in potassium and other nutrients.

The third morning she woke naturally and her temperature was nearly normal. We needed the Labour ward so we moved the family into the Maternity ward, which was quieter than the General ward at that time. Matti's parents were delighted with her recovery and nursed her devotedly until she was well and strong again.

A Midwifery Nightmare

Towards the end of the month we admitted a pregnant woman who had come from a distant inland village outside our District. We had never been there on patrol and I did not discover how Nini heard about us. Very unusually she came alone, without any relatives, which was almost unheard of in Papua. "She has no husband," said Mary as if that was sufficient explanation. Nini spoke a different language but had some English so she had obviously been to school. This was her first pregnancy and I judged her to be between 30 and 35 years of age, which is late for a first pregnancy in Papua. Nini was also unusually short, being only four feet four inches tall, with very small feet, which was not a good sign, as people small in stature often had a correspondingly small pelvis.

When I examined Nini, I estimated that she was almost at full term, probably about 38 weeks, as the baby's head was already engaged in the pelvis. I wondered how she had found her way down the mountain alone, carrying her food and belongings. As it was late evening when she arrived and she was very tired, I asked the nurses if they would cook her some food as she looked too exhausted to start cooking a meal for herself.

I was concerned that all the factors added up to possible complications with the delivery. The next day, after she was rested following a good night's sleep, I suggested to her that it would be better if she were to go into the Hospital in Samarai, where a doctor would be on hand if there were complications. There was some urgency as the boat was due, but Nini flatly refused to go, saying she was too frightened, as she had only seen the sea in the distance, and did not want to get on a boat. I realised what a big event it was for her to travel alone to our Hospital and although Mary and Walo tried to persuade her, she was adamant that she would not go. We had no option but to accept her decision, but it left me feeling uneasy.

Five days later Nini went into labour. All went well during the first stage, but when she reached the second stage of labour and was ready to give birth, we ran into problems. As I suspected there was disproportion between the baby's head and the pelvic outlet. The head was deflexed (the baby's head extends, looking in a upward direction, rather than tucked in towards its chest) and in that position was too big to rotate through the bony opening of the pelvis. I attempted to flex the head to no avail, as there was very little room to get my hand in. We could just see the head but it was stuck and could not move. Nini was very distressed as the contractions were coming thick and fast and she implored me to help her.

It was now around 6 PM and too late to radio Samarai to ask them to send a boat for Nini, as labour was obstructed and the baby could not be born normally. I knew that Mike P, the doctor, would agree to send a boat for such an emergency, but I also realised that it was unlikely that we could save the baby. The mother's life was also in danger from a ruptured uterus, exhaustion and dehydration. We had at least twelve hours to go before I could even contact Samarai and it would take another six to eight hours for the boat to arrive. So the chances were very slim indeed, but I put up a drip to counteract dehydration and made Nini as comfortable as possible.

I made a final attempt to deliver the baby with forceps but I could only get one blade in, as the space was so tight. It was also very uncomfortable for Nini and I abandoned the attempt, feeling sick in the stomach as I contemplated the night that lay ahead. Mary and I decided we would both need to stay with Nini during the night and to try and get some rest when we could. Around 10 PM the baby's heartbeat, that had been getting progressively weaker, stopped altogether. I had not expected the baby to survive but even so it was a sad event. However, the baby's death meant that we could give Nini heavier sedation, to make her more comfortable and possibly to reduce the strength of contractions. We moved her into the empty Maternity ward onto a more comfortable bed and she fell into a restless doze.

Mary and I took it in turns to watch Nini and at 3.50 AM she spontaneously delivered the baby into the bed. It was a little girl and her head was elongated and misshapen. At death the baby's skull bones had collapsed and this had allowed the head to reduce in size and finally slip through the pelvis. Mary and I were vastly relieved at this unexpected turn of events. Nini was drowsy but she was not shocked or bleeding and she seemed relatively well considering the ordeal she had gone through. We were waiting for the placenta to deliver when Nini suddenly collapsed and died. We were both so shocked we could hardly believe what had just happened. We tried to resuscitate her but were unsuccessful and at 4.30 AM we had to admit defeat. We laid the baby girl next to her mother on the bed and covered them both with a clean sheet.

Mary was upset and I was devastated. We did not know what was the cause of Nini's sudden death unless it was a pulmonary embolism (a clot of blood, which blocks the pulmonary artery). She had been conscious and had not complained of any pain so we had no indication that this would be the outcome. We went up to the house and I wanted to escape into a deep well of sleep but could only lie in bed going over and over events and wondering if we should have done anything differently.

I got up again about 6.30 AM and sent a message to Kwalahu to ask if he could arrange for a coffin to be made. As Nini had no relatives with her I thought we might have to bury her at Fife Bay, as we had no facilities to keep a body in the tropical heat. Kwalahu came over and said prayers for Nini and the baby and for us. We washed and dressed her and the baby, and by the evening two men appeared with a rough wooden coffin. Kwalahu was very supportive and helped us place Nini and the baby inside and said that we would have the funeral service the next day. However, much to my surprise several men appeared about 8 PM who said they had come from Nini's village to take her home. I could only assume that someone had gone to the village to tell them about her death. Because of the language barrier we were unable find out the exact details. They did not seem unduly surprised or upset by her death, but I felt terrible about what had happened especially as she was the first person who had ventured down to Hospital from that village.

Fortunately Kwalahu was still around and was able to speak with the men who knew a little Police Motu. He said they were pleased that a coffin had been made for her. They would probably bury her in a mat and use the wood for something else, but that did not seem important. They left at first light next morning and I tried to imagine the scene when they arrived in the village. I wondered who there would be to mourn her passing, as she had been so alone in such an uncharacteristic way for a Papuan.

Certainly, for me, this was the most traumatic experience I had encountered in my time at Fife Bay. It was the first time I had been involved in a maternal death in a Hospital. I felt as if it would be forever etched into my consciousness and although life returned to normal fairly quickly, it took me quite a long time to recover.

CHAPTER 28: AIRBORNE INVADERS

During February we were plagued by large numbers of flying ants. They usually arrived in the house at dusk in droves, and headed for the Tilley light that hung suspended over the table. Then they fell to earth in huge numbers, shedding their wings and leaving bodies about an inch thick on any surface. They got into our food, inside our clothes and hair, and onto the table. I never understood what drove them to swarm in the way they did, but it was only possible to deter them by turning out the lamp and sitting in the dark. This was inconvenient to say the least, but there was little we could do but sweep up bodies next morning.

Maiola

Maiola had been looked after at the Hospital when she was a baby, as her parents had not wanted her. She was 'mentally sub-normal' (the medical term used at that time) and had severe behavioural problems. Pastor Joel and his wife, Tele, adopted her as they were childless, and brought her up as their own child. When Maiola was nine years old the family came to the Hospital as Tele felt unwell. When I examined her I found she had a large abdominal mass, which was most likely a tumour. There was little I could do and I suggested that Joel take his wife into the Hospital in Samarai for treatment. Subsequently, Tele was transferred to Port Moresby Hospital for major abdominal surgery.

Joel and Tele did not feel that they could take Maiola with them and asked if we would care for her, which I agreed to, knowing it would be difficult as we were still looking after Lebohai and baby Peri but we could not find a viable alternative. Maiola was naturally upset at being parted from her mother and kicked and screamed a great deal, until she became a little more used to us. She was a handful and needed one nurse's sole attention during her waking hours, as she could not be left unsupervised. My admiration for Tele and Joel, who had cared lovingly for this disturbed child over the years, grew by leaps and bounds. Fortunately, the tumour in Tele's abdomen was benign but it took a long time for her to recover from the operation and we ended up looking after Maiola for several months.

One Night's Events

One evening there was a commotion on our veranda and when I went out to investigate I found a small group of schoolboys who had brought a sick friend up for treatment. This lad was about 15 years old and was quite noisy and irrational. He also had a temperature and I surmised that he probably had cerebral malaria. I asked the boys to take him back to their house and followed with the necessary medication. Unfortunately, the noise had woken Maiola who started screaming. I sat with the lad until 11 PM when he finally went to sleep, but when I returned to Middle House, Maiola was still very upset and everyone in the house had been kept awake by her noise. I decided to sedate her so that we could all get some sleep and be fit for work or school in the morning.

However, my sleep was short lived because I was woken again at about 1.30 AM by two men from Isudau, a village in the bay about three-quarters of an hours walk away. They told us that a woman in labour had given birth but the placenta had not been delivered and she was bleeding heavily. I grabbed my midwifery bag and Mary, who had heard the noise and got up, said she would come with me in case I got lost in the dark, which was very likely. The two men had gone on ahead to let the family know that we were coming. Walo was back from patrol so would hold the fort until we returned. As she was sedated, Maiola slept through the disturbance and therefore did not wake up other nurses or schoolgirls.

We set off rather grumpily because we expected all pregnant village women who lived within Fife Bay to come to Hospital to have their babies. Although we did not mention it, we were both aware that this was the first delivery since Nini had died and we did not want any more complications. It took us over an hour to reach the village because it was high tide and we had to skirt around a lagoon as the water was too deep to wade through. When we did arrive we found that the placenta had been delivered but the woman was still bleeding. I expelled some blood clots and Mary gave the mother an injection of ergometrine to help the uterus to contract. Fortunately, this was effective and she began to recover, so we did not need to put up a drip. I gave her an injection of long-acting penicillin to prevent infection and some folic acid and iron tablets, as she was anaemic and had had considerable blood loss.

We were then able to turn our attention to the baby boy who was small but seemed healthy enough, if a little cold. We wrapped him in a blanket and gave him to his grandmother to keep warm, but he was hungry and readily took to the breast when his mother felt well enough to feed him. We looked up our village records and found that this lady had never been to our antenatal clinic, during this, her fourth pregnancy. I was not sure how she slipped through the net but both she and her husband got a ten-minute lecture from Mary about not attending clinic or coming to Hospital for delivery. "You could have died," said Mary severely "what would your baby have done then?" They both looked suitably shamefaced and made us some tea before we left to return home. We got back about 5 AM and both went to bed. I slept until lunchtime but felt dopey all day. The following night we were not disturbed so could sleep all night, which was a bonus.

Unexpected visitors

About a week later, much to everyone's surprise, a small group of people straggled in from an inland village. The two men and four women had minor ailments, mainly coughs and sores that required treatment, but they were very curious about everything that was done at Hospital. The women were particularly interested in the beds in the Maternity ward and the babies' cots. It transpired that they were from Nini's village. At first I wondered if they were seeking reprisals but their manner was anything but aggressive. They fingered my hair and exclaimed at my blue eyes and it occurred to me that they had not seen many white people before. However, the star of the show was young John W who visited the Hospital at the same time. He also had blue eyes and very blond hair and they all got on famously. John was not at all fazed by their close scrutiny; in fact I think he rather enjoyed it!

The women all wore grass skirts and were bare-breasted. That was not unusual, but they looked longingly at the cotton dress material in the trade store. As they had no money, we used a barter system and traded a piece of cloth for each of them, for some food. They gave us some sago, which the nurses had and some sugar cane that I ate. I had become rather fond of sugar cane and enjoyed its sweet crisp taste. It required strong teeth to bite through the outer covering to the flesh beneath but with practise I got quite good at it. The men wore ragged shorts but they were more interested in our bush knives than clothes. We let them have a bush knife each, for some mangoes, and they were very pleased with the exchange. I had a feeling that they had picked the mangoes from off our tree, but decided to ignore it. They stayed about four days, inspecting everything, and I came to the conclusion that they were just curious to see the place and what went on there. I hoped that they would not be afraid to return again.

Now, that we were fully staffed and Geoff and Shirley W were established in the Big House, Kwalahu agreed that I could take the local

206

leave that I had not been able to take last year. I made arrangements to visit Alan and Wendy in the town of Rabaul, as it was a good opportunity to see something of the island of New Britain. I felt quite nervous about leaving Fife Bay, as apart from short visits to Samarai, I had been there for 18 months, virtually cut off from the outside world. Although we listened to BBC World Service on the radio, sometimes it felt as if the rest of the world did not exist. I tried to imagine life in London but I was surprised at how easily the reality of those memories faded, so it was just as well that I had the chance to visit a town once more. I felt sure that once I was back where there were shops and traffic it would all fall into place!

CHAPTER 29: VISIT TO NEW BRITAIN

I HAD ARRANGED TO BEGIN MY LOCAL LEAVE by travelling to Iruna to catch the plane to Port Moresby, before flying on to Rabaul to stay with Alan and Wendy, but as always there were delays and hitches to contend with. Our usual boat, the MV Laurabada, had run aground in a storm and damaged her hull, so was out of action. Another boat, the MV Papua, arrived instead, a day late, on a Thursday, to begin the 24 hour journey to Iruna travelling west up the coast. The MV Papua took two days and two nights to reach Iruna, instead of the usual 24 hours, but as I was the only European on board, I was given the only passenger cabin. It was over the engine room and was very hot and noisy but at least I could lie down. The crew were very kind and kept bringing me platefuls of rice and fish to keep me going, as we spent one whole day loading and unloading copra, which contributed to the delay.

General Election

The other reason for the delay was that a General Election had been called and ballot papers were off-loaded from the boat. They had to be signed for and the right person, usually someone in local government, was not always available and had to be found and brought onto the boat to take charge of the papers. The election process was very drawn out as boxes of ballot papers also had to be sent by plane or canoe to remote villages and then returned after voting, which often took several days to complete. The electoral officers had to travel all over the country to ensure that those entitled to vote were given opportunity to do so. Some papers were lost when a canoe was swamped in bad weather, and others apparently never reached their destination. Subsequently, I heard of one village that wanted to vote for President Johnson (the American President, Lyndon B Johnson) but eventually the process was completed, and Michael Somare, a popular politician, and leader of the Pangu Party (Papua and New Guinea Union Party) was elected to the House of Assembly. The Pangu Party had only ten members and saw themselves as being in Opposition, as the Independent Australian members were in the majority. The 1968 election was only the second election to have taken place in the Territories of Papua and New Guinea. The first in 1964 elected individuals, but there were no clearly defined political parties.

The road to nationhood for the people of this country was complex; they had been precipitated from a tribal culture into a democracy almost overnight. Initially Australia had ruled the country through their Governor and his Legislative Council. In 1964 when the House of Assembly was set up, six notable Papuans were elected, one of whom was Mr John Guise, (later Sir John Guise, knighted in 1975 when he became Papua New Guinea's first Governor General), who led a working party on Constitutional Development as the first step towards self government.

I was to have stayed with Jan and Nick on the Friday night to catch the Saturday plane out but we did not arrive until Saturday morning. To my surprise the MAF plane was waiting on the airstrip. So it was a matter of saying hello and goodbye to Jan and Nick, before jumping aboard the single-engine Cessna for the one and a half hour flight to Port Moresby. I had arranged to stay with Vi and Bill Bache, two Australian missionaries, who lived in Koki, a suburb of Moresby, for four days, before flying up to Rabaul. It was a strange feeling to be in a town again, walking on pavements and smelling traffic fumes when cars and buses travelled past.

*   *   *   *

Rabaul

I had sent a telegram from Port Moresby with my expected time of arrival, but when I arrived at the airport in Rabaul there was no one there to meet me. I did not have an address for Alan and Wendy as they had moved into a different flat whilst I was in Moresby and there had been no time to let me know their whereabouts. Whilst I was wondering what to do, I saw a face I thought I knew. It was Doug Hoskins, who had been at All Saints' College in Sydney with me, two years earlier. He was very surprised to see me suddenly pop up from nowhere, but I was very glad to see him. Doug was working for the Methodist Church in Rabaul (now the United Church since church union) and he was able to take me to Alan and Wendy's new flat. Now it was Wendy's turn to be surprised, but fortunately they had just about finished unpacking. It was not the best time for a guest to arrive! Alan stayed at Raronga Theological College during the week and came home at weekends. Raronga was 25 miles outside Rabaul along a hot and dusty road. The telegram I had sent from Moresby, four days earlier, arrived the next day!

Rabaul was a pleasant town situated in the volcanic hills of the northern tip of New Britain in the Bismarck Archipelago, lying off the northeastern New Guinea coast. The local people spoke Tok Pisin, originally a trade language made up of many different languages. On the Sunday after I arrived I attended the United Church in Rabaul, with Alan and Wendy. There were a large number of expats in the congregation, and the hymns were in English and Tok Pisin. There was even a choir and organ to lead the singing, which was wonderful. The opening verses of St Mark's gospel sounded strange to my ears: *Guitnuis bilong Jisas Kraist, pikinini bilong God* – This is the Good News about Jesus Christ the Son of God (English version *Good News Bible*, 1994, St Mark Ch 1, v1, p45).

It was lovely to see Wendy and Alan and the children again. Wendy and I went shopping in town, and I bought some dress material, a new pair of sandals and a bedcover. The town was quite small with only two streets, but there was more choice of shops than in Moresby. During the few days of my stay, I enjoyed fish and chips, milkshakes, and chocolate éclairs, but not all at once! We went for a drive over the mountains and down to the coast for a picnic, which was a novel experience for me, as I had not ridden in a car since I arrived in Papua.

I also visited Raronga College and the George Brown High School where I met several ex-Lawes College students, and Methodist colleagues from All Saints'. The students seemed to have settled in well, and it was great to renew friendships with All Saints' folk. Rabaul was previously a centre of Methodist missionary endeavour, and it felt good to be part of the same fellowship now we were the United Church.

Raronga College was set in beautiful grounds. The College Principal was an expert grower of hibiscus and the garden was full of hibiscus flowers in a variety of colours, some single and some double blooms. I had never seen such a wonderful display. At Fife Bay we had hedges of red hibiscus and the girls often picked flowers to put in their hair (plate 12), but I did not know that there were so many other varieties. Whilst I was in Rabaul there were several earth tremors. It was a strange sensation to feel the earth shuddering under my feet. Earthquakes were not uncommon, and there were two rumbling volcanoes that sometimes erupted and I was told that Rabaul itself was built on the site of an ancient crater.

Many smaller islands in the Archipelago surrounded New Britain. I took Andrew to Duke of York Island for the day, where they had a small Hospital and a Nurse Training School. We went on a copra boat and the sea was like blue silk. Andrew seemed to enjoy himself and was quite a hit with the nurses at the Hospital. We had lunch there before returning to Rabaul. It was interesting to see a Hospital run on similar lines to Fife Bay, although it was larger and, in spite of being on an island, it was not so isolated, as several boats called there each week.

On my last full day in Rabaul, we went to the opening of Gaulim Teacher Training College on the Gazelle peninsula. Several families crammed into two cars, including nine children (Health and Safety had not been heard of) and we arrived in time for the opening ceremony. The church service went on for two-and-a-half hours and the children became restless, as did I because I found it difficult to sit for so long cross-legged on the floor! Eventually we were released and went down to the beach for a picnic lunch, before returning to Rabaul.

Return Journey

Before my flight left in the afternoon, I managed to squeeze in a visit to the hairdresser to get my hair cut properly. I had kept it short with Margaret's help but a professional haircut was a real luxury. I emerged feeling a lot better, as this time my hair was properly shaped and did not look as if some creature had been nibbling at it. After my trip, I felt refreshed and was glad that I had been able to spend time with Alan and Wendy. It was also a good experience to have seen another Mission Station, albeit one very different from Fife Bay. Having been free of the responsibility of running the Hospital for a few days, I was a little reluctant to return, but I knew that I would soon get into the swing of things again.

Last Lap

I flew from Rabaul to Port Moresby, then transferred to a Cessna for the next leg of my journey. When I boarded the small plane at Moresby, I discovered that one of my fellow passengers was a Samoan pastor travelling back to the islands. He was a very large man and took up at least two seats, overlapping both of them. The pilot moved us around several times in order to distribute the weight evenly. I was not fond of travelling on small planes and was even more disconcerted by this turn of events. However we had a safe if bumpy landing at Gurney airstrip in Milne Bay where the pastor had to be helped out of his seats as he had been wedged into two seats in the tail section. I think he was also glad to get off the plane, as I was! I then travelled by truck from Gurney airport to Alotau and caught the launch to Samarai and from there to Kwato.

I had to stay at Kwato for a few days as the boat to Fife Bay was delayed by bad weather. It was just before Easter and I spent Palm Sunday, 7th April 1968, at Kwato, and the morning service was partly in English. The church was decorated very effectively with palm branches. The Kwato Church building was unusual, built in the style of a traditional Suau Meeting-House. The sides were open but the roof sloped down almost to the ground.

I also heard that Shirley W had had her baby, a girl, in Samarai Hospital, whilst I had been on holiday, and mother and baby had already returned to Fife Bay. I looked forward to meeting the new arrival who had been named Diane Ruth. I managed to get a boat to Fife Bay at 6 AM, on the Monday of Holy Week, but we had a very difficult trip back that took over ten hours, instead of the usual six. We sailed into a head wind all the way and it was a very rough sea. Almost everyone was seasick, including me, and we all lay around on the deck trying to find a dry spot out of reach of waves and spray that lashed the deck, but most of us were soaked by the time we arrived. Not for the first time, I wondered why this ocean was named the Pacific, when it was anything but peaceful!

It was surprisingly cold and I arrived at Fife Bay feeling much the worse for wear. I headed straight for Middle House and a cup of tea and a shower, but when I got there, I found that the Malaria Control Team had arrived from Iruna and were waiting to speak to me. I managed to change into dry clothes and Margaret made us all some tea, but I had to spend the evening discussing mosquitoes, blood slides and logistics as the team were due to leave at first light, on the boat I had just got off. It was good to know that we were included in the Malaria Control Programme, which meant spraying all houses and

Hospital buildings with DDT. It was the timing of the preliminary visit that was the problem, as I was definitely not at my best, but as usual the message telling us of the team's visit arrived after they did.

CHAPTER 30: SNAKES ALIVE!

Fortunately, it had been relatively quiet whilst I had been away, and Mary and Walo had managed any problems. Toby nearly bowled me over when I returned. He had lost weight and Margaret said he had been reluctant to eat, probably because he missed me, but he soon perked up.

An Unwelcome Visitor

I was in the bathroom on my second day back when out of the corner of my eye I saw a sudden movement. I turned around to investigate but froze in amazement as coiled around the stand holding the water tank was a large black snake. The Papuan black, which was what I thought it was, along with the taipan, was a highly dangerous, venomous snake. I backed slowly toward the door whilst I contemplated what I should do. I liked snakes and admired their sleek beauty, but I knew that this was unusual in expats and Papuans alike. By choosing our bathroom to investigate, the snake had signed its own death warrant and I felt quite sad, as I could think of no alternative.

I located Toby and the cat and shut them into Margaret's bedroom out of harm's way. Margaret had already gone down to the school and Mary and other nurses were at the Hospital, but Walo was still in the house. It was unlikely that she would go into the bathroom but I told her about the unusual inhabitant and she went visibly pale. "I will get a man from the Hospital to kill it" was all she could say, before disappearing down the hill.

215

I waited until two men appeared with sticks and a bush knife looking quite nervous. I showed them into the bathroom, and said "be careful," before making myself scarce, as I did not wish to witness the snake's demise. It was not long before they appeared with the body, looking triumphant. I asked the men to bury the snake in the bush, which they agreed to do. I gave them each some money for helping us out and they went off to buy tobacco at the trade store, well pleased with themselves. For a few weeks Margaret and I were extremely vigilant when we went into the bathroom. We also looked carefully before putting on any footwear, as it was not unknown for snakes to inhabit a warm pair of slippers.

Easter 1968

We celebrated Easter as usual, with special services on Maundy Thursday, Good Friday and Easter Day. During the celebrations on Easter Sunday, I met Shirley and Geoff W's new baby girl, Diane. She was a bonny baby and schoolgirls resident at the Big House loved to help Shirley look after her. I still missed spring flowers that we associated with Easter at home, daffodils and primroses in particular that do not grow in the tropics, but there were other things to be enjoyed. It was very hot and we had a bumper crop of mangoes, and on Easter Monday we all went to the waterfall for a picnic. We ate a lot of mangoes and washed the juice off in the water when we went in for a swim. I had a letter after Easter from my friend Stella, who said they had had snow at the beginning of April. It was hard to imagine it as we sweltered in the heat.

A Welcome Visitor

Russell, a young American, arrived on the next boat. He was a research student and had come to study the Suau language. I thought that when he had mastered it he might be able to help me learn more Suau. He was staying at the Big House, which was bursting at the seams, as there were five adults and two small children plus school-girls. It meant a lot of cooking and work for Shirley, although Kala helped out after she had finished teaching. Russell had to sleep on the veranda, as there were no spare rooms. He was married and if his wife joined him they could move into one of the student houses. He had to spend a lot of time in villages, which meant he would be away a lot and this might not suit a young American wife unused to the isolation of Fife Bay.

Hospital Matters

The Department of Health brought out a syllabus for training our Nurse Aides, which was useful and I implemented it straight away. It was a year-long course that was meant to have started in January, but we only received it in April, so had quite a bit to catch up with as there was an exam at the end of it. Our girls were keen to learn and we had a session most afternoons, if we were not busy. The course covered basic anatomy and physiology, common diseases and their treatments, first aid and simple midwifery. We did not have a classroom, so used the veranda, but if I had been up in the night, I had to cancel the class to catch up on sleep. I hoped the girls would use that time to revise, but I suspected that they found other ways to use their time.

As was the way of things here we were suddenly busy after Easter. One very sad event occurred when a women who was eight months pregnant was fishing in the sea when she was stung by a stingray fish. She came into the Hospital feeling unwell and the site of the sting was clearly visible. I was not sure what to do, so treated her with antihistamines after consulting with Dr Mike P at Samarai. The swelling and inflammation around the sting site subsided but her baby who had been alive and well when she was admitted, died 24 hours later *in utero*. I could only assume that the toxins from the fish sting had gone through the placental barrier and caused the death of the baby. Mike P confirmed this. He thought it was a very unusual case, and as there

217

were not many recorded deaths of this nature, he sent the details to the British Medical Journal.

I did not have the means to induce labour so had to wait for nature to take its course. Two weeks later the mother gave birth to a stillborn baby boy. Both parents were naturally very upset and blamed the *puri puri* man for sending the fish to sting the mother. I asked Kwalahu to come and speak to the parents, which he did, but they were not consoled and took their baby back to the village for burial.

Eastern Patrol

My next patrol to the eastern side of the District was long overdue, so I arranged to travel to Bonarua Island on the boat that left at 5 AM on Sunday, with Margariti. I felt slightly off colour on the Saturday, but went ahead as planned. It was a rough sea and I was seasick all the way to Bonarua, so that did not help matters. The pastor's house where we stayed was unusually comfortable; Margariti and I had our own room, which had a low bed where I spent the rest of the day. The next morning I felt better and after breakfast we ran a well attended clinic, but by the time it was finished I felt very unwell and retired to bed shivering with a temperature of 103°F. I stayed there all day and the pastor's wife kindly made me a jug of *sipora* to drink, as I was too nauseated to eat anything. Margariti amused herself by walking around the island.

I didn't feel any better the next morning and I could hear the pastor and his wife talking about what they should do. As I knew the Bonarua people owned a small boat, I asked them to take me to Samarai, so that I could consult the doctor there. The people were only too happy to oblige, as having me visit them on patrol was one thing, but having me languishing in their village with fever was another. The Bonarua boat always reminded me of a much smaller version of the pictures of Noah's Ark, in that it was like a large rowing boat with an engine under a square box in the middle. I laid down on an old

218

mattress under an awning on the deck and felt sorry for myself. There were heavy seas and the boat took four hours to reach Samarai and inevitably I was seasick.

Samarai Hospital was on a hill and normally there was an ambulance waiting on the quay to transport passengers to Hospital. However, on this occasion the road was being repaired and I had to walk up the hill. I staggered up the steep incline, wrapped in an off-white sheet I had borrowed from the village, over my nightshirt, which is the way Papuans dress if they are ill. As I passed people on my way up I could imagine them saying "she has gone native," a description applied to anyone who did not behave in a manner expected of an expat. Margariti accompanied me looking embarrassed. By the time we reached the top I was quite breathless, and as I turned the corner, I saw Mike P and his wife in their garden watching my progress in surprise.

Mike P quickly sprang into action and procured a wheelchair. I was admitted to a single room, and Mike P examined me. He put up a drip, took some blood tests and gave me a sedative, and the result was I slept for about ten hours. Margariti said she would visit her cousin-sister, and as she seemed keen to do so, I agreed provided that she come back in the morning to see how things were.

I had convinced myself that I had malaria, but the blood tests were negative, so a diagnosis of PUO (pyrexia – fever – of unknown origin) was made, which was common in the territory. After a couple of days my temperature returned to normal, although I still felt nauseated and had little appetite. Mike P suggested that I spend a few days at Kwato to recuperate and wait for the next boat to Fife Bay. It was a good thing that the Kwato folk were always ready to receive strays like Margariti and myself, and never seemed to mind when we turned up unexpectedly. We stayed at Kwato for three days and had a good trip back to Fife Bay, as the sea was calm. Mary left two days later by sailing canoe to finish the patrol that I had started. She visited the hamlets and two villages that I had missed, Modewa and Ilo Ilo.

I thought I had better stay at home for a few days and she was quite keen to go which was helpful.

Visiting Snakes

I don't know why the snakes were particularly active at this time of year, but we had two more visit us. One attempted to crawl through my bedroom window, but I was able to push him back with a long stick. There was a lot of bush outside my window and he slithered away unharmed. He was a non-venomous python and I was glad he had escaped. He had been seen curled up in the pit toilet a few times and that put people off using it especially at night. Our cat found the second snake coiled up asleep in our storeroom. The cat, ever curious, strolled into the storeroom, but flew out at such speed that her feet did not appear to touch the ground. She was fluffed up to three times her size and when I went to investigate, I realised why. I quickly came out and shut the door, but as the snake, which I thought was a taipan, did not budge, it had to be dispatched. I sincerely hoped that we would not encounter any more.

When I told Kwalahu, he said he would send some men to cut the grass around our house and Hospital, as snakes liked to hide in long grass. Keeping the grass cut back was a constant problem, because it grew so fast. The patients' relatives sometimes helped but it was too big an area for them to manage. True to his word, Kwalahu organised over twenty men who came from Savaia, a village just outside the bay, to cut the grass. They spent the morning in what I called no man's land clearing away grass and weeds with their bush knives. We made them tea and they seemed to enjoy the whole process. I, for one, was very pleased with the end result.

CHAPTER 31: SICK CHILDREN

My BIRTHDAY FELL AT THE BEGINNING OF THE MONTH, and Shirley arranged a birthday party for me, which was very kind of her. All the staff came and we had a really enjoyable evening. It was a good way to begin the month, especially as I was feeling a little homesick.

We had been unusually busy at the Hospital after I arrived back, with six sick children admitted in one day with chest infections and/or malaria. One baby's temperature was 106°F but he responded well to treatment. An elderly man was also brought in during the afternoon but he died the next morning before I had time to make an accurate diagnosis. I thought he had pneumonia and had started him on antibiotics but it was too late. I think he had been ill for a few days and the family had delayed bringing him in. They carried him home again, their wails echoing into the distance. I always felt bad when someone died, even though there was nothing more that I could have done. I felt even worse when people had travelled a long distance to reach the Hospital and had hoped for a good outcome.

Things that go bump in the night

We had been up for three nights with sick children and on the fourth night, when they were all recovering, I was looking forward to several hours of uninterrupted sleep. About 1 AM, the quiet of the night was shattered by blood curdling screams and my bedroom door flew open and three schoolgirls landed on my bed. In the dark it took a while to extract everybody from the mosquito net; the girls were shaking in fright and babbling away in Suau. By this time Margaret and the nurses were awake, but we could not get any sense out of the girls. I thought we must have burglars or that a snake had got into their room, but eventually they calmed down enough to tell the full story.

Apparently, Daionesi and Lahela had got up to go to the toilet without a torch although it was very dark. The vibration of their feet on the floorboards caused a cupboard door to swing open and hit Daionesi in the back. Yelling loudly they ran back into their room and fell over Doreka, another schoolgirl, who sat up shrieking with fright, whereupon they all got up and ran screaming into my room. When we worked out what had happened they fell into fits of giggles, which only schoolgirls of thirteen know how to do. I took them back to their room and they laughed and jabbered away in Suau for another hour, before finally falling asleep. So much for a peaceful night!

Midwifery Problems

In the morning we admitted a woman who was already in labour. Her three previous pregnancies had all resulted in stillbirths due to disproportion (where the woman's pelvis is too small or the wrong shape for the baby's head to pass through). Previously I had examined her at the antenatal clinic in her village, and had encouraged her to go to Samarai for a caesarean section, but she was too frightened and instead had come to Fife Bay. This baby was quite small, but as labour was slow and prolonged we worried about her and monitored her very closely. Not unnaturally she was very anxious, but we had to be very sparing with sedation because of the effect on the baby.

Later that evening another woman was admitted in advanced labour. It was her seventh child and when I examined her, I found she had a transverse lie, which meant that the baby's body was lying across her abdomen, with the head under her left ribs instead of where it should have been – in the mother's pelvis. The danger in that situation was that the baby's shoulder would enter the pelvis and labour would be obstructed, causing the death of the baby and probably also of the mother. I attempted to turn the baby through the mother's abdomen but this was unsuccessful. I just had time to consult Dr Peter Calvert on the radio, before she reached the stage when normally the baby would have been born. Following Peter's advice, I ruptured the membranes, and attempted to turn the baby internally. Fortunately, I was able to grasp a foot and bring down a leg, and eventually I managed to deliver the baby, a barely-alive boy, as a breech. I have never been more thankful to see a pair of feet!

I was just resuscitating the baby when the first woman, who was being looked after by Walo, delivered her child, also a live boy, with a very moulded head where it had been squeezed through the pelvis. He was barely breathing and we worked on both babies for what seemed an eternity, before they both began to look pink instead of blue and breathe on their own. We said prayers of thanksgiving all round as both mothers, who had recovered quite quickly from their ordeal, proudly fed their baby boys.

Problems with Indispensable Household Items: the Fridge

Sometimes it felt as if inanimate objects conspired against us! The handle came off our kerosene fridge door, which meant that we were unable to shut it. This caused us great difficulty, as we needed to keep our vaccines cold. In the end we kept the door closed by winding copra string around it and securing the string to the kitchen wall. This meant that every time we need to go to the fridge we had to undo it and then repeat the process. It was frustrating and caused tempers to be frayed! The fridge was ancient, about 13 years old, and I wrote to the United Church office in Moresby requesting a new one, as this one was beyond repair. I knew that money was short but this was an essential item and I hoped that the administration would be sympathetic. We took some items up to the Big House to store in their fridge, although Shirley didn't have a lot of room as they had a house full, and it was nearly as much hassle trekking up and down every time we needed something.

While we waited for a reply from Port Moresby, help came from an unexpected quarter. The Patrol Post had a spare fridge that they leant us until we were able to get a new one. It was quite a performance getting it over to us, as it had to be carried by the prisoners from the local jail. Two policemen escorted them, but the fridge was heavy and the men had to stop and put it down at frequent intervals. I hoped that none of them would suffer a back injury. When the fridge was installed on our veranda, I gave the men some fruit juice as they were sweating freely. We had to wait 24 hours for the fridge to get cold before we could transfer our goods, but it was a great relief when we were able to do so.

Problems with Indispensable Household Items: the Toilet

About the same time, our one luxury, the WC under the house, stopped working. Further investigation revealed a broken water pump, and as it had been installed a long time ago, hopes of finding a replacement faded rapidly. My attempts to explain what we needed to a couple of local workmen were met with an air of mystery and incomprehension, so after a bit I gave up. Throwing buckets of water down the toilet was wasteful and ineffective, so there was nothing for it but to return to using the traditional *small house*. The one designated for Middle House was worthy of inclusion in *The Specialist* (1929), a little book about unusual toilets by Charles Sale, illustrated by William Kermode.

It was situated some way from the house, down an overgrown path, which made visits at night somewhat hazardous and never to be attempted without a large torch. The walls of the *small house* were built of corrugated iron, and placed over a large hole in the ground. Inside was a large box with three holes, side by side, but as far as I knew it was only ever occupied by one person at a time. For some reason, to get into it you had to step up on an old oil drum. As the door did not close properly it was necessary to indicate your presence if you heard another person approaching down the path. It was a favourite haunt of a variety of lizards, some rats, and a pair of bandicoots, who lived in the bush nearby.

Toilet paper was at a premium, and we supplied each nurse with her own roll. We all had to carry our own supply back and forth, as if left in the loo it would disappear. Local people who did not have such luxuries used coconut husks, and a supply of this commodity was available for anyone who forgot to take in their own toilet roll! Newspapers were scarce and if available were used to roll tobacco into cigarettes, not wasted as a toilet paper.

After a few weeks of struggling with the facilities available, Margaret and I decided to ask Kwalahu if we could have a new *small house* built, in a more convenient position. We were already waiting for a new water tank, but as the wet season was rapidly approaching we felt we needed a more up to date convenience, as paddling down that path in darkness and torrential rain was not an appealing prospect.

CHAPTER 32: IMPROVEMENTS IN
MEDICAL CARE

W E WERE FORTUNATE TO HAVE A VISIT FROM NICK from Iruna
this month, so I was able to get him to take a look at several of our
patients. I was glad to have him to deal with the dentistry, as he was
much less squeamish than I was. We did not have any complicated
midwifery cases during his brief stay, but the big news was that he
came to introduce a contraceptive device that had been supplied by
the Department of Health. It was known as a Lippes loop and when
inserted into a woman's uterus it was meant to prevent further pregnancies. Although we could not be 100% certain of its effectiveness, it
was a great improvement on nothing at all.

I called in several mothers that had had ten children or more and
offered them the device, which they were very pleased about. Nick
explained the success rate and potential risks but they all opted to
have it. The husbands who accompanied them were also enthusiastic.
The more children a woman had, the greater the risk of complications, and we hoped to extend the opportunity to all women in due
course. Nick showed Mary, Walo and me how to insert the device and
left us a supply to use in the coming weeks.

I took advantage of Nick's visit by asking him to check my
wheezing chest, which had been causing me some problems. One of
the difficulties was my allergy to grass and tree pollens, which grew
in abundance at Fife Bay. The advice from my Allergy Consultant
to "Eliminate allergens from your environment," was a non-starter.

Nick gave me some tablets to take at night, which did improve the situation.

Malaria Eradication

The DDT spraying team descended on us that month. Every wall and ceiling had to be sprayed in an attempt to eradicate the female Anopheles mosquito that carried the malaria parasite. It was a huge job to remove everything from Hospital, including patients, who had to sit outside in their beds. Fortunately it did not rain and no one was seriously ill at the time. The same procedure had to be carried out at Middle House, where we stowed everything under the house. The cat and Toby had to be kept well out of the way, as DDT was poisonous to animals. In fact all our little lizards and geckos died, which I was sad about. There were still a few cockroaches about afterwards; they seemed to be immune to everything! The team also took blood from a section of the population in an effort to determine the extent of malaria in the area. If the spraying helped to reduce the incidence of malaria, all the hassle it caused would be worthwhile.

The house and Hospital reeked of DDT for days afterwards, and one unforeseen side effect was an increase of rats in villages. This was because the village cats ate lizards and geckos when they fell out of thatched roofs of village houses, and then died from DDT poisoning. Suddenly our cat's kittens were much in demand, but we only let them go to a village if we were sure that their owners would feed them properly, or the same fate would await them.

We were alarmed when some of our 'burnt out' patients with leprosy (where the disease is no longer active but the nerve damage and lack of feeling persists) came in from the villages with wounds on their feet from rat bites. They normally went bare foot, although they had been issued with sandals. On this occasion we redoubled our efforts and made sure that they had suitable footwear, which had to be worn day and night, as the rats would bite their feet while they slept.

227

New Equipment

Kwalahu kindly arranged for some village men to build us a new *small house*. Corrugated iron for the roof and timber for the wall posts arrived on the boat, but we supplied the nails that we purchased from the trade store. I had no idea that so many nails would be needed and suspected that the temptation was too great and some found their way into the men's pockets! It was probably expected as a perk of the job.

Our two new water tanks, one for Middle House and one for the Hospital also arrived from Samarai. We were keen to collect more water during the coming wet season, to avoid having to take our personal and Hospital washing to the river during the next dry season. However nothing in the Territory was straightforward. The Hospital tank was already assembled but there was no hole at the top for the water to flow into! For some reason the tank for Middle House had not been assembled, which meant we had to find someone who had equipment and ability to solder it together, no mean feat where we were living!

One of the men building our toilet said he could cut an inlet hole into the Hospital tank, which he did manage to do after a fashion, but it was too big and had to be covered with wire netting to prevent contamination. Eventually with much huffing and puffing the tank was erected on its concrete base and I heaved a sigh of relief. Our tank had to wait until a skilled man could come down on the boat from Iruna to weld the pieces together. It was a better option than returning the already paid for tank to Samarai, as we thought that if we sent it back we might not see it again. It was difficult not to get frustrated by this sort of thing, but it achieved nothing, except to relieve our feelings. I realised even the simplest tasks could produce problems and that it was better to expect things to go wrong, as then we were surprised if they didn't!

To cheer myself up I decided to make a new dress from the pink material I had bought in Rabaul. I rarely wore pink, so I thought it would be a change. The pattern, though simple to follow, was different from the usual shift in that it had a zip fastener and I was unable to finish the dress until I could get the right sized zip from Samarai. At least I made a start and I was quite pleased with the result. My sewing skills improved through necessity, as there was very little to buy in the way of ready-made garments in Samarai.

Sunday Afternoons

If possible we all tried to have half-an-hour's rest after lunch, but on Sundays, if we were not busy at Hospital, we extended the time to an hour or more. In June the temperature started to drop from 80-90°F to between 65°F and 70°F, which felt quite cool so that we needed a blanket to be comfortable.

At 3.30 PM on Sundays we held a service at Hospital for staff and patients. It lasted about three-quarters of an hour and was usually taken by one of the college students. They usually spoke in Police Motu as they all came from outside the Suau area. Most men understood well enough but some women, including me, did not, but I went along to support the efforts of the students.

Western Patrol

I had been due to go on patrol last month but it had to be postponed owing to Nick's visit, which I did not want to miss. We left Fife Bay on the Pipi Gari (named after a famous Papuan sailor and first Papuan captain of a coastal steamer, in Johns, 1937) the coastal boat that replaced the MV Laurabada. Ruta, one of our experienced Nurse Aides and a Suau speaker accompanied me. The boat was due to leave at 6.30 AM so we got up early and were on board just after 6 AM. However er the boat did not leave until 9.30 AM largely due to the time it took to land a fully-grown pig, which took exception to being unloaded onto a dinghy. The vessel capsized when the pig was lowered into it, but the pig was fortunately still suspended in a sling, and could be winched back on deck. It was making a great deal of noise and its new owner had to go back to the beach and launch a large sailing canoe to collect it. This was even more precarious, as the man had to hang onto his prize possession to prevent it from escaping from the canoe into the open sea. Eventually order was restored and the rest of the cargo was unloaded and we were able to set off.

We headed for Gadaisu, the westernmost point of our District, from where we would make our way back, stopping at villages on the way. I had sent messages over the local radio station letting people know we were coming, so the clinics were well attended. This was the most effective way of communicating with people in villages, as someone in a village, often the pastor or a teacher, had a radio and would let people know when to expect us. If they had not known when we were coming, most of the women would be away working in their gardens, and would probably miss the clinic.

We wanted to check the progress of all babies and keep up to date with their BCG and triple vaccines, in order to maintain adequate immunity. As I had done this patrol on previous occasions, I knew most mothers and babies, which was an advantage in assessing their health. The pastors and their wives, whose hospitality we enjoyed, were also more relaxed as they knew me and we had an enjoyable time. All the same I found it difficult at times, in the midst of routine work, to hold on to a sense of God. I worried sometimes about not fulfilling my missionary calling. At other times I was too busy to think about it at all!

On this patrol we also wanted to explain to women and their husbands that contraception was now available. Ruta was invaluable in explaining the options to the mothers and could answer their many questions. The women had to come to Hospital for the Lippes loop to be fitted and in the ensuing months several couples turned up. The husband, looking sheepish would sidle up to me and ask for "the stop the baby medicine". Both parties had to be in agreement that this was what they wanted, but as many couples had large families, with enough surviving children, they were quite keen.

As there were no pension arrangements, most families wanted to have several healthy children who would be able to care for them in their old age. Every old person that I met was cared for by their family, in the home of one or more of their children. It was often their grandchildren who attended to their needs, going to a lot of trouble to obtain their grandparent's favourite food, such as shellfish. The elderly were revered for their age and experience of life, and this system was built into the culture.

The only drawback of this patrol, from my point of view, was the need to travel a lot by canoe, as there were so many waterways to negotiate to reach the next village on our route. I had become quite nervous of travelling by dugout canoes. The people, although experienced sailors, had apparently never heard of the Plimsoll line and they loaded their canoes until they were very low in the water. If it got rough and we took on water, we had to bail like mad with a coconut shell and sometimes men would have to jettison some of the goods they were carrying to lighten the load.

One particular day we were due to move on to the next village, and the canoe was so small, that I lost my nerve. It was already about 4 PM and it would have meant venturing out into the open sea around a headland, and I could see waves crashing on rocks. Local people thought my refusal to go by sea was very funny, and rolled about laughing. I did not like to ask the pastor to put us up for another night, and anyway we were expected in the next village. It was too far to walk inland before it got dark which was why the canoe had been suggested in the first place. However a local man with a wicked grin on his face, which should have warned me, said he would take Ruta and me by a short cut.

We set off at a pace that I could hardly sustain, but worse was to come. The short cut involved clambering up and over a fast-flowing

231

waterfall. The rocks were slippery as we ascended and I hung on for dear life. We reached a point when I had to be hauled up by the guide or I would have slid all the way to the bottom. Ruta and our guide were chattering away in Suau, no doubt commenting on the folly of the *dim dim* Sister they had to heave over rocks as she had refused to travel by canoe! To make matters worse it began to pour with rain. I was just glad that my mother, who had worried about my travelling in London, could not see me suspended several feet from the ground, clinging onto a wet rock face, whilst water deluged all around me. Soaked to the skin, we eventually reached the other side of the waterfall and after about an hour's walk over rough terrain we saw the village in the distance, for which I offered up a prayer of thanks.

It was nearly dark by this time and the thought of a plate of hot sweet potato cooked in coconut that I knew would be ready for us, seemed unusually appealing. I was relieved to reach the pastor's house in one piece and thanked our guide for delivering Ruta and me safely to our destination. The canoe, which had carried our medical box and personal belongings, had arrived ahead of us! After I had washed and changed into dry clothes, I began to recover. I was ready for sweet potatoes, which we ate by the light of a hurricane lamp. Prayers followed during which I nodded off, but I hoped that the pastor hadn't noticed. I fell asleep very quickly that night on my mat on the floor, and hardly heard rats scuttling about in the roof thatch.

Next morning I was stiff, but, as mothers came early for clinic, we got up and got going. Our guide had left even earlier to return home, well pleased with the tea and tobacco I had given him. This was the penultimate village that we visited and the rest of our journey home was uneventful. Ruta could not wait to tell the nurses and schoolgirls about our adventures, and I could hear them all laughing as I drifted off to sleep that night.

CHAPTER 33: DOUBLE TRAGEDY

I BECAME ACUTELY AWARE OF HOW DIFFICULT IT WAS to give appropriate treatment to very ill people in the absence of laboratory facilities, during July (1968). Two people were admitted to the General ward, one of whom was an eighteen-year-old girl in a coma, and the other was an older man with fever and very little incentive to live.

Nina

Her family brought Nina into Hospital on a stretcher, as they were unable to rouse her. She had been unwell for a day or two before this. When I examined her, she had neck stiffness and a high fever, and groaned when she was moved, which indicated pain or cerebral irritation. A blood slide would have indicated if malarial parasites were present and the results of a lumber puncture would have told us if she had meningitis, but we had neither. I moved Nina into the only single room we had, which was on the Maternity ward, in order that she could be in a quiet environment. Fortunately, we had no mothers or babies in the Maternity ward at that time, so there was no danger of cross infection.

I spoke to Dr Peter Calvert over the radio, and he confirmed that I should treat her for both cerebral malaria and meningitis, as her symptoms indicated that she was suffering from one or other condition. Nina was also very dehydrated but her veins were collapsed and I could not insert a needle into a vein to put a drip up. Peter suggested intra-peritoneal fluid as an alternative. I had used this method with young children but not with an adult. It was relatively easy to insert a small needle into the subcutaneous tissues of Nina's abdomen and run a drip through, where it was slowly absorbed through the peritoneum (the membrane that lines the abdominal cavity). We sponged Nina regularly with cold water to reduce her temperature, but in spite of giving her massive doses of antibiotics and antimalarial drugs, her condition worsened and she died after 48 hours.

Naturally her family were upset. In fact we all were, and many tears were shed at the loss of such a young life. I thought long and hard as to whether there was anything more we could have done, and familiar feelings of frustration at having to work in the dark returned. It was difficult not to feel that we had let the family down by failing to arrest Nina's illness, yet I knew that these things still happened in Hospitals where they had every facility available. I think I was always afraid that if we were not more effective in our treatment, people would boycott the Hospital and turn to the *puri puri* man for help.

These feelings were reinforced some time later when Mary and I went to a nearby village for a school visit. As we passed by through the village on our way to school, loud wails came from inside one of the houses. I asked Mary why this had happened. "It is Nina's family home," she said. "Seeing us has reminded them of their sadness." We continued with the school visit, but I could not easily forget Nina's family's distress.

Dioni

The second sad situation occurred about a week later, when Dioni, a man we had been treating for TB was admitted. He had been unwell in the village for a month, then his family decided to carry him to Hospital. However Dioni was convinced that he was a victim of *puri puri*. He lay in bed with his eyes closed, refusing to eat or drink. His only physical symptom was fever, and he reluctantly allowed me to treat him for malaria, but he refused to allow me to put up a drip to correct his dehydration. I consulted Peter over the radio and he suggested starting him on a course of antibiotics, in case he had TB meningitis, which was a definite possibility and might account for his symptoms. Peter discounted psychiatric illness, such as severe depression, which I had wondered about. We gave him regular injections but his condition did not improve. I was aware that fear will weaken resistance to disease, and I thought that this was a major factor in Dioni's case.

Mary told me that "He had done something bad," although she did not elaborate. He now felt guilty and thought that the person he had wronged had sought revenge. I asked Kwalahu to come over and talk to Dioni, which he did willingly, spending over an hour talking to him about God's love and forgiveness. But it made no difference and Dioni just got weaker and weaker. Both Mary and Kwalahu said that Dioni was convinced that the strong magic prepared by the sorcerer would kill him and nothing would dissuade him, so he turned his face to the wall and waited for death. Dioni's wife was distraught and we tried to help her, but we were all helpless in the face of such powerful belief, and I was unable to offer an alternative diagnosis.

After a week Dioni's family decided to take him home again, and I heard later that he had died three days later. This was the first time that I had experienced such powerful psychological forces at work. We would never know if Dioni's death had a physical cause, but his state of mind certainly caused him to lose the will to live and hastened his end.

Brief Visits

On a brighter note, we were very pleased to receive a visit from Avis Martin, who was working at Iruna and her niece Jackie, who was over from England. They arrived on the boat and were on their way to Kwato for a few days' holiday. Avis was one of the first nursing Sisters to work in Papua, having arrived post-War in 1948, and had set up Hospitals and started Nurse Training Schools, including the one at Fife Bay under the auspices of LMS. Avis was a pioneer of the church's medical work, and was recognised as such by the Papuan Health Authorities, who set the examinations for nurses whom Avis trained. In her memoirs Avis (Martin, 2007, unpublished) records that all the nurses passed and were awarded badges. The visiting Sister from the Department of Health, Sister Bignold, was "very impressed with how well the nurses at Fife Bay had done in their practical examinations." The nurses were all local Suau girls and when they left to get married, as they invariably did, they set up clinics in their villages. Fife Bay was considered to be too isolated to continue as a Nurse Training School, so it was moved to Iruna, where more facilities were available. Avis also set up nurse training at Kapuna Hospital in the Gulf. Avis had spent nine years at Fife Bay, but had not been back for a number of years, so she was very keen to look around and see everything. The boat was only in the bay for three hours so we did not have a great deal of time together.

Strangely, as we had not seen any visitors for some months, another boat sailed into the bay that afternoon; it was a trimaran and caused great excitement. The boat was crewed by two families, one from Australia and one from New Zealand. They were friends on holiday, sailing along the Papuan coast. Some schoolboys came running up to Middle House, as Shirley and Geoff W were over at Isuleilei, to tell us that a number of *dim dims* had landed. Margaret went down to the beach to meet them while I prepared tea. Fortunately we had made some biscuits in honour of Avis and Jackie's visit, but we had little else.

I had not seen so many white people together for a long time. The visitors seemed very surprised at the set up at Fife Bay. I showed them around the Hospital and they were suitably impressed. However the tide was on the turn and as quickly as they had arrived they left, and Avis and Jackie went with them too, as their boat was getting ready to leave.

Tropical downpour

The wet season brought with it a lot of coughs, colds and chest infections. One of our teachers, Mehea, was greatly troubled by severe asthma attacks, often waking in the early morning and sending a note with a schoolboy for us to come to his aid. During July he was in *status asthmaticus* (an asthma attack that lasts for 24 hours or more) four times, which was very exhausting and frightening for him and taxed our resources to the limit. After using all the drugs for asthma that we had available we had to resort to giving him hydrocortisone. Mehea was too breathless to come to into Hospital, where we had oxygen, but as we only had one cylinder I could not let him have it in his house, as we often needed it to resuscitate newborn babies. Another village man was also admitted with *status asthmaticus* and he too needed an injection of hydrocortisone to bring him out of it. It did not help that I was also coughing and wheezing and needed to treat myself at the same time as the patients.

Helpful Toby!

I had to wash my mosquito net on the one dry day we had, as Toby had come in one night, muddy and soaking wet. He had used my net as a towel, rolling himself up in it whilst I was at the Hospital with a patient. I had to endure the smell of wet dog and mud for a few nights until we had a dry day. I hung the net under the house, but it was difficult to keep it off the muddy ground, because of its shape. It wasn't quite dry when I reinstated it over my bed, but I dare not sleep without a net, as mosquitoes were out in force because of the rains.

Surprises

Margaret had to go into Samarai on the Pipi Gari, to visit the dentist. I was glad that I was not called upon to attend to her teeth. She had developed toothache whilst on patrol and had also been upset by the spectacle of a group of village folk on their way to a funeral feast. That in itself was not a problem, but she had been disturbed as three women were carrying whole cooked dogs. Schoolboys who accompanied her told her it was the custom at a funeral feast. I was glad I had not seen it, although I would at least be prepared for a future occurrence. Margariti had gone into Samarai for her holiday, on a previous boat, to visit her mother. Margaret saw her at the dentist and apparently she had got married to one of the dental assistants. Margariti told Margaret that she had met him when she had accompanied me into Samarai after I was unwell on patrol. She had told me she was visiting her cousin and had kept very quiet about her visit to the dentist! Margariti would be unlikely to return in the circumstances, which meant we would have to replace her.

At the end of July 1968 I had completed two years at Fife Bay. In some ways it had seemed longer than that, but mostly the time had flown by.

CHAPTER 34: WORDS AND NUMBERS

Two Guide trainers came from Port Moresby, on their two-yearly visit and I was passed as a fully-fledged Girl Guide. At a ceremony held one Wednesday afternoon, I was invested as Guide Commissioner for the Suau District. I had to borrow a uniform and felt a bit of a fraud as Guiding wasn't something I had previously been very interested in. However nurses and schoolgirls took it all very seriously and I could see how important it was for them to belong to a world-wide organisation.

Group of Guides and Trainers

In the evening we had a campfire and the local Scout troop joined us. It was quite fun as we roasted sweet potatoes and everyone enjoyed them. It was a beautiful moonlit night, with a brilliance of stars that I loved to see. The Brownies, who didn't wear blouses and tied their ties around their necks, sang *Happy Wanderer*. Although they had

239

practised the song, they went wrong in the chorus and dissolved into giggles, much to the consternation of their Brown Owl who wanted to impress the trainers from Moresby. In spite of my misgivings about my Guiding abilities, it was a happy evening.

Learning Suau

Every missionary was expected to pass a language examination at the end of his or her first term and although this did not often happen in Papua, I was concerned at my slow progress in learning Suau. I was frequently told that it was one of the easier of the Papuan and New Guinean languages of which there were over 800. This was because Suau was an Austronesian language in common with most of Milne Bay area, as opposed to a Papuan language found in other parts of the Territory. I decided to ask the Station Head pastor, based at Isuleilei, and from Suau Island, if he would teach me.

Pastor B readily agreed, and I presented myself at his house one wet afternoon. It soon became evident that he was at a loss where to start, but eventually he began by deciding to translate the Ten Commandments. This was quite a feat as only the New Testament had been translated into Suau, but he had attempted to translate them from English into Suau. It revealed an interesting system of counting. The Suau numbers only went up to five, after which they counted five plus one, five plus two and so on. There was a number for ten, then it was ten plus one, ten plus two, and so on. Number twenty in Suau was *tau esega ea pei*, literally in English, man one is dead. The subject always comes first in a sentence, I had learnt that much. Numbers higher than twenty were 'one man dead' plus one, and so on. I was so taken by this method of counting that we did not get very far with the lesson that day.

Children in school were taught in English as their teacher was often of a different language group. They learned to count in English so generally it was not a problem for them. I decided that for future lessons it would help if I wrote out some English words and phrases that I could ask the pastor to translate for me. I could then learn them and he could correct my pronunciation. This was more helpful, but we did not meet very often, as we were both busy with our various duties.

I had been presented with a Suau New Testament, *Riba Harihariuna*, by the District Church Council in October 1966, when I first attended that event, and I had learnt the Lord's Prayer in Suau:

9   *"Ina doha au uura, au ene:*

        Tamamai e galewa eai,

        Esam se hetabuei,

10   *Em basileia bena i laoma,*

        Em nuatu tanoubu eai ta bena se lauwatai

        Doha galewa eai laulauna,

11   *Aiai ama wau-ta u leama;*

12   *Ema baaea u nuatugabaedi,*

        Doha hinage ai, tauhebaaeamai edi baaea ai nuatugabaedi;

13   *Ena noho ai hearo tabu u hesagugabaemai,*

        Na baaea eai mo u hesaguhaimai.

        (Basileiana enam, gigiborina enam, tepo saesaena enam,

        ana huia, ana tasi, Amen.)"

Riba Harihariuna, 1962, Mataio 6 vv9-13, p16

It was interesting that there were no words for *please* or *thank you* in Suau so English words were used in church services: *Thank you, Iesu Keriso* (Jesus Christ). The Suau universal greeting *agutoi* was often substituted in conversations between people for *please* or *thank you*.

Farewell Party

It hardly seemed possible that Chris had completed nearly a year as a VSO, but his time was up and we had arranged a farewell party for him. We had been very fortunate in our VSOs, first Brian, then Chris. They had each made an important contribution to the life of the station. VSO was a British organisation, which assessed and sent suitable young men and women to work in developing countries for a minimum of one year. They were given board and lodging by the host country and received a small allowance to sustain them. Their Australian counterparts, who also worked in Papua and New Guinea, were known as AVAs. The party was held at the Big House, as this was easier for everyone, particularly Shirley and Geoff W, as their baby was still under a year old. Margaret and I helped with the cooking for the thirty or so guests, not counting children. All the College and District staff came, plus their spouses. We curried fifteen tins of what we called Chinese cow, corned beef made in China, accompanied by masses of local vegetables. It was quite popular as it all disappeared, although I could only manage a small amount. We followed this with coffee, biscuits and several cakes that Shirley had made. Papuans do not eat pudding, but they did like cake and not a crumb was left, mainly because the older children kept coming back for more.

Mimisina's Mother

We had only been in bed for a couple of hours when, true to form, at 2 AM we were called out to a woman in labour. I was surprised to find that it was Mimisina's mother, Mari. Mimisina was the two-and-a-half pound baby we had looked after at the Hospital for five months, until she weighed enough to go home (Chapter 21). She had been admitted in August 1967, and had only gone home in January 1968. When I enquired after her I was told Mimisina had died, apparently on the way back to the Hospital. "She had diarrhoea," said her father "and breathing problems." I thought she possibly had had pneumonia, and I felt very sad, but had to turn my attention to the mother in labour.

Mari must have become pregnant when Mimisina was around four months old, as it appeared that her current pregnancy was full term. So much for the notion that a woman who is breast-feeding a baby will not become pregnant! Had she lived Mimisina would have been barely a year old. It would have been difficult for Mari to raise two babies under 18 months, and Mimisina would immediately have been at risk of malnutrition if she had to come off the breast when the new baby was born. Unfortunately, the family lived at the extreme edge of the District and it was three days' journey from their home to Hospital. Little Mimisina didn't stand a chance as diarrhoea can kill a child in 24 hours. I felt really upset, as we had all become very fond of Mimisina, whom we had called Mimi for short.

Face Presentation

When I examined Mari, she was well on in labour but the baby's head was extended and it was coming face first. I had not delivered a baby in that position before, and had to take a quick look at my midwifery textbook. I knew that one of the causes of a face presentation was an abnormality in the baby. I hoped and prayed that this was not the case. Mercifully, the baby's head was in the anterior position, which meant that the baby's chin, and not the forehead was the leading part. (If the forehead is the leading part, it becomes impacted and cannot be delivered). I had to do a large episiotomy to deliver the head, but the rest of the delivery proceeded normally. The baby girl's face was bruised and swollen, otherwise she appeared healthy and weighed in at over seven pounds. Both parents were very happy although they had been worried at first by their daughter's appearance, but by the next morning the swelling around the baby's eyes and mouth had started to go down and she was able to feed normally.

Hospitalisation

I had not been feeling well for a while, as I could not get rid of a persistent cough. I was wheezing all the time and getting very breathless, and although I did not have a raised temperature, my pulse rate was higher than normal. The time came when I was so breathless that I had to sit down half way through having a shower, so I decided something more had to be done, as self-treating had its limitations. I had given myself a course of penicillin but did not like to repeat it without further consultation.

I needed some shopping in Samarai and as the MV Pipi Gari was due in on Sunday, I decided to stay at Kwato for the weekend and see Dr Mike P whilst I was there. I contacted Margaret and Kevin Douglas, who were now in charge at Kwato, and they said it would be fine. Mike P told me that he would see me when I arrived on Sunday as he was going on patrol in Milne Bay on the Monday and Tuesday. Both Mary and Walo were managing well so I decided I could leave them for a weekend, as I intended to get on the return trip of the Pipi Gari. I wanted to be back by Tuesday as the District Church Council was due to meet on the Thursday of that week and I had been invited to attend.

The boat didn't get into Samarai until 8.30 PM on Sunday evening, by which time I had missed the last launch to Kwato. I struggled up to the Hospital and asked one of the Sisters if I could have a bed for the night in the nurses' quarters. We were just discussing this when Mike P appeared. I explained my symptoms and he examined my chest with his stethoscope. "Have you listened to your chest lately?" he said, passing me the stethoscope. It sounded like an out-of-tune orchestra, but I could not interpret the sounds. "You have got broncho-pneumonia," he almost shouted, "with only one-third air entry in one lung, the other one solid, no wonder you are breathless – it's bed for you my girl," and he went off muttering.

I was taken aback as I was totally unprepared for being admitted, but I was soon installed in a single room in Hospital and started on tetracycline, an antibiotic, and aminophylline, six-hourly, for the wheezing.

I had no idea that it would be the end of October before I was able to return to Fife Bay.

CHAPTER 35: ON BEING A PATIENT

I HAD NOT EXPECTED TO REMAIN IN HOSPITAL at Samarai, especially as I did not feel very ill. Wheezing and breathlessness were the main problems but, in spite of treatment, my lungs stubbornly refused to improve. Tests revealed an abnormally high level of cells called eosinophils in my blood and Mike P became quite excited as he thought I might have Tropical (Pulmonary) Eosinophilia, which normally affected young, indigenous males. It was caused by a parasite called *filaria*, a nematode (small worm like creature) causing an allergic reaction resulting in wheezing. Mike P said that if his diagnosis proved to be correct he would write up my case for a medical journal, as the condition was so rare in European females. I was duly treated for the parasite with a drug called Hetrazan, alongside antibiotics and asthma drugs. I also had postural drainage twice daily in an attempt to clear my lungs. This was accomplished by hanging over the side of the bed, to drain lungs of fluid, but it was not very effective.

I began to worry about the cost of my treatment, as CCWM would be asked to pay the bill, which was added to daily. I had only packed enough clothes for a weekend so Mike P allowed me to go into Samarai to do some essential shopping. After ten days I was able to spend a weekend at Kwato, which was a welcome break for me. However, I woke about 4.30 every morning with episodes of severe coughing, waking other people in the process, as the walls were so thin. So it was not much fun for any one else.

It was good to have two visitors who came to see me in Hospital; the first was Father Cope who was an Anglican priest, working in Samarai, and the second was Margaret who came in to see the dentist.

She was able to bring me up to date with news of Fife Bay and I was glad to hear that Mary, Walo and the rest of the team were coping well.

My blood count slowly returned to normal but the chest symptoms failed to improve. I had a reaction to the Hetrazan tablets and had to come off them, which was a relief. I also stopped the antibiotics and antihistamines, although I continued with drugs for asthma.

Strange Experiences

I was into the third week when something took place that would only happen in a country like Papua. Samarai Hospital had a visit from a surgeon, who came to perform some of the more complicated surgery on patients on the waiting list. That morning Mike P came to see me and asked how I was feeling. I said I had had a lot of rest and was feeling relatively well, apart from the coughing fits. Mike P said they were short of a theatre nurse and he asked me if I would scrub up and assist Dr B in the theatre. I was aghast, as it was some years since I had worked in theatre, but he said they had a theatre nurse but needed a second. He would be the surgeon's assistant and he was sure I hadn't forgotten the basics! Suddenly, I was transformed from a patient into a theatre nurse, with the *proviso* that if I started to cough I would leave theatre immediately. I felt nervous as I scrubbed up, as I was sure that two years in the bush had not prepared me for this experience!

The first patient was a middle-aged woman with an abdominal mass that she had had for some years. When she was opened up the mass was revealed as an extra-uterine pregnancy. The baby had been conceived in one of the two fallopian tubes but instead of travelling down into the uterus it had been expelled into the abdomen, where it had developed until about thirty weeks. Foetal life could not be sustained in those circumstances and it had become calcified and was as hard as a rock. The outline of the head and limbs were definable and I realised I was witnessing the removal of a so-called stone foetus as described in textbooks. What was so extraordinary was that the woman had had a successful pregnancy and a live birth after the tubal pregnancy, whilst the stone foetus was *in situ*. Because she lived in a remote village she had not sought medical help before, and had endured years of fear and discomfort.

The surgeon was an experienced man in his sixties, and took it all in his stride. I heard later that the surgeon's wife, also in her sixties, had travelled by canoe to visit one of the nearby islands. On the way home there was a storm and the canoe was swamped, and his wife was tipped out of the canoe into the sea. Fortunately she was hauled in again, without coming to any harm. It is likely that the couple would not forget their visit to Samarai! The rest of the operating list passed smoothly but I was very tired afterwards, although glad of the experience.

Port Moresby

Mike P was concerned about my lack of progress and decided to transfer me to Taurama Hospital in Port Moresby, where I would be under the care of chest specialist Dr Ian M. I arrived at the Hospital on 12th September 1968, after quite a complicated journey from Samarai. It was a four-hour boat journey across Milne Bay, followed by half an hour's journey by truck to Gurney airstrip near Alotau. The flight to Port Moresby took an hour and a half, but I finally arrived at Hospital, where I was admitted to a single room, a concession to my status as a nursing Sister. I saw Dr M the next day and he prescribed a new drug and intensive physiotherapy, as well as various tests. I had a lot of visitors from church folk in Moresby, including Ravu, who was surprised to see me in Hospital.

Eventually, after minimal progress, I was put onto steroids and I began to improve. Dr M decided that the diagnosis was allergic asthma, exacerbated by stress. He thought it was unlikely that I was infected with *filaria* although it was endemic at Fife Bay, as it was in all the coastal regions. As I felt so much better, I started to help around the ward, as they seemed to be permanently short of staff. The ward took both medical and surgical patients, and in the room opposite mine was a 74-year-old Roman Catholic nun, who had had both eyes operated on for cataracts. I sat with her for most of the afternoon, as with both eyes covered she was a little confused. Some other nuns from her order visited her and we had quite a chat about life from our respective experiences.

Dr Peter Calvert came into the Hospital to talk about my future, which sounded ominous. My UK leave was not due until April 1969, and earlier Peter had said that it might be delayed because there might not be anyone available to replace me. Because of my medical problems he felt that they would have to reconsider that decision, and it would be discussed at the next Medical Standing Committee. At the end of the month Dr M allowed me to leave the Hospital to stay at Metoreia (the United Church headquarters) so that I could attend the outpatients department.

Ravu and Lahui were living in the main house, which was full, and I went to stay with Daphne Watt, in the Girls' Hostel, where she had been the warden since May. I had stayed with Daphne in Sydney, so that worked very well. I had to stay in Moresby until I was off the steroids that had to be reduced gradually. Whilst I was there the Mainland Region Synod meeting was held, and it was a good opportunity to meet everyone again. I spent the weekend at Ruatoka, the church's teacher training college, at Kwikila outside Moresby. It was very

Ruth in Port Moresby 1968

249

hot and dry and subsequently very dusty. I was glad that I did not live there permanently.

Sixty-five people came to Synod and as I was not an official delegate, I helped Glad Butler, one of our senior missionaries, with the catering. That meant providing morning and afternoon tea, lunch and dinner. Being mostly men at the Synod they were all hearty eaters. Tables were set up under the house at Metoreia, which was my domain. It meant a lot of running up and down stairs, but I was thankful that I could do that with out becoming too breathless. A month earlier I could not have done so.

Whilst in Moresby, I took the opportunity to buy some cotton material to make two new dresses, as I had so little with me. I also went into Boroko, the shopping centre in the Moresby suburbs where I bought two dresses, as mine always looked homemade, and I needed something a little smarter. Geoff W came in from Fife Bay for the Synod meeting so I was able to catch up with news. He said that Mary and Walo were managing very well, in my prolonged absence. This relieved me of some of the worry and feelings of guilt that I had left them to cope alone for so long.

Committee Decisions

The Medical Standing Committee met during Synod and Peter came to give me their verdict. It was decided that I should go on leave early for health reasons, and, as Sally Green wanted to delay her leave until later next year so she could go to New Zealand with a friend, she would be available to relieve me. Peter suggested that I return to Fife Bay as soon as Dr M signed me off, and then go back to the UK in time for Christmas. I had not been keen to return home in the middle of winter, but realised that this was probably the best option. Although I felt sad at the thought of leaving Fife Bay, it would be lovely to be at home for Christmas and I knew my parents would be pleased.

Dr M told me to stay on the steroids until November and then gradually reduce them before stopping altogether. If I started to wheeze again I was to go back onto them until I went to see him in Moresby on my way back to the UK. The drier climate in Moresby seemed to suit me better than the humidity of the southeast coast.

I had to make all my travel arrangements to the UK before I left Moresby on 18th October to return to Fife Bay. I flew back by the same route that I took when I left Samarai. It was quite a rough flight and I was relieved to land at Gurney airstrip. The contrast in the climate was very noticeable. Moresby had been hot, dry and brown, whereas Milne Bay was lush green and very wet. I was seasick on the boat from Alotau to Samarai but I arrived eventually at Kwato, where I fell into bed and slept heavily.

Whilst waiting at Kwato for the boat to Fife Bay, I visited Mike P, the doctor at Samarai. He was very pleased to see me looking so well. It was a case of hello and goodbye, as it was unlikely that I would be travelling back via Samarai. Mike P had been a good friend and a great support to me, and I would certainly miss our contact. Geoff W arrived from Moresby while I was still at Kwato, so we were able to travel back together. We left Kwato at 11.30 PM and sat on the wharf at Samarai waiting for the boat until 1.30 AM. However it was a bigger boat than usual and Geoff W and I had a cabin each, so we were able to sleep most of the way. We arrived at 8 AM, and climbed into the canoe that had been sent out to fetch us. Toby swam out, about 150 yards, and clambered into the canoe, then shook himself all over us. He was so pleased to see me, I was afraid he would capsize the canoe by jumping around. The nurses and Middle House schoolgirls came down to the beach to meet us. The girls were so pleased to see me they were quite overwhelmed and started crying. I think they thought that I would not return.

It took me a while to settle down into the normal routine, there was a backlog of mail to sort out and patients to catch up with. I felt quite engulfed by it all. Mary and Walo had managed remarkably well, but

Mary had lost a stone in weight, which was a testament to the heavy responsibility she had carried. I had to tell them that I would be leaving them in December and there were more tears, but they were glad to hear that Sally would arrive before my departure.

CHAPTER 36: FAREWELL FIFE BAY

It was not all that easy, settling back into the work at Fife Bay at the same time as packing up to leave. I found it difficult to disengage from the work and concentrate on the task of what to take and what to leave behind. The weather was also very hot and dry and the sky was cloudless and blue. We sweated all day but as usual we were short of water. I could not spare time to go to the waterfall to cool off. One advantage of this season was that the kapok trees were bursting with well-filled pods. Walo took the opportunity to make some extra pillows for herself and the nurses, as well as for the Hospital. Mary went off for a well-earned two-week break. Walo went for her leave after Mary returned. They were both really tired after having to manage everything on their own for so long.

Our cat had her third litter of kittens in a year. Toby was excited by the new arrivals but I am not sure if the mother cat greeted them with the same enthusiasm. There was no possibility of getting her spayed to prevent further pregnancies and I worried about her future health. The village people were always keen to have a kitten but they were not good at looking after them, often leaving them to fend for themselves, so the outlook for the kittens was not great.

The Girl Guides invited me to go for a picnic with them to an island in the bay. Normally I would have enjoyed going but, with Mary away and so much to do, I regretfully said no. Margaret went on patrol to visit three village schools soon after I got back. When she returned she told me that one of the teachers at Savaia couldn't find his dog. However, he had found a large python sleeping under a tree with a suspicious bulge. He killed the snake and inside he found the whole body of his dog. I felt sorry for both dog and snake, but I was told that the snake had made a tasty meal for the meat-hungry village people.

Medical Emergency

Early one morning, a young man was carried in on a stretcher. His father, one of the stretcher-bearers, said he had been ill in the village for six days. When I first saw him I thought he was already dead, but then I detected a faint pulse. His father told me that George had been vomiting blood and passing black stools, all indicative of internal bleeding. He also had a high fever, was very jaundiced, and so anaemic as to be almost exsanguinated. What he needed was blood, which I did not have, but I put up a dextran drip to replace his fluids before calling the doctor at Samarai. Fortunately Mike P was available and agreed to send a boat out as soon as he could. For once the sea was calm and the boat arrived at 11 PM that night with a medical orderly and three units of blood on board. We took George out in the dinghy in a semi-conscious state and loaded him on board. The orderly put up the first unit of blood and, once that had run through, a little colour returned to his lips. I stayed on board until the boat left at first light, hoping and praying that this eighteen-year-old would make it to Samarai.

I heard later from Mike P that George had a bleeding duodenal ulcer. This was very unusual in such a young man. He was given nine units of blood in all before being flown to Port Moresby for further treatment. Eventually, George made a reasonable recovery, but continued to have stomach problems for some years. As a result of his experiences, he decided to train as a medical orderly so he could help other people in similar circumstances.

Unfortunately, I started coughing and wheezing soon after I returned to Fife Bay and had to start back on antibiotics. I couldn't go back on steroids until I saw Dr M again in Port Moresby. This turn of events was disconcerting, as I had hoped to remain well for the rest of my time at Fife Bay.

Wedding Bells

When Mary came back from her holiday she announced that she was getting married on 1st January 1969. I was really sorry to miss her wedding, but it could not be helped. She was going to marry a teacher and was very happy about it, but would have to leave the Hospital to live in the village where Misi, Mary's husband-to-be was teaching. I wished them both well. Mary had been such an asset with her knowledge of the local area and the language, and a great support to me. It meant that Sally would be starting here without Mary's experience to help her, but Walo was very reliable and Ruta and Nancy, both local girls, would be able to help with the language.

Parties

Margaret was due to go on leave so we decided to give a party, as I would be leaving not long afterwards. We invited about 25 people but were short of meat, so had to get one of the men to kill two of our roosters. One of the nurses plucked them for us but, when it came to the meal, I didn't fancy eating them. We curried some corn beef and I stuck to that. The poultry soon disappeared and there was plenty for everyone. True to form we had a woman in labour, but fortunately there were no complications and I was able to leave Walo and Nancy to manage the event.

The following Sunday, after church, the people of the District held another party as a farewell gesture for me. We sat down on the grass to enjoy piles of food laid out on banana leaves. I was given several baskets and some carvings as farewell gifts. One or two people came up and thanked me for helping their families when they were ill, including the mother of the baby born with a club foot, who by then was running around normally. I felt sad to be leaving the people

255

whose lives had been interwoven with mine for the last two and a half years, but as most of my asthma symptoms had returned with a vengeance, I realised that I had little alternative.

Crocodile Incident

I had not seen an injury caused by a crocodile the whole time I had been at Fife Bay, but the week before I left, a man was admitted who had been attacked by a freshwater crocodile, when he crossed a small creek not far from Fife Bay. He was carried in with extensive wounds to both legs from the crocodile's claws, and a bite on one arm. He was also, not surprisingly, suffering from shock, but he was lucky to be alive. I put up a drip and started him on antibiotics to counteract infection, after I had dressed his leg wounds and sutured his arm, which was bleeding badly. This event caused quite a stir and people came from some distance to visit him and marvel at his survival. There was some muttering about sorcery as the crocodile had escaped and people were very wary of going near the creek, which was understandable and wise!

Sally arrived two days before I left on the MV Pipi Gari, so there was just time to introduce her to the staff and to hand over the rest of the work. It was good to know that the Hospital would be in safe hands. I said a sad farewell to my friends and to Toby before boarding the boat to Iruna. I stayed with Jan and Nick for a couple of days before flying to Port Moresby. After another round of farewells, I left, on 19th December 1968, on a Qantas flight to Hong Kong (plate 47). The administrator in Port Moresby had given me a single ticket instead of the usual return ticket supplied to people going on leave. When I queried this he said I did not look well enough to return, which upset me, but I could do nothing about it then as the ticket had already been bought.

I stayed one night in Hong Kong, with Daphne W, a friend I had met at Carey Hall. My flight to London did not leave until midnight and as Daphne was a teacher and at school that day, I went out in the morning to look around the area, with directions as to which bus to get back to my friend's flat. It took me three attempts to board the bus as the local people did not queue, and I was nearly bowled over in the rush. Eventually I realised that I had to push my way onto the vehicle, along with everyone else. I did not venture out in the afternoon, as I needed to recover and repack before being driven to the airport.

I arrived in London on 21st December, feeling a little under the weather, as I was still coughing and wheezing, although I was back on steroids. It was very cold and grey, but I looked forward to Christmas with my family, after being away for three years. The sudden transition felt very strange, especially the rapid move from the tropics to a grey, cold and wet England. The UK weather matched my mood, as I was unsure as to what my next step would be. When my father heard me coughing he was convinced that I had contracted TB, although I did all I could to reassure him that this was not the case. After celebrating Christmas and spending another week resting at home I began to feel a little better, with sufficient energy to think about the future.

EPILOGUE

In January 1969, I began a long round of medical consultations with various consultants to whom I was referred in London. I spent a week in the Hospital for Tropical Diseases where they were able to rule out the likelihood that I was suffering from a tropical disease.

I had several interviews and discussions with Mary Cumber and other staff at Livingstone House, who said that I could only return to Papua if the doctors that I had seen agreed. Unfortunately, the doctors were all of the opinion that even if I were fit to return, I would most likely suffer a reoccurrence of the condition, now diagnosed as allergic asthma.

However, I was not happy about this, as I knew in my heart of hearts that I had not finished my work in Papua. I also thought that now I knew what the problem was I would be able, given the right circumstances, to manage it. So I argued my case with those in authority, although at the same time I recognised that they had my best interests at heart.

Finally, with some exasperation on the part of my senior colleagues, it was agreed that I could see another consultant physician, who specialised in asthma. I can still remember the words that he wrote in the letter, following the consultation: "I see no reason why this young women should not return to the tropics, provided that she is not sent to work alone in another isolated outpost." I was elated to receive this news, and with some reluctance, my colleagues agreed that I could return.

Letters flew between London and Kapuna. Dr Peter Calvert was happy to have me back especially as a vacancy had arisen at Iruna, the Hospital that had not only a doctor, Nick Thomson, but was situated on an airstrip. Iruna was also a Training School for nurses, where I could teach, as well as be involved in the everyday work of the Hospital. CWM agreed and I was very happy to comply. My parents were less happy as they had hoped that I might be content to stay in the UK. However, I had been able to spend quite a lot of time with them and I had visited my brother and his family as well as various friends and I was ready to leave.

I did a refresher course in Midwifery at a teaching Hospital in Birmingham that was very useful and prepared to leave the UK. I flew back to Port Moresby via India, and stayed for a few days in Bombay (now Mumbai) and Calcutta (now Kolkata) with colleagues. I was fortunate to be able to attend a local wedding whilst in Calcutta, but made an awful mess of eating rice with my right hand, which was the custom.

Almost exactly a year since I had left Fife Bay, I arrived at Iruna on 22nd December 1969, ready for my second term. Dr Nick Thomson and his wife Jan, together with their three children, gave me a very warm welcome. I soon settled into the work and enjoyed the teaching. Iruna Hospital was new, having been built in 1968, by the Presbyterian Church of New Zealand. It had room for 30 patients and 18 trainee nurses, 14 girls and four boys, who between them spoke twelve different languages.

I shared a house with Heather Armstrong, an Australian teacher, and we became good friends. I got to know her family who lived in Queensland, on my occasional visits to Australia. Heather accompanied me to England on one leave and later, after I returned to the UK, several of Heather's family members visited me in London.

Nick and Jan moved in December 1970, to Lopomu, an island in Amazon Bay, for Nick to do translation work updating the Mailu New Testament. Dr Peter Strang and his wife Marion and their three

259

children followed Nick. Peter stayed until February 1973, when he was headhunted by Dr Hakan Hellberg, from Finland, to work for the World Council of Churches' Christian Medical Commission based in Port Moresby. Peter was the liaison officer between the Churches' Medical Council and the government's Public Health Department.

From June until December 1973, we were fortunate to have the services of Dr Frances Guard, a Methodist volunteer from Queensland, Australia, who provided medical cover. No other doctor was available after Frances left but Sister Shirley Pyper from New Zealand joined me in January 1973 and together we ran the Hospital and Nurses' Training School. Shirley left in December 1974 and Sister Sally Green took her place. So we had come full circle. Sally and I worked together until I left in February 1976, to return permanently to the UK.

I spent seven happy and productive years at Iruna and remained well. I often reflected on my time at Fife Bay, when I had sometimes felt that I was hanging by a thread. However that thread had tremendous tensile strength, and enabled me to accomplish some of the things I set out to do.

In 1975 the Territory achieved Independence from Australia and was officially called Papua New Guinea. We had many excellent trained nurses who could take over the running of the Hospital. I felt it was the right time for me to return to England as my parents were both getting older and were in need of more help.

Before I left Iruna, my good friend Stella Smith was able to come out from England on a three-month visit. She had recently had a major operation for bowel cancer and arrived with a suitcase full of dressings. Stella had supported me by staying in touch throughout my time in Papua, so it was really good to be able to show her everything at first hand. As she was a trained nurse, Stella was able to give us a hand in the Hospital, go with me on a couple of short patrols and generally get the feel of the place. We all enjoyed her stay very much.

I knew however that when I finally returned to England I would suffer from reversed culture shock, and find it difficult to settle down, so I kept in mind a prayer used in Papua.

O Jesus, Be the canoe that holds me in the sea of life.

Be the steer that keeps me straight.

Be the outrigger that supports me in the time of great temptation.

Let the spirit be the sail that carries me through each day.

Keep my body strong, so that I can paddle steadfastly on,

Through the long voyage of life. Amen

HISTORICAL BACKGROUND

On ARRIVAL AT FIFE BAY one of the most striking things to see were the letters LMS that were painted on the roof of one of the buildings. The letters were so large that they would have been easily visible from the air and I was told that they dated back to the time when the Catalina sea plane used to land in the bay. To the people of Fife Bay however the lettters were of historical significance and a symbol of the beginning of their church. The letters stood for London Missionary Society and it was under their auspices that I had been sent out to Fife Bay. Although by the time I arrived the name had been changed to CCWM (Congregational Council for World Mission). Not that the local people knew or cared about that, it remained LMS to them for many years.

I had grown up in a Congregational church in Essex, and recognised the congregational form of Church Order in Papua Ekalesia. From its earliest days, LMS had sought to plant indigenous churches in the countries it worked in, and training local ministers and pastors had been a priority from the start. The two best-known early British missionaries to Papua were WG Lawes who was the first European to settle in Port Moresby (1874), and James Chalmers, known in Rarotongan as *Tamate*. Rarotonga, one of the Cook Islands, was where Chalmers worked for ten years from 1867, before he arrived in New Guinea in 1877 and travelled extensively throughout the Territory. They gave their names to the two ministerial training colleges, Lawes College at Fife Bay and Chalmers College at Veiru in the Delta region. However the first missionaries were from the South Seas, from churches that had grown from the work of LMS. They began to arrive in 1872 in the Western and Central Districts. Many of the South Seas and Samoan pastors were killed by the local people or died of various diseases and at Fife Bay there was a small graveyard that contained the graves of several Samoan families, both adults and children.

In 1901, Ruatoka, the veteran Raratongan missionary, opened a memorial chapel at Vatorata, near the village of Gabagaba, some 40 miles southeast of Port Moresby. A teacher/pastor training college had been set up at Vatorata by WG Lawes, but it was later moved to Fife Bay. In the chapel a memorial window listed the names of 82 South Sea missionaries who died between 1871 and 1899.

Tamate settled at Suau Island in December 1877, and when I visited the Island on patrol I met a very old lady who said that she remembered his visits to the Island. For more than 20 years *Tamate* travelled up and down the coast from Milne Bay in the east to the Mai Kassa River in the west. Then in 1901, *Tamate* and a colleague, Oliver Tompkins, were killed by the Goaribari people in the Gulf. Ruatoka, who had already given many years of service wanted to replace him but in the end it was the Revd Ben Butcher who came to continue the work in that area.

Then followed a list of distinguished men and women who carried on the work that went from strength to strength. Initially, the European ministers and their wives were given a basic medical training at a Medical Missionary College to enable them to carry out some essential medical work. Eventually the need for qualified medical staff became apparent.

The church established medical work along the coast including a Hospital for people with TB and leprosy on Gemo Island just off Port Moresby. This was set up by Constance Fairhall, in 1937. Rachel Leighton followed her and Joan Phillips and Myra Kennedy later joined the Gemo staff. Avis Martin served in Papua from 1948 until 1976 and pioneered much of the medical work along the south coast. She also began a nurse-training programme, which was accepted and developed by the government. Lillian Holden, who arrived in Papua in 1957 worked mainly in the Gulf area, and completed fourteen years service. I became one of a long line of nurses and midwives. Contemporary with me were Sally Green, Margaret Sharman and Sheila Reali, all from the UK. Secondary school teachers were also sent from the UK by the LMS, Isabel Hathaway and Sheila Rudofsky among others. There were also nurses and medical staff from Australia and New Zealand, all of whom made notable contributions. The four doctors, and their families working for the church, were all sent from the Presbyterian Church in New Zealand. Dr Peter and Dr Lyn Calvert were stationed at Kapuna, and Dr Nick Thompson was stationed at Iruna (Mailu). Nick was succeeded by Dr Peter Strang when he left the Hospital to do translation work on the Mailu language.

Other Christian groups established themselves, including the Methodist, Anglican and Roman Catholic Missions. In 1890, Sir William McGregor, the Administrator of British New Guinea called the Mission leaders together and suggested that they agree to work in different areas of the country. WG Lawes agreed to this on behalf of the LMS, George Brown agreed on behalf of the Methodist Overseas Mission, and AA McLaren on behalf of the Anglican Mission. The Roman Catholic Mission felt unable to agree to this arrangement, but the comity agreement was very successfully maintained by the other three churches. Each church worked in their designated area, to avoid confusion and make the best use of their limited recourses. The LMS worked on the south coast, both west and east of Port Moresby.

Of course none of this happened in isolation (map 4). Both Portuguese and Spanish explorers had a hand in discovering New Guinea in the 16th century. The first recorded sighting of the western aspect of the island was by a Portuguese explorer in 1526; he called it Os Papuas. In 1545 the Spanish explorer Ynigo Ortiz coined the name Nueva Guinea (New Guinea). The Spanish explorer, Luis Vaez de Torres, was the first to make contact with the south coast of Papua. In July 1606, Torres called at Sideia Island where he encountered some hostility. Sailing further west Torres arrived at Mailu Island in August 1606 where he and his crew had a serious encounter with the Mailu

264

people. There was a massacre and 16 children were taken to Manila as hostages.

Other well-known names followed, Abel Tasman sailed along the coast in1642 and gave his name to the Tasman Sea. The Dutch mounted an expedition in 1705 and The British East India Company took formal possession of part of the island in 1793 but this was not recognised by Britain. Then in 1828 the Dutch formally annexed the western half of the island. Dutch administration continued in the west until 1962 when it became a United Nation's protectorate, in the move towards independence. In 1969 western New Guinea was annexed by Indonesia, becoming known as Irian Jaya for a while, before being administered from 2002 as the two Indonesian provinces of Papua and West Papua (see Ricklefs, 1993, for an excellent history of west New Guinea).

In1842, Captain Blackwood in HMS Fly discovered the mouth of a vast river, which he named the Fly and charted the Gulf of Papua. He was followed in 1846 by Lieutenant Yule in HMS Bramble who also attempted to take possession of the southeast coast for Britain. In 1873, just a year before WG Lawes arrived, Captain Moresby, sailing in HMS Basilisk discovered and named the port on the central south coast, Port Moresby. The Australian States' government began to fear that Germany would take over the whole island and in 1883 Queensland government, supported by the other states, sent one of their magistrates to Port Moresby, where he claimed New Guinea for the British Empire. However, Britain repudiated this action, as it had done on the two previous occasions, rather than add another black colony to its empire. The Australian colonies were keen to acquire Papua for economic and security reasons, feeling that a non-British power on their doorstep would bring an enemy to their door.

When Germany hoisted its flag in 1885, having annexed northeast New Guinea and the Bismarck Archipelago, it prompted Britain to declare the southeastern part of the island a British Protectorate. It was also a move to protect the indigenous people from exploitation by 'blackbirders' from the sugar plantations of Queensland, and those looking for land, timber and gold. In 1884 Sir William McGregor formally annexed British New Guinea for the Crown and Commodore Erskin raised the British flag on Metoreia hill in Port Moresby, in the presence of WG Lawes and *Tamate*. The government of Queensland was given responsibility for the administration of the territory. In 1901 it was transferred to the newly formed Commonwealth of Australia, and it was then officially called Papua.

Thus the island was divided into three by colonial powers; what the indigenous people thought of this is not recorded. In 1914 German New Guinea was occupied by Australian troops, and after the First World War, in 1921, the United Nations gave Australia a Mandate to administer German New Guinea, so that effectively Australia was responsible for the administration of both the northeast and southeast half of the island. When I arrived I had little notion of the history of the country, but some of the older folk could remember the war, and on walking through the bush I saw the remains of an Australian Air Force plane.

During the Second World War, in 1942, the Japanese invaded Papua and occupied the northern part of the territory. In 1943-44 after fierce fighting, Australian and American forces, assisted by the local people, who were conscripted to act as stretcher-bearers, defeated the invading army and reclaimed the territory. This involved the troops climbing up the notorious Kokoda trail to cross the Owen Stanley mountain range, which took a heavy toll on their resources. One strategic battle was fought in Milne Bay area. The Japanese attempted to take Gurney airstrip, which had a concrete runway, but they made a geographical error and landed seven to eight miles away, near to Alotau, where they were driven back by the allied army. This proved to be a turning point in the war in the Pacific.

The country remained under Australian army control (ANGAU, Australian New Guinea Administrative Unit) until 1946 when it was handed over to the civil authorities. In 1949 a bill was passed that formerly constituted the administrative merger of the territory to be known as the Territory of Papua and New Guinea. In 1953 the Legislative Council was inaugurated and in 1963 an amendment to the Papua and New Guinea Act provided for the House of Assembly of 64 members to replace the Legislative Council. This paved the way for Independence. The country became self-governing on 1st December 1973, and achieved Independence on 16th September 1975 when the Assembly adopted the name of Papua New Guinea (plate 48). It also elected to have Queen Elizabeth II as their Head of State. I was glad to be present to share in the celebrations.

LIST OF COLOUR PLATES

Between pages 85 and 86

1   LMS painted on Lawes College School roof in the rainy season, with Margaret under red umbrella

2   CWM logo

3   MAF plane in which Ruth flew to Mailu, refuelling at Popondetta, July 1966

4   Owen Stanley mountain range with village on ridge

5   General and Maternity wards back view

6   Patient arriving on double hulled canoe

7   Moving Maternity ward water tank for repairs!

8   Fife Bay from Isuleilei Point

9   MV Moturina delivering oil drums to Fife Bay

10   Bertha and Tavita, with Miriam and Andrew

11   Middle House with kapok tree in foreground

12   Middle House schoolgirls, one playing cat's cradle

13   Ruth's certificate of Papua Ekalesia membership

14   Papua Ekalesia logo

15   Ruth enjoying coconut milk

16   United Nations Day celebration - schoolgirls dancing with Brian in foreground

17   Schoolchildren performing traditional dance in evening light

18   Tavita conducting Lawes College School choir on United Nations Day

19   Margariti, Ruth and Eileen (L to R) starting out on patrol

20   Ruth on patrol - Women's Fellowship group outside village church

21   "Sail Oh!" Boat in the bay

Photographs of Ruth's shells from Papua at the end of chapters taken by Helen Scoging

GLOSSARY

agutoi	greeting, please, thank you
aioni	goodbye
Buka Wana	Suau Hymn Book
Casuarina	evergreen tree
copra	dried meat, or kernel, of the coconut used to extract coconut oil
dim dim	European, foreigner, white person, expat
hemarai	ashamed
kam kam	chicken
kipa	woven bark of nipa palm (*Nypa fruticans*), used to make walls
Motu	language of the Motu people
Pandanus	palm-like, dioecious trees (male and female flowers produced on different plants)
Papua Ekalesia	Papuan Church, from the Greek ἐκκλησία (Ekklesia) meaning Church
peroveta	Papuan choral tradition, prophet song

Police Motu	sometimes called Hiri Motu, a trade language, which was easier to understand, bridging the gap between speakers of different regional languages
puri puri	belief in sorcery originating from the *puri puri* man, who could cause illness that might lead to death
rami	Papuan skirt made of a piece of cloth wrapped around the waist, reaching to the ankles, and worn by the men and boys
Riba Harihariuna	Suau New Testament, translated as New Word
sela sela	small animal with prehensile tail
sipora	local citrus fruit, like lime
Suau	language of the Suau people
Tok Pisin	form of Pidgin
wontok	relative or person who belongs to the same language group or village

Abbreviations

ANGAU	Australian New Guinea Administrative Unit
AVA	Australian Volunteers Abroad
BBC	British Broadcasting Corporation
BCG	Bacille de Calmette et Guérin, a vaccine against tuberculosis
BMS	Baptist Missionary Society
CCWM	Congregational Council for World Mission
CWM	Council for World Mission
DDA	Dangerous Drugs Act
DDT	dichlorodiphenyltrichloroethane, insecticide
GV	Gentian Violet
LMS	London Missionary Society
MAF	Missionary Aviation Fellowship
PANGU	Papua and New Guinea Union Party
PNG	modern, independent country of Papua New Guinea
TB	tuberculosis
VSO	Voluntary Service Overseas
WCC	World Council of Churches

Conversions

inches to millimeters mm	1 inch x 25.4 mm
feet to metres m	1 ft x 0.3048 m
pounds lb to kilogrammes kg	1 lb x 0.455 kg
miles mi to kilometers km	1 mi x 1.609 km
temperature °F to °C	(°F - 32)/1.8 °C

Bibliography

Abel, RW, 1934, Charles W Abel of Kwato - *Forty Years in Dark Papua*, Revell, 255pp

Ashton, C, 1975, *Papua New Guinea*, Editor, Published on the occasion of Papua New Guinea's Independence by the Office of Information, Papua New Guinea

Buka Wana: Hymn Book in the Suau Language of Papua, 1967, Stanmore Missionary Press, 90pp

Good News Bible, 1994, Bible Societies/HarperCollins, 1325pp

Gospels of St Matthew, St Mark, St Luke, St John in Neo-Melanesian (Pidgin English, Tok Pisin) for the Territory of New Guinea, 1963, British and Foreign Bible Society, 311pp

Gray, L, 1988, *Sinabada, Woman Among Warriors: A Biography of Rev Sue Rankin*, Joint Board of Christian Education of Australia and New Zealand, Melbourne, 147pp

Johns, E, 1937, *Pipi Gari of Elevala* (Famous People of PNG series), Pearson Education Australia, Longman, 26pp

Lambourne, RA, 1963, *Community Church and Healing*, Darton, Longman and Todd Ltd, 192pp

Macey Kennedy, M, 2008, *Gemo, Memories of a Happy Island in the Sun*, Edited Alison Savage, Typeset Jo Grant, Made in Ink, Tasmania, 194pp

Maynard, OM, 1960, *Be Prepared - The Official Handbook for Girl Guides*, C Arthur Pearson Ltd, London, 331pp

Martin, A, 2007, *Memoirs*, unpublished, 116pp

Myles, MF, 1961, *Textbook for Midwives*, Churchill Livingstone, Edinburgh, London, 776pp

Riba Harihariuna, The New Testament in Suau Language 1962, British and Foreign Bible Society in Australia, 627pp

This was translated by Charles Abel, and after his death revised by his son, Russell. It was subsequently published in 1998 by The Bible Society of Papua New Guinea, and is also available online at http://pngscriptures.org/swp/index.htm

Ricklefs, MC, 1993, *A History of Modern Indonesia* since c.1200, Stanford University Press, 496pp

Sale, C, 1929, *The Specialist*, Specialist Publishing Company, St. Louis, Missouri, 31pp

Thomson, N, 2013 *Memories of Papua*, Fisher Print, Feilding, NZ, 235pp

Ward, RG and DAM Lea, 1970, *An Atlas of Papua and New Guinea*, Department of Geography, University of Papua and New Guinea, Collins and Longman, 101pp

OTHER SOURCES

Reference must be made to the following Internet websites for invaluable help in identifying place names and locations, especially in the preparation of Maps 1, 2, and 4.

Googlemap	www.google.co.uk/maps Map data ©2014 GBRM PA, Google, MapIT
iTouchMap	www.itouchmap.com © iTouchMap.com 2007-2014
MapCarta	www.mapcarta.com Map data ©2014 Google Imagery ©2014 TerraMetrics
Mappery	www.mappery.com
Wikimapia	www.wikimapia.org, Imagery © DigitalGlobe, Landsat, NASA ©2014 TerraMetrics

Wikimedia
www.commons.wikimedia.org/wiki/Category:Papua_New_Guinea
www.commons.wikimedia.org/wiki/Atlas_of_Papua_New_Guinea

Wikipedia
www.wikipedia.org
www.en.wikipedia.org/wiki/Outline_of_Papua_New_Guinea

276